The Storyteller and the Garden of Eden

The STORYTELLER *and the* GARDEN of EDEN

ELLEN A. ROBBINS

☙PICKWICK *Publications* • Eugene, Oregon

THE STORYTELLER AND THE GARDEN OF EDEN

Copyright © 2012 Ellen A. Robbins. All rights reserved. Except for brief quotations in critical publications or reviews, no part of this book may be reproduced in any manner without prior written permission from the publisher. Write: Permissions, Wipf and Stock Publishers, 199 W. 8th Ave., Suite 3, Eugene, OR 97401.

Pickwick Publications
An Imprint of Wipf and Stock Publishers
199 W. 8th Ave., Suite 3
Eugene, OR 97401

www.wipfandstock.com

ISBN 13: 978-1-61097-539-1

Cataloging-in-Publication data:

Robbins, Ellen A.

    The storyteller and the garden of Eden / Ellen A. Robbins.

    xiv + 180 p. ; 23 cm.—Includes bibliographical references and indexes.

    ISBN 13: 978-1-61097-539-1

    1. Bible—O.T.—Genesis II–III—Criticism, interpretation, etc. 2. Plays on words. I. Title.

BS1237 R60 2012

Manufactured in the USA.

What a piece of work is a man! how noble in reason! how infinite in faculty! in form and moving how express and admirable! in action how like an angel! in apprehension how like a god! the beauty of the world! the paragon of animals! And yet, to me, what is this quintessence of dust?

—SHAKESPEARE, *HAMLET* II 2 303–8

If we change the stories we live by, quite possibly we change our lives.

—BEN OKRI, *A WAY OF BEING FREE*

Contents

Acknowledgments ix
Abbreviations xi

1. Zeno in the Garden of Eden 1
2. Introduction to the Text 15
3. What's in a Name? 23
4. Crime and Punishment in Eden 55
5. Mortal or Immortal? 81
6. The Snake 105
7. On the Characters and Their Motivation 120
8. The Storyteller and His Story 144

Genesis 2:4—3:24 The Text in Translation 157
Bibliography 163
Index of Subjects 173
Index of Hebrew Words and Phrases 176
Index of Authors 177

Acknowledgments

My deepest gratitude goes to my teacher Baruch Levine, who provided unflagging support throughout my studies; to my student David Harris, who critiqued many drafts of the manuscript; and to Derek Beattie, whose work inspired my own and whose encouragement made this work possible. Last, I wish to thank all those who have labored in this field before me and from whom I have learned so much. Any errors and infelicities are entirely mine.

Abbreviations

BIBLE TRANSLATIONS

ASV	American Standard Version
BKAT	Biblischer Kommentar, Altes Testament
ESV	English Standard Version
JPS 1917	Jewish Publication Society Bible (1917)
KJV	King James Version
NAB	New American Bible
NASB	New American Standard Bible
NEB	New English Bible
NIV	New International Version
NJB	New Jerusalem Bible
NJPS	Tanakh: The Holy Scriptures: The New JPS Translation according to the Traditional Hebrew Text
NKJV	New King James Version
NRSV	New Revised Standard Version
REB	Revised English Bible
RSV	Revised Standard Version
TEV	Today's English Version (Good News Bible)
TNIV	Today's New International Version

ANCIENT SOURCES

Ancient Versions

LXX	Septuagint
Tg. Onq.	*Targum Onqelos*
Tg. Ps.-J.	*Targum Pseudo-Jonathan*
Vulg.	Vulgate

Abbreviations

Apocrypha and Old Testament Pseudepigrapha

Apoc. Mos.	*Apocalypse of Moses*
Bar	Baruch
2 Bar	2 Baruch (Syriac Apocalypse)
Sir	Sirach/Ecclesiasticus
Wis	Wisdom of Solomon

Babylonian Talmud and Rabbinic Works

b. Ber.	*Berakot*
b. Nid.	*Niddah*
b. ʿErub.	*ʿErubin*
b. Šabb.	*Šabbat*
b. Soṭah	*Soṭah*
Rab.	*Rabbah* + biblical book (e.g., *Gen. Rab.* = *Genesis Rabbah*)

JOURNALS AND REFERENCE WORKS

AB	Anchor Bible
ABD	*Anchor Bible Dictionary.* Edited by David Noel Freedman. 6 vols. New York: Doubleday, 1992
ABRL	Anchor Bible Reference Library
AnBib	Analecta Biblica
BDB	Francis Brown, F. S. R. Driver, and C. A. Briggs. *A Hebrew and English Lexicon of the Old Testament.* Oxford: Clarendon 1907
Bib	*Biblica*
BibOr	Biblica et Orientalia
BRev	*Bible Review*
BZAW	Beihefte zur *ZAW*
CAD	*Chicago Assyrian Dictionary*
CBQ	*Catholic Biblical Quarterly*
ER	*The Encyclopedia of Religion.* Edited by Mircea Eliade. 16 vols. New York: Macmillan 1987
ExpTim	*Expository Times*
FAT	Forschungen zum Alten Testament

Abbreviations

GKC	*Gesenius' Hebrew Grammar*. Edited by E. Kautzsch. Translated by A. E. Crowley. 2nd ed. Oxford: Clarendon, 1910
HBM	Hebrew Bible Monographs
HSS	Harvard Semitic Studies
HSM	Harvard Semitic Monographs
IBC	Interpretation: A Bible Commentary for Preaching and Teaching
IBS	*Irish Biblical Studies*
ICC	International Critical Commentary
IDBSup	*Interpreter's Dictionary of the Bible: Supplementary Volume*. Edited by Keith Crim. Nashville: Abingdon, 1976
ITC	International Theological Commentary
JAAR	*Journal of the American Academy of Religion*
JBL	*Journal of Biblical Literature*
JFSR	*Journal of Feminist Studies in Religion*
JJTP	*Journal of Jewish Thought and Philosophy*
JSNT	*Journal for the Study of the New Testament*
JSOT	*Journal for the Study of the Old Testament*
JSOTSup	Journal for the Study of the Old Testament Supplement Series
JSS	*Journal of Semitic Studies*
LTQ	*Lexington Theological Quarterly*
NCBC	New Cambridge Bible Commentary
NIDB	*New Interpreter's Dictionary of the Bible*. Edited by Katherine Doob Sakenfeld. 5 vols. Nashville: Abingdon, 2006–2009
OBT	Overtures to Biblical Theology
OED	*Oxford English Dictionary*
OTL	Old Testament Library
OTS	Old Testament Studies
RB	*Revue biblique*
RHR	*Revue de l'histoire des religions*
RTP	*Revue de théologie et de philosophie*
SAAS	State Archives of Assyria Studies
SBLBSNA	Society of Biblical Literature Biblical Scholarship in North America
SBLSymS	Society of Biblical Literature Symposium Series
SR	*Studies in Religion. Sciences religieuses*

Abbreviations

STAR	Studies in Theology and Religion
TD	*Theology Digest*
Them	*Themelios*
ThTo	*Theology Today*
TynBul	*Tyndale Bulletin*
VT	*Vetus Testamentum*
VTSup	Vetus Testamentum Supplement
WTJ	*Westminster Theological Journal*
WUNT	Wissenschaftliche Untersuchungen zum Neuen Testament
ZAW	*Zeitschrift für die alttestamentliche Wissenschaft*

ONE

Zeno in the Garden of Eden

It's what we think we already know that often keeps us from learning.
—Claude Bernard

Everyone knows the story of Adam and Eve, the hapless couple who ate an apple from a tree forbidden by God, Eve having been tricked by a snake (who may have been Satan in disguise), and then, because of their disobedience, were expelled from their earthly paradise where we'd still be if it weren't for all the foregoing. This is the plot line of a story that is best known as the Fall of Man, although it is often mistakenly referred to as the Garden of Eden.

In the actual biblical story of the Garden of Eden the kind of fruit is not mentioned (there's no apple), the human beings remain unnamed (there's no Adam or Eve), and the snake's motive is unclear (there's no Satan either). The biblical account is plainly at odds with the story as it exists in the popular imagination. Because these first chapters of the Bible introduce the reader to God in His first interactions with human beings they function as a template for understanding that relationship and so cast a long shadow over Western civilization itself. This makes a sound reading of the biblical story imperative.

As important as the story is, no one has managed to come up with a way to read it that differs in its entirety from the Fall of Man, one that provides a unified account of all its scenes and results in a systematically different take on what the story is about. In large part, the problem is that we think we already know the answer, that Genesis 2–3 is the tragic first act in the history of the human race. This idea follows understandably from the context in which the story was placed when the book of Genesis as we have it was pieced together, and in all likelihood represents the view (and certainly the intention) of whoever made the compilation.[1]

We now come across the Garden of Eden story in a context, as part of what is called the primeval history (Genesis 1–11), a collection of originally unrelated narratives strung together very roughly (leaving some rather inelegant seams) to form a chronological thread leading up to the patriarchal stories and the beginnings of Israel in Genesis 11–50. Before being brought together to serve as an introduction to the history of Israel and its people, each of these stories had its own source, style, and original purpose.

When the Garden of Eden narrative was incorporated as prologue to the prehistory of Israel, whoever was responsible had a "theological plan"[2] and so put it into a context that strongly affects the way we read it.[3] As a result of this editorial process, the story of the Garden of Eden found itself set between the cosmic creation narrative in Genesis 1 and the story of Cain and Abel in Genesis 4.

Placing the story on the heels of the creation narrative gave it a definite spin. The events described there now seem to explain how the perfect world presided over by godlike humans in the first chapter of Genesis turned into the vale of tears we know today. On the far side of Genesis 2–3 we have the story of Cain and Abel. When the Garden of Eden story is followed by that of the first murder we get the impression that God's creation is continuing to go downhill. This impression is further reinforced when (after the genealogical interruption in Gen 5) we find the story of the Flood, where God, fed up altogether with human misbehavior, rues having created living creatures and only at the last moment determines

---

1. Familiarity with this idea is already evident in Ezekiel 28, where the expulsion from Eden is used as a metaphor for the prince of Tyre's tragic fall from perfection and power; see Gowan, *When Man Becomes God*, 69–92.

2. Westermann, *Genesis 1–11*, 195. See also van der Toorn, *Scribal Culture*, 137–40; Dahlberg, "Unity of Genesis."

3. "J's history, accordingly, is the gradual unfolding of the resultant dialectic between Yahweh and the sons of Adam" (Kawashima, "Sources and Redaction," 56); also Clines, "Theme"; Blenkinsopp, "P and J."

to bring about a new beginning. In this sequence of events, it's almost impossible to read the Garden of Eden story as anything but the first step on a slippery slope, perhaps even one that is determinative for what will follow.[4]

When we look at the halfhearted way the story was integrated into its context, it's clear that little care was taken to reconcile its contradictions with the creation story in Genesis 1 (the order of creation of the animals, to take only the most obvious example). And, as far as what immediately follows, Genesis 2–3 is only weakly linked to Cain, Abel, and Seth through their identification as the children of Adam and Eve.[5] They play no role whatsoever in the narrative of their children's lives; as parents they are noticeably silent on the murder of their supposed son by his own brother.[6] After the birth of Cain (Gen 4:1), Eve is never mentioned again anywhere in the Hebrew Bible. In Gen 4:25 Adam is referred to by name for the first time, as the father of Seth ("Adam knew his woman again and

---

4. E.g., reading Genesis 2–3 in its larger context, Savran concludes, "Man's reversion to his original dust foreshadows God's undoing of his creation, a process of 'anti-blessing' which reaches its climax in the flood story" ("Beastly Speech," 43). Pfeiffer sees Gen 1–11 as a "pessimistic view of human life" ("Wisdom and Vision," 96–97); "the sin of the generation of the flood climaxes the history of human sin" (Clines, "Noah's Flood," 134). See also Blenkinsopp, *Creation, Un-creation*, especially 54–55, 80–81. Cf. Sandys-Wunsch, "Before Adam and Eve."

5. Gen 4:1–2 (only Eve is mentioned by name as the mother of Cain and Abel); Gen 4:25 (only Adam is mentioned by name as the father of Seth). In these passages, as is common to the later stories in Genesis, the names of Cain and Seth are provided with etymological connections to the story in which they are found. The etymology of Cain's name in Gen 4:1 reflects perhaps the earliest interpretation of Genesis 2–3, similar to and perhaps based upon the etymology of Eve in 3:20—one that takes procreation as analogous to divine creation or at least as a replacement for it. Since 3:20 is a later addition, it's possible that 3:20 and 4:1 were added by the same source in order to make this point; see Skinner, *Genesis*, 86. We may also note the discrepancy in the woman's use of ʾelohîm in the Garden of Eden story and Eve's use of Yahweh in 4:1. Bal notes a possible pun on *Hawwah/Yahweh* in 4:1 as a "functional analogy between the two creative forces," which would explain why "the mother of all life" is mentioned there by name and Adam is not ("Sexuality, Sin," 40). This certainly would be the case if we took *qanîtî* from the root *qîn* to mean "I made (a man)," to which we might compare Gen 14:19, where God is described as *qoneh šamayîm wa-ʾareṣ*, understood as "maker of heaven and earth." On Gen 14:19, see Westermann, *Genesis 12–36*, 186–87.

6. This problem is solved in *The Life of Adam and Eve*; there the parents are aware of the danger and try to avert it (22:4–23:2). On *The Life*, see below, pp. 107–8, 140–42.

she gave birth to a son and named him Seth").[7] Adam appears for the last time in Genesis in the so-called Priestly genealogy in Gen 5:1–5 ("This is the book of the generations of Adam. On the day God created Adam/a human being, in the likeness of God He made him"). This refers back not to Genesis 2–3 but to the creation story in the first chapter of Genesis, where the human being (ha-ʾadam) is made in the "image" and in the "likeness" of God.

It appears that when the Garden of Eden story was drummed into service as part of a longer history, its characters had to be provided with personal names. As a result of this new function, now beginning the broader history described in Genesis and in the Bible as a whole, Adam and (to a much lesser extent) Eve were reconfigured to serve as the earliest ancestors of the people of Israel, the organizing principle of the book of Genesis.[8] It's probable that it was then that "the human being" became Adam and "the woman" became Eve; the way that they're identified in the story, "the human being" (ha-ʾadam) and "the woman" (ha-ʾiššah), suddenly proved insufficient for the progenitors of the entire human race in the context of a genealogy where everyone else had a personal name. It was easy enough to turn ha-ʾadam into Adam, but to provide the woman with a name it was necessary to introduce a verse into the text (3:20), although the verse sticks out from its context.[9]

Besides its two human protagonists and their integration into the genealogical framework of Genesis, what about the story itself? How was it fit into the rest of the Bible and the history of Israel as the biblical writers portrayed it? A curse on the soil (recalling Gen 3:17) is mentioned twice in the story of Noah,[10] although the idea that the ground was cursed because

---

7. The Hebrew text is unambiguous in 4:1; the subject is "the man" (ha-ʾadam). Yet many translations render ha-ʾadam as the personal name Adam (among them, LXX, Vulg., KJV, NKJV, ESV, NIV and TNIV, TEV, RSV; corrected in NRSV). The father of Cain is not referred to by name in the text, leading to much speculation as to his identity, often focusing on the snake or Satan/Samael (from *Tg. Ps-J.* 4:1–2, 5:1–3 to the present day).

8. The late recapitulation of Israelite history in Chronicles begins with Adam (1 Chr 1:1), followed by that in Luke, who traces the ancestry of Jesus back to Adam (Luke 3:38).

9. On Gen 3:20 as a later addition, see below, pp. 65, 94–96, 127–29.

10. In Gen 5:29 and, in language recalling Gen 3:17, 8:21. "And he called his name Noah saying, he will give us rest from our work and from the toil (ʿiṣṣabôn, as in Gen 3:17) of our hands from the soil (ha-ʾadamah) that Yahweh has cursed" (5:29); "Yahweh smelled the sweet odor and Yahweh said to Himself, never again will I curse the soil (ha-

of something human beings had done may have been an independent and traditional idea among the Israelites that was taken up by the author of the Garden of Eden story as he adapted so many others. "As exceptional fertility was ascribed to divine blessing (27^{38} etc.), and exceptional barrenness to a curse (Is. 24^6, Jer. 23^{10}), so the relative unproductiveness of the whole earth in comparison with man's expectations and ideals is here regarded as the permanent effect of a curse."[11]

The Flood story and Ezekiel 28 contain the only associations with ideas found in the Garden of Eden narrative in the entire Hebrew Bible, and these concern images that may have been in common use.[12] Other than the limited connections in the genealogies and the Flood story, the inhabitants and events of the Garden disappear from Genesis entirely.

Given the gravity of the accusations against the first human beings for occasioning punishments that affected human life forever after, we might expect some reference to the events in the Garden of Eden in the rest of the Hebrew Bible, yet such references, if such they are, are surprisingly rare and concern a place (Eden or a Garden of God) rather than an incident with momentous ramifications.[13] Just as with the notion of a curse on the ground, it's equally possible that our storyteller adapted the concepts of Eden and a Garden of God that were current in his time as that these biblical passages refer back to the story that now finds itself in Genesis 2–3.[14]

We do find the biblical context useful in one respect, the pivotal theological preconception that the story is about sin, in particular the

---

ʾadamah) on account of the human being (ba-ʿabûr ha-ʾadam)" (8:21).

11. Skinner, *Genesis*, 83–84.

12. Fishbane, *Biblical Interpretation*, 372–73, sees a "typological link between Adam and Noah" that would resonate as irony for the audience of the Flood story (assuming one preceded the other).

13. Besides the references to a curse on the ground, all other apparent allusions refer to a place (Gen 13:10; Ezek 28:11–19; 31:2–18; 36:35; Isa 51:3; Joel 2:3); with one exception, all are found in the prophets. On their relation to Genesis 2–3, see Stordalen, *Echoes*, 321–56; Neiman, "Eden"; Westermann, *Genesis 1–11*, 208–11; Gowan, *When Man Becomes God*, 78–84. Of these only Ezek 28:11–19 may reflect an awareness of the story in Genesis 2–3. That Hos 6:7 refers to Adam rather than to a place name is highly uncertain.

14. How the original audience responded to "Eden" depends on its historical situation and familiarity with its (apparent) connection with 'pleasure.' The possibilities have been explored thoroughly in Stordalen, *Echoes*; also Blenkinsopp, *Creation, Un-creation*, 61–67.

sin of disobedience.¹⁵ Although it has been often observed that there's no mention of sin in the story itself, the belief that it describes the first sin is pervasive.¹⁶ Yet, despite the focus on human sinfulness throughout the rest of the Hebrew Bible, it's remarkable that there is not a single direct reference back to the people or events of Genesis 2–3.

The historical books of the Bible abound in examples of the Israelites' disobedience to God's commands and subsequent punishments, culminating in exile from the promised land, but these are never traced back to some original sin or compared to that of the first human beings. Although the story of the expulsion from Eden would have resonated among the Israelites in exile (assuming it was known to them), it is never explicitly employed as a metaphor for that experience, nor is there a single reference or analogy to the supposed first sin as precursor to the many sins documented in the historical books of the Bible. As important as the Garden of Eden story became in postbiblical theology, especially in terms of the "original sin" of the first man, it seems to have made virtually no impression whatsoever on biblical writers attempting to interpret their own history.

Viewing the story in the larger context of Genesis and of the Hebrew Bible in its entirety leads us to consider the date when the story was written relative to other biblical texts. Just because the Garden of Eden story is situated at the beginning of human history and so appears early on in the larger narrative we can't automatically assume that the story it contains was composed earlier. Biblical scholars are now in the midst of rethinking when the independent sources were compiled into the book of Genesis, and since I don't believe it necessary to resolve that particular issue in order to understand the story as we have it, I gladly leave it to others.¹⁷

---

15. Most recently, Mettinger, *Eden Narrative*, 57. For an excellent summary of this interpretation in the simplest possible terms, see Humbert, *Études*, 192–93. On its early development, Malina, "Some Observations." Bal calls the assumption that a story is about good and evil "the moralistic fallacy" ("Tricky Thematics," 143).

16. To get around this, Miller claims "The key term in the description of the sin is the verb ʾākal" (*Genesis 1–11*, 28), based on Walsh ("Genesis 2:4b—3:24"). However, although the disobedience and two of the punishments involve eating, it doesn't necessarily follow that eating *per se* (and not what was eaten) was the problem as perceived and addressed by God.

17. The long-held theory that the Yahwist's work (which is assumed to incorporate the Garden of Eden story) dates to the early monarchic period is now openly challenged, and the time of its composition remains an open question. See Ska, "Genesis 2–3";

Complicating the attempt at dating is the possibility that the story was written down long after being passed along orally.[18] Its use of language, especially wordplays, points to an audience that was *hearing* the story, whether recited or read aloud. "The great civilizations of antiquity were oral cultures... The transmission of cultural lore—stories of origins, legends of ancestors and heroes, dos and don'ts, professional skills and wisdom—was nearly always accomplished by word of mouth... Written texts reached their audience through oral delivery by a speaker."[19]

When we read silently, in the original language or in translation, we miss verbal cues that appeal to the mind directly through the ear. Not only was the Garden of Eden story once independent of the other stories in the book of Genesis, it likely originated as an oral composition that was meant to enlighten and entertain its audience. If it was passed down orally there's no telling when it might have been composed.

The trajectory in which the Garden of Eden story is now found in Genesis 1–11 imposes (or at least facilitates) an interpretation that accords well with reading the story as the Fall. "The ironic theme in these chapters is that of man's failure to live up to the aim of his creation. Whatever the process through which the separate stories were combined into one, the passage is finally intended to have a thematic unity. The final editor (or editors) was far more than a mere compiler, but was in a true sense an 'author.'"[20] When we take the story out of the matrix into which it was later integrated and consider it as a stand-alone work, it sheds the implication of catastrophic change from a perfect creation of godlike humans by a sure-handed creator. Removing it from the larger context allows us to read the story on its own terms, before its integration into the book of

---

LaCocque, *Trial*; Blenkinsopp, "P and J"; Wyatt, "Interpreting the Creation"; Winnett, "Foundations." According to Mettinger, the Deuteronomistic History "constitutes one great etiology for the loss of the land," universalized in Genesis 2–3 (*Eden Narrative*, 58). LaCocque stresses expulsion from Eden as a metaphor directed to the exilic community, thereby dating the composition to the exilic period (*Trial*, 18–21); also Mendenhall, "Shady Side of Wisdom," 326–30 (on the basis of content and vocabulary). Stordalen argues for an even later date also based on the vocabulary in Genesis 2–3 (*Echoes*, 206–13), as also Blenkinsopp (*Creation, Un-creation*, 57–60; *Pentateuch*, 63–67).

18. "The failure of all attempts to break up the J narrative of the primeval history into two literary strands points inescapably to the conclusion that the author derived his material from oral sources" (Winnett, "Foundations," 3); also Niditch, *Oral World*, especially 31–38, 125–27.

19. Van der Toorn, *Scribal Culture*, 10–13.

20. Good, *Irony*, 82.

Genesis and the slant this puts on it. This results in a dramatically new reading that departs significantly from the entire history of interpretation.

The following pages deal exclusively with the text of Genesis 2–3, itself a shorthand way of referring to Genesis 2:4—3:24 (even here there's an ongoing discussion of whether to include all of 2:4).[21] The Bible was broken up into chapters in the Middle Ages, and some of these divisions are now routinely ignored in Bible translations. The chapter division between Genesis 2 and 3 tends to obscure the way they are linked by means of a very significant choice of words. What we have is a single story (with a few scattered later additions).

Some find in the story two independent sources, but even if that were the case, the two have been so completely integrated into the story as we now have it that we're required to deal with it as it is, as was intended by whoever combined the original sources (if indeed that was what happened).[22] As we'll see in the following pages, the author of the story did use and transform common language and images, and therefore it isn't far-fetched to claim that he did something similar with preexisting narrative material, although we have no direct evidence that he did so or even that such material existed.

How we approach the task of interpretation can have a significant impact on what we find. Because we're dealing with a story that everyone knows (more or less), the first step in interpretation is to exclude all preconceptions, ancient and modern, just to see how far we can get without superimposing any a priori assumptions or complex analyses that would never have been employed in the creative process (or by its intended audience). Given the sophisticated approaches to the narrative in the past, this may appear simple-minded, but simplicity has certain advantages. A simple argument is easy to comprehend and easy to critique. The goal is to recapture the experience of the original audience in hearing the story for the first time. The "real story" is not a new but an old one, indeed the oldest one, the story as its author composed it.

21. See below, pp. 50–51. On the history of the question of the unity of Gen 2:4 and a new proposal, see Stordalen, "Genesis 2,4"; also Kempf, "Introducing the Garden Of Eden"; Hess, "Genesis 1–2."

22. On this controversy, see Wallace, *Eden Narrative*, 101–30; Westermann, *Genesis 1–11*, 186–90. To my mind the most coherent view is that of Humbert, *Études*, 48–81, who argues that the author of Genesis 2–3 (whom he still considers to be the Yahwist) used extracts from a traditional creation myth as the backdrop for his story of disobedience and expulsion.

Zeno in the Garden of Eden

Every interpretation seeks to answer the question, what happened in the Garden of Eden? Does this question imply that the events in the Garden actually took place sometime in the past?[23] For many readers, what the story describes are the first facts of human history; the notion of original sin stands or falls on this assumption.[24] For others the story is just that, a story.

Luckily for us, we can avoid this controversy in its entirety by simply restricting our inquiry to the text itself and asking, what is the story of the Garden of Eden about? Whether it is a fictional story or the report of an historical event, choices have been made, details added or omitted, to lead the audience to see the events and characters through the eyes of the storyteller. He is the one interpreting the story for us. "Not only do the characters serve as the narrator's mouthpiece, but also what is and is not related about them . . . all reveal the values and norms within the narrative, and in this respect it makes no difference whether the characters are imaginary or whether they actually existed."[25] What happened is what the text says happened, nothing more or less. Whether the author intended to report actual historical events has to be determined as far as possible from the story itself.

So, what *does* the text say? What *is* it about? Even after we clear preconceptions from our minds, we're left with a story that is silent on key issues (for example, the motivation of the snake). Then there's the problem of language and translation. The original audience of the story had a competence in its own language. It could respond immediately to words, idiomatic expressions, and cultural references that thousands of years later we can only attempt to approximate. This is the challenge we face as we seek to understand perhaps the most influential story ever told.

How will we know when we have reached a satisfying interpretation, or at least are on the right path? We must first be aware of the assumptions we bring with us as we read. The basic assumption made by virtually every reader is that what we have before us is a sad story in which

---

23. The idea that Adam was actually the forefather of all human beings has been taken quite seriously. The Nuremburg Chronicle (1493), one of the first printed books, begins human history with Adam. For a fascinating account of this idea and its vicissitudes, see Livingstone, *Adam's Ancestors*.

24. For an attempt to redefine historical accuracy in order to preserve original sin, see Alonso-Schökel, "Sapiential and Covenant Themes."

25. Bar-Efrat, *Narrative Art*, 46.

The Storyteller and the Garden of Eden

humankind has fallen from a previous paradisiacal state. If only the first humans hadn't chosen to disobey God's injunction, we'd all still be living in Eden, happily ever after. There'd be no suffering, no food insecurity, maybe even no death.

And this wouldn't just apply to us. As the story of the Fall took on a life of its own, the events in the Garden of Eden took on tragic consequences for the entire natural world. In *Paradise Lost* Milton describes the scene in which Adam, following Eve, first tastes the forbidden fruit,

> Earth trembled from her entrails, as again
> In pangs, and nature gave a second groan,
> Sky loured, and muttering thunder, some sad drops
> Wept at the completing of the mortal sin
> Original, while Adam took no thought,
> Eating his fill.[26]

The initial letters of the last three lines spell out *woe*.[27] Woe aptly summarizes the Fall story, reading the events in Eden not only as the first act in the tragedy of the human race but as ruin for the natural world as well.[28] Before the fall, the sky never darkened, nor was there thunder (often taken as a sign of divine displeasure). In this (let's admit it, depressing) interpretation of the biblical story, we constitute a fallen humanity inhabiting a fallen world. The consequences of this way of seeing ourselves are beyond measure.

Milton's image of the suffering of the natural world as a result of the fall appears as early as Paul's letter to the Christian community in Rome: "For we know that the entire creation laments and suffers as in childbirth

---

26. Milton, *Paradise Lost* IX 1000–1005. Milton's imagery of cosmic repercussions is borrowed directly from biblical passages where God's anger affects the entire universe (Judg 5:4–5; 2 Sam 22:8; Ps 68:9; Job 26:11). This idea is especially present in prophetic hyperbole (Isa 13:9–13, esp. v. 13; 34:1–5; Jer 4:23–28; Joel 2:30–31; Hag 2:6, 21). On the use of hyperbole by the prophets, see Caird, *Language*, 113–17.

27. Here Milton adapted the biblical acrostic tradition that used the Hebrew alphabet in order as the initial letters of poetic verse (Ps 25; 34; 37; 111; 112; 119; 145; Prov 31:10–31; Lam 1; 2; 3; 4). During the Renaissance, acrostics were a popular means of encoding meaning. On acrostics as a literary device, see Goody, *Interface*, 272–73.

28. For Milton the entire cosmos was affected by the fall; this idea also appears in rabbinic midrash, which Milton knew well (e.g., "As soon as I had eaten, the leaves showered down from all the trees in my part, except the fig tree alone," *Apoc. Mos.* 20:4); see Werman, *Milton and Midrash*, 213.

up to the present time."²⁹ In the passage quoted above, Milton follows Paul in drawing a direct analogy between the condition of the world and the woman's punishment to suffer in childbirth ("Be assured that I will increase your toil and your pregnancies, in pain you will bear children"). The difference between the two is that Paul, by using this metaphor, implicitly acknowledges that a curse on the natural world was inflicted by God.³⁰

It is no accident that both Milton and Paul compare the suffering we see throughout nature to the pain of women in labor. Since Adam was given the forbidden fruit by the woman that God had provided to be his helper, the buck stops with Eve, and reflects, as generations of Christian theologians have argued, on all women, upon whom guilt and suspicion would forever rest. "And don't you know that Eve is you? The sentence of God on your sex lives on in this world, the guilt still must live too. You are the devil's entryway, you who opened the seals of that tree, you the first to violate the divine law, you who so easily persuaded man, the image of God, whom the devil didn't dare to attack directly. Because of what you merit, which is death, also the son of God had to die."³¹

For many it was the very existence of a woman that caused the good life in the Garden to come to an end. In Michelangelo's portrayal of the creation of woman on the ceiling of the Sistine Chapel in the Vatican, the sleeping Adam rests at the foot of a dead tree as God conjures a woman from his body. Here, in the image of the tree, death enters the world simultaneously with the woman. This is based on an allegorical interpretation of Genesis 2–3, dating back to the first century in both Jewish and Christian traditions, in which the woman is understood to be that part of the person that ties us to the material world with all its temptations and pleasures.³² If it were not for the creation of a woman, the man would have lived forever in perfect obedience to God, and the natural world wouldn't

---

29. Romans 8:22. The connection with the pains of childbirth is preserved in the Vulgate translation (*parturit*). On labor pains as "proverbial for the extremity of human anguish," Skinner (*Genesis*, 82).

30. Also Isa 24:1–6

31. Tertullian, *De Cultu Feminarum* I 1 (c. 200 CE); author's translation.

32. Early on, under the influence of Greek philosophy (which had its own problems dealing with myth), the story was understood as an allegory, with Adam representing mind and Eve sense perception through which the mind is tempted to sin (Philo, *On the Creation of World* 151–52; Philo, *Questions and Solutions on Genesis* 1:33, 37, 43, 45, 49; cf. Origen, *Homilies on Genesis*, Homily 1:15).

have experienced suffering and death. Taken this way, most of the story is irrelevant; the fall takes place when a woman first appears.

Within the context of the Fall story this remains the most grievous accusation: that a woman brought death into the world, whether because she was the first to eat the forbidden fruit or by her very existence. Reading the story as a catastrophe has had catastrophic repercussions for individuals and society, particularly for women who have been held responsible for human suffering and death.

One way to keep "the fall" from influencing the way we read is to trace how it developed in the postbiblical period. Once we know how an idea develops historically, we can no longer assume that it had always existed. In the "fall" scenario, the chief culprit is the snake. It is taken for granted that the snake behaved maliciously toward the humans and acted with the intention of deceiving them. Because the story is silent on *why* the snake would be hostile to them, it became convenient to introduce yet another assumption, that the snake was either an agent of Satan or Satan in disguise.

When Satan was identified with the presumed malevolent snake, he became the enemy of humankind par excellence. I hope that by showing how, when, and why Satan came to be read into the Garden of Eden, we can and should take him out of it. Removing him from the story of human origins may help to blunt the power that the figure of Satan has held over the religious imagination for millennia.

We've inherited many other preconceptions from the long history of interpretation. For example, take Gen 3:7 ("And the eyes of both of them were opened and they knew that they were naked, and they sewed fig leaves and made coverings for themselves"). It has long been assumed that this verse refers to the origin of sexual awareness, which is thus viewed as an effect of disobeying a divine command. Assuming that sexual desire is a consequence of sin reinforces an attitude towards human sexuality that is ambivalent at best.[33] It comes from a time when the body was opposed to the soul, and all bodily desires were suspect.[34] The opposition of body and soul provided the foundation on which the allegorical interpretation

---

33. Augustine argued that as a result of eating the forbidden fruit, the first human covered his genitals to conceal an erection he could no longer control, for which he felt shame (*Literal Meaning of Genesis* XI 32 42; *City of God* XIV 17–26).

34. Brown, *Body and Society*.

was built and in which women, identified with the body and sensuality in all its forms, became the source of all physical temptation.

Claus Westermann noted, on this introduction of sex and sexual shame into the interpretation of Gen 3:7, "This explanation is in accordance with a very traditional Christian conception of the story of the "fall." It is a telling example of how fixed and firm ideas can influence the understanding of the text."[35] Many other "fixed and firm ideas" frame the way we read the story. No magic wand can make them disappear. In order to read afresh, we simply have to hold open the possibility that we still have lots to learn. "Noticing in a new way a single detail or pattern in a work of art may begin to modify one's response to the whole."[36] The aim of this study is to supply many such details, and present an opportunity to see the story in an entirely new light.

According to one version of Zeno's paradox, a runner will cross half the distance to the goal, then half the remaining distance, and so on in an infinite series of fractional advances, and thus never be able to reach the goal at all. Biblical interpretation suffers a similar predicament. As we read closely we'll discover many details in the story that either have never been observed or have been proposed but generally ignored. I trust that one or more of the insights in these pages will provoke a reassessment of what the Garden of Eden story is about. At the end of this journey the reader is called upon to judge the degree to which the goal of a cogent coherent interpretation has been reached. To do less is to fail to honor the author of the *real* story of the Garden of Eden, whoever he may have been.

"The precise intention of the author in all of its plenitude, strictly speaking, may be irrecoverable, but every act of criticism is nonetheless an attempt to attain it – like an asymptote one forever approaches but never reaches."[37] Throughout the present work we'll discover the extent to which attention to detail, patience, and an open mind yield a fresh perspective and a new appreciation of the storyteller and his work. We'll have to read and reread the story, looking at it through many lenses, putting to it a variety of questions, to see what it has to say about each of its charac-

---

35. Westermann, *Genesis 1–11*, 235. That a noted twentieth-century theologian put quotation marks around *the fall* and describes it as conventional indicates a new reading of the story is long overdue.

36. Boyd, *Origin of Stories*, 391.

37. Kawashima, "Sources and Redaction," 50.

ters and why they do what they do. The purpose here is to weave together the insights of many who have worked on Genesis 2–3, while adding some new observations, in order to construct a thoroughly revamped interpretation based on those clues within the story that provide a clear indication of *how the text itself asks to be read*. The storyteller embedded these clues in myriad details of tone, syntax, and especially in the choice of words, and at times relied on the plain common sense of his audience and on its facility with its own forms of expression. Certain of these details will be familiar but they have never been taken in their totality to provide a radically new way of reading the Garden of Eden narrative. The aim of the present work is to show that, overall, these clues converge to reveal a story that is not intended to explain the fall of man, but rather our *rise* to full humanness, to our status "little lower than a god."[38]

---

38. Ps 8:6. Like Genesis 1, this psalm attributes our exceptional status to God's initial design for human beings; on Gen 1 and Ps 8, see Bird, "'Bone of My Bone,'" 521–22.

TWO

Introduction to the Text

Omnis traductor traditor. (Every translator is a traitor.)

IN THE PAGES THAT follow we'll read the story of the Garden of Eden on its own terms, steering clear of the major lines of interpretation that have persisted since antiquity.[1] The approach here will differ from previous interpretations in its focus on the story's unique use of language. Considerations of style and language point to a storyteller distinct from other biblical authors and sources in his methods, interests, and purpose. For the sake of recognizing his contributions, let's call him the Storyteller.

In order to understand his methods we're obliged to pay close attention to the language in which the story was composed. As we'll see, the narrative was built upon a series of puns that its original audience would have gotten immediately. As readers we can begin to approximate the sensibility of Hebrew speakers in ancient Israel by recognizing the ways in which the story has been constructed on such wordplays.

To see how meaning has been embedded in particular words we're obliged to pay attention to the story in its original language. This turns out to be much simpler than might at first appear. All relevant Hebrew words have been rendered into the English alphabet.[2] We can appreciate

---

1. On the earliest tendencies in interpretation, see Kugel, *Traditions*, 93–144; Malina, "Observations."

2. All translations of biblical texts are my own, and transliterations follow a simplified system that generally ignores vowel length.

The Storyteller and the Garden of Eden

the interconnection of words when we see them written phonetically, as they sounded when heard. However, staying so close to the original language of the story makes for some inelegance in the English translation. For this I apologize.

Most awkward to represent in translation are the names of the characters in the story as they actually appear in the biblical text. One of the main characters is of course God. There are two predominant ways in which the Hebrew Bible refers to God. The first, the Tetragrammaton (the four consonants *Y-H-W-H*, which modern scholarship presumes was pronounced *Yahweh*), is the personal name of the god of the Israelites. The second, *ʾelohîm*, is the generic word for a deity that is used for Yahweh, for members of the Israelite pantheon,[3] and for the gods of other peoples.[4]

In virtually every English translation of the Bible (following the methods of representing the divine name in early translations into Greek and Latin) *Yahweh* is rendered as "the Lord" and *ʾelohîm* as "God," while small-g "god" is used for *ʾelohîm* when it refers to deities other than Yahweh.[5] In Genesis 2–3 we find a rather unusual way of referring to God with the composite *Yahweh ʾelohîm*, which in translation becomes "the Lord God."[6] In English this seems to make perfect sense, if only by familiarity; however, in Hebrew it entails real grammatical problems. In translation the two names exist in apposition, both seemingly parallel in meaning, but this is impossible in the grammar of biblical Hebrew.[7]

---

3. The plurality of such gods is assumed in Gen 1:26; 3:5, 22; 6:2,4; 11:7; Ps 82; Job 1:6, not to mention in the numerous references to other heavenly beings called messengers (*malʾakîm*), later translated via the Greek *ángeloi* ("messenger") as "angels" (Gen 18–19; 32:1), as well as to the heavenly army (*ṣebāʾ ha-šamayîm*) of which Yahweh is the military leader, hence His title, "Yahweh of hosts" (*yhwh ṣᵉbāʾôt*). On the history of monotheism in ancient Israel, see Mark S. Smith, *God in Translation*; Smith, *Early History of God*; Smith, *Origins of Biblical Monotheism*; Morton Smith, *Palestinian Parties*; on the divine assembly, Kee, "Heavenly Council"; Lenzi, *Secrecy and the Gods*, 237–40; Sandys-Wunsch, "Before Adam and Eve."

4. Common when referring to non-Israelite deities, Gen 35:2,4; Exod 20:3; Deut 31:16; *passim*. Yahweh is specifically "the god of Israel," or "the god of Abraham," that is, the tutelary god representing the interests of a particular people.

5. Translating YHWH as "Lord" (Gr. *kyrios*) dates as far back as the third-century BCE Septuagint version.

6. On the divine name in Genesis 2–3, see below, pp. 121–22. On other occurrences of Yahweh *ʾelohîm* see Humbert, *Études*, 41–46; L'Hour, "Yahweh Elohim," 525–28, without uncritically accepting his conclusions on its meaning.

7. If *ʾelohîm* modified the divine personal name ("Yahweh the god") à la "Nathan the

There are two aspects of the problem of the divine name that *do* affect the way in which we read the story. Translating Yahweh as "the Lord" smoothes over a distinction that was clear in ancient Israel between Yahweh and the gods of other peoples. Yahweh was the specific name of the god of the Israelites; "Lord" on the other hand is a generic term based on a socio-economic relationship ('lord of the manor'). The translation "the Lord" replaces a personal divine name with an abstract title that makes God seem somewhat less of a character in the story, undercuts the extent to which He is represented anthropomorphically, and obscures the connection of this particular deity to His Israelite audience.

The most satisfactory explanation for the double name Yahweh 'elohîm is that it serves to emphasize Yahweh as a deity over against the other characters and so should be translated as "Yahweh, a god." "It is important to retain J's 'Yahweh, a god,' because it focuses attention on the distinction between the categories of divine and human."[8] In fact, as we'll see, the distinction between mortal and divine is the central focus of the events in the story.

There is also the difficulty of the two ways in which the story refers to the deity. The narrator uses Yahweh 'elohîm throughout, but in the dialogue between the snake and the woman (Gen 3:2–5) both characters refer to Him simply as 'elohîm (God). Thus 'elohîm replaces Yahweh 'elohîm in Genesis 2–3 only in spoken dialogue, perhaps to avoid having even the characters in a story pronounce the divine name aloud.

In order to get a more precise impression of the actual text, in biblical quotations the reader will find Yahweh 'elohîm, a literal transliteration of the divine name fleshed out with vowels, despite its stylistic clumsiness, rather than the generic impersonal "the Lord God." In Genesis 2–3 the narrator treats Yahweh 'elohîm as another character in the story, although with unique powers. In general discussion, for simplicity's sake, I'll revert to the more familiar way of referring to the deity as God.

It cannot be emphasized strongly enough that the key to understanding the story lies in the way that the Storyteller refers to the human characters. Consistently throughout, they are called "the human being"

---

prophet," one would expect the definite article, which is added in the LXX version (*kyrios ho theòs*, when it doesn't just replace Yahweh 'elohîm with "the god" (*ho theòs*). Everett Fox's literal translation "Yahweh, God" merely points to the difficulty.

8. Coote and Ord, *Bible's First History*, 51 (still assuming J to be the author of Genesis 2–3).

(*ha-'adam*), "the man" (*ha-'îš*) and "the woman" (*ha-'iššah*). While the personal divine name *Yahweh* is usually translated as the generic "Lord," the reverse happens in the customary way of referring to the main male character as "the man" or even "Adam" rather than the more generic "the human being"—the actual way the character is named in Genesis 2–3. The use of the rather unusual *ha-'adam* is so significant to the structure of the story that we have to follow the language of the text and translate *ha-'adam* as "the human being" or, in short, as "the human."

Just like the English word *man*, in Hebrew the word *'adam* can indicate the collective humanity (humankind as a whole) or a single person. Despite the fact that "the human being" isn't specific as to gender, it seems clear that in the story *ha-'adam* is male,[9] contra those ancients and moderns who consider the first human being androgynous (only becoming male after the woman is made).[10]

Although "the human" is consistently referred to with male pronouns (since the noun *'adam* is gendered male in Hebrew), it's not just a matter of pronouns. It strains the imagination of the audience to have a human character whose sex is ambiguous.[11] Moreover, when the Storyteller refers to the protagonist as *ha-'adam* ("the human"), he is entirely motivated by the wordplay with *ha-'adamah* ("the soil") that is so central to the story. This wordplay determines the choice of *ha-'adam* rather than the specifically male *ha-'îš* ("the man"). To keep faith with the Storyteller, I'll render *ha-'adam* as "the human" in quotations from the biblical text and when relevant to the discussion, although elsewhere "the man" will do.

While it is somewhat misleading to translate *ha-'adam* as "the man," it is even more so to replace *ha-'adam* with the personal name Adam. While translating the personal divine name Yahweh as "the Lord" acts to *depersonalize* the character of God in the story, referring to the human (*ha-'adam*) as Adam and the woman (*ha-'iššah*) as Eve, as is commonly

---

9. See, for example, Stratton, *Out of Eden*, 95–108; Watson, "Recovery," 93–97; Clines, "What Does Eve Do to Help?", 40.

10. On whether the first human was male, see Barr, "One Man," and de Moor's reply, "First Human Being." The notion of an androgynous Adam appears in early Jewish midrash (*Gen. Rab.* 8:1; *Lev. Rab.* 14:1; *b. Ber.* 61a; *b. ʿErub.* 18a) and was revived by modern feminists (Trible, "Depatriarchalizing," 37–39; Trible, *Rhetoric*, 80, 94–99; Bal, *Lethal Love*, 112–19).

11. For critiques of the idea of a genderless character, Kawashima, "Revisionist Reading"; Lanser, "(Feminist) Criticism in the Garden," 69–74.

done, has the opposite effect. It *personalizes* them beyond what the text calls for, turning generic characters into individuals.[12]

In Aesop's *Fables* the characters are simply designated by their species (the fox, the hare, and so on). This allows them to act, speak, and think without giving the reader a sense that they represent individual animals involved in events that may have actually taken place. They are like the animals that the human names in Genesis 2 by the names of their species. Similarly, the main characters in the Garden of Eden are generic members of their species, "a human being" and "a woman." They are everyone and no one in particular. When we refer to them as Adam and Eve, we feel closer to them as individuals. This removes us from an engagement with the intelligence and wit of the Storyteller that is essential to a close literal reading and its ultimate goal, a proper understanding of his work.

It may come as a surprise that there is no character named Adam in the story of the Garden of Eden. The first clear-cut use of Adam as a personal name in the Bible occurs in Gen 4:25 ("Adam knew his woman again and she bore a son").[13] After that the name Adam appears only in two passages in the Hebrew Bible and there only in genealogical material.[14] With the integration of the Garden of Eden story into biblical history, *ha-ʾadam* as the first father had to be given a personal name and so became Adam.

"The human" (*ha-ʾadam*) occurs twenty-two times in the course of the story. In only three verses in Genesis 2–3 is it possible to read the personal name Adam and, given the consistent use of *ha-ʾadam* when the Hebrew syntax is unambiguous, it's now generally recognized as unlikely that these verses use a personal name. The tradition of replacing *ha-ʾadam* with the personal name Adam in Gen 2:20, 3:17, 21, traces back to the third-century BCE Greek translation known as the Septuagint (which

---

12. Personalizing all the characters in the story, attributing to them full emotional lives, reaches lofty heights in Milton's *Paradise Lost*, the source of its great charm.

13. The word *ʾiššah* (woman) comes to also mean "wife," although "wife" has no meaning prior to the social institution of marriage (as a result, those interpreters who read the text as endorsing marriage view "God brought her to the human" (2:22) as the deity performing a wedding ceremony). We would still be loath to refer to a man and woman living together as husband and wife.

14. Gen 5:1–5; 1 Chr 1:1. It's uncertain whether the use of *ʾadam* in Gen 5:1 refers to a person named Adam or more likely to the collective humankind, as the verse alludes to Genesis 1:26–27, where "humankind" is clearly intended. In Gen 5:2 *ʾadam* is a collective. The transition to Adam as a personal name occurs in Gen 5:3.

The Storyteller and the Garden of Eden

also has "Adam" elsewhere in its translation of Genesis 2–3), and its use of "Adam" in these verses is followed in the Old Latin and then in the Latin Vulgate, the basis for most Christian translations until the modern period.[15] Given the simplicity of using personal names rather than the generic "the human" and "the woman" (and, as the personal names have already appeared in Genesis 4–5), by the first century the tradition of using Adam and Eve for the characters in Genesis 2–3 is fully established, as we can see in various letters in the New Testament.[16]

The way that the Storyteller refers to his characters (in the case of God, personalized and identified as a deity; depersonalized in the names of the humans) suggests that we begin the process of taking the particular words of the story seriously. The focus on language gives us an opening into the kinds of choices he made, providing a window into his personality. The great joy of a close reading lies in the discovery of this person, this mind.

A major benefit of recognizing the Storyteller and his method is the ability to spot later additions to the text as we now have it, passages that, on stylistic grounds alone, cannot be ascribed to him.[17] These leap out at the reader attentive to his voice. Which leads us to the question of authorship: who composed the narrative of the Garden of Eden? By this I mean what can the text itself tell us about the Storyteller; what does it reveal about his interests, his point of view? What is his voice, and in what way can any of this contribute to the way we interpret the story?

The answer to these questions links together insights from the entire history of interpretation, steps along the way that converge to create a composite portrait of sorts. We all have favorite authors, threading our way through their works primarily because we appreciate their minds in all their particularity. We revel in individual authorial voices, we know them through their creations. This is the Storyteller I hope to identify in these pages.

This is not to deny that the author of the story of the Garden of Eden has made use of traditions with which he and his audience were famil-

---

15. For a survey of ancient and modern translations, see Lussier, "'*Adam*"; York, "Adam," 15.

16. Rom 5:14; 1 Cor 15:22, 45; 1 Tim 2:13–14.

17. On 2:10-14, see below, p. 28; on 2:24, pp. 31n23, 34–35; 64n19, 71–75; on 3:20-21, pp. 65, 94–96, 127–29.

iar, images and turns of phrase that we'll be able to identify as we come across them. By incorporating what was familiar and interweaving his own ideas, he has created a new and unique work, playing with tradition and language in a manner that transcends the reduction to "sources" and reflects an identifiable intelligence.[18]

An early effort to conjure the mind of the storyteller in Genesis was Harold Bloom's *The Book of J*. There he characterized the author as "an immensely sophisticated, highly placed member of the Solomonic elite, enlightened and ironic," very possibly a woman.[19] Whatever the value of his conclusions, as a literary critic Bloom introduced into the reading of Genesis a sensibility to the author's voice that was new and worthy of attention. Following the thinking current in his time, he assumed that "J" (the Yahwist) was the author/compiler of much of Genesis; that is no longer the case.[20] It seems to me that the singularities in the Garden of Eden story point to an original composition that shares few if any features with the rest of Genesis, least of all with the patriarchal narratives (Genesis 11:10—50:26).

When a writer employs a strong voice, when his work is stamped with a novel point of view and a particular use of language, we intuitively recognize it and have little difficulty in distinguishing that voice from others. This is much easier when we're dealing with more contemporary writers, but we might do well to pay the same kind of attention to ancient texts. In addition to a new interpretation of the Garden of Eden story that this sensitivity offers, it's my hope that readers will have the joy of discovering the Storyteller and giving him the recognition he deserves.

Because the Storyteller appealed to his audience through a very deliberate use of language, our first task is to explore the story from this angle. In the next chapter, we'll look at basic issues in the language of the story that show how the Storyteller went about composing it by playing with words, common expressions, and images. Once we have a firm un-

---

18. For a rather dated survey of comparative ancient Near Eastern material, see McKenzie, "Literary Characteristics," 152–56.

19. Bloom and Rosenberg, *Book of J*, 9–10. On this suggestion, see Bledstein, "Was Eve Cursed?"; Troost, "Reading for the Author's Signature."

20. For recent discussions of the J source, see Dozeman and Schmid, *Farewell to the Yahwist?*, where the disintegration of J does not yet extend to the primordial history (Genesis 2–11); also Levin, "Yahwist"; Wyatt, "Interpreting the Creation."

derstanding of his methods, we can move on to the narrative content and try to determine what he set out to accomplish, what the story is about.

THREE

What's in a Name?

In the beginning was the pun.
—SAMUEL BECKETT, *MURPHY*

IT IS VIRTUALLY IMPOSSIBLE to arrive at a correct appreciation of the story of the Garden of Eden without understanding the role that language plays in it. When we get a good handle on the ways in which words are the focus of the story, many of the problems of interpretation simply vanish.

To illustrate this, let's begin with the most peculiar episode in the story: the scene that opens when God remarks that "it is not good for the human to be alone" and ends with the creation of the woman (Gen 2:18–22). From the beginning of this scene we know where the story's going, we expect the introduction of a woman, but the narrative takes a long detour to get there.

The actual solution to the human's problem is interrupted by the creation and naming of the animals. Too little attention has been paid to this scene, certainly the most inexplicable in the entire story. The modern reader asks, what was God thinking? Did He really believe that the animals might suffice to assuage the human's solitary existence? And what sort of helpers might they prove to be? Was the woman simply plan B? And, moreover, what's the deal with the naming? Why does God present the animals to the human "to see what he would call them"? Everyone

The Storyteller and the Garden of Eden

assumes, no doubt correctly, that these are species rather than personal names. But what's the point here?

This episode takes up roughly as much space as the all-important scene between the snake and the woman. In the economy of the text, it's clearly there for a reason. The scene begins as God observes "it is not good for the human to be alone." We don't know whether it's not good from His point of view, perhaps realizing that the human can't procreate alone, or from the point of view of the solitary human being. In order to solve this problem, God forms the other animal species as He had the human "from the soil" (*min-ha-'adamah*), creating them in the same manner and from the same matter as He did the human[1] and "brought them to the human to see what he would call them."

The narrator seems to go out of his way (in terms of the main story line) to list the kinds of animals that the human names ("all the land animals and all the birds of the heavens"). After the human gives them names, the narrator informs us that "as for the human (*l-'dm*),[2] he/He did not find a counterpart helper (*'ezer kenegdô*)." It's unclear whether the subject of this sentence is God or the human; since it's the human who is doing the naming, one might surmise that he is also the one making the judgment call. On the other hand, as it was God who made the initial observation of a problem, it's possible that He was monitoring the effect of His attempt to solve it. (We'll consider this question a bit further on.) Despite their being made from the same material as the human, the animals fail to suffice as counterpart helpers. How does this become apparent? The answer must lie in the only thing that has transpired since their creation, God's request that the human name them. It's in the process of naming the animals that it becomes clear that they don't satisfy the criterion for counterpart helper.[3]

It is generally accepted that this episode is about the human rather than about the names that he bestows. His role in the scene has been

---

1. We can't make too much of the sole difference, the addition of the divine breath for the human; see below, pp. 87–89, 91–92, 126.

2. See below, p. 159n6.

3. How the human comes by the names is not provided in the Genesis text, but a later tradition has it that he was taught the names by God. In the Qur'an God teaches Adam the names in order to demonstrate to the angels (who have not been taught them) that in this respect he is worthy to be God's earthly representative, despite man's violent nature (Sura 2:31–35). On the angels' ignorance of the names, see *Gen. Rab.* 17:4; on their objections to the creation of human beings, *Gen. Rab.* 8:5.

What's in a Name?

taken to be a sign of dominance, a prequel to his naming (and therefore his authority over) the woman. However, the point of the text lies in the *contrast* between the scene where the human names the animals and the following scene in which he names the woman (as with the animal species, also with a generic term). It is only the latter scene that reveals the connection between the man and the woman *by means of the words that designate them*.

Here the author must deviate briefly from his otherwise consistent use of "the human" (*ha-ʾadam*) for the man throughout the story, replacing *ha-ʾadam* (with its implicit male gender) with the explicitly gendered "the man" (*ha-ʾîš*).

> **2:23** And the human (*ha-ʾadam*) said:
> This one, this time, bone from my bones and flesh from my flesh,
> As for this one, it [*her name, not the woman herself*] will be called woman (*ʾiššah*) because from man (*me-ʾîš*)[4] this one was taken.

It is only when the man (now *ha-ʾîš*) names the woman with a word (*ʾiššah*) that appears to derive from his does it become clear that she will be the counterpart helper, the requisite *ʿezer kenegdô*. This necessitates a shift in the word for the male character in the story; for the play on words to work, "the man" (*ha-ʾîš*) must replace "the human" (*ha-ʾadam*) because the Hebrew word for *woman* is not *ʾadamah* (the word that would be the feminine form of *ʾadam*, already in common use for "soil") but *ʾiššah*.[5]

Language plays a critical role in the composition of the story.[6] If "words are phonic compositions—their sound symbolism is inseparable from their meaning patterns,"[7] this is especially the case when words are actually the substance of the story. When we fail to see how words form the foundation for the narrative, interpreting is like steering a boat with-

---

4. LXX and the Samaritan Pentateuch are based on Hebrew *me-ʾîšāh*, "her man," which would have made the pun even stronger. On this as more likely original, see Louw, *Transformations*, 140–41.

5. Trible's argument that *ha-ʾadam* becomes male (*ha-ʾîš*) only when the woman appears misses the point of the naming episode. She accepts the dominance explanation for the naming scene, which renders the story and its author hopelessly patriarchal (Trible, "Depatriarchalizing").

6. Galambush made many similar observations, although with quite different conclusions, and otherwise following the main lines of the traditional interpretation ("*ʾādām* from *ʾādamā*"). See also Naidoff, "Man to Work the Soil."

7. Glück, "Assonance," 69.

out a rudder. Reading the text in translation makes attempts at interpretation futile. By unpacking the use of language in the eventual creation of the woman, we can come to appreciate the composition of the story in an entirely new way. With this in mind it's useful to go over the argument made here in detail.

The sequence of events in Gen 2:18–23 is as follows. First the deity observed, "It is not good for the human to be alone." He then formed the animals and "brought them to the human (*'el-ha-'adam*) to see what he would call them" and when the human completed the task of naming, the narrator informs us "as for the human, he/He did not find a counterpart helper." Although the syntax here does not allow us to determine whether it was the human or the deity who comes to this realization, it can only be that one or the other comes to this conclusion on the basis of the names that the human gives to the animals; the names don't fit. How do we know they don't fit? Because they bear no apparent etymological connection, no aural relationship. It isn't enough that the animals and the man are made in the same way from the same material; they just don't resonate together.

We can go further than syntax to determine whether it is God or the human who comes to the conclusion that the animal experiment has failed. First of all, it is God who makes the initial observation that the human is alone. If this was a problem for the human, the story doesn't bother to mention it. When presented with the animals, he names them as he is told, just as he eats when the woman gives him the fruit. If *ha-'adam* in Genesis 2 epitomizes what it was to be human before eating from the Tree of Knowing, we can be assured that his condition afterwards was greatly improved.

When he fails to name the animals with words corresponding to his own name, it's likely that it is God who notices the failure and therefore was the one who determined that the names of the animals didn't fit. This explains the addition of *l-'dm* ("as for the human") to indicate the change of subject in 2:20 ("And *the human* named every kind of livestock and every bird of the sky and every animal of the field, but, *as for the human*, He did not find a counterpart helper"). If the human had been the subject of both verbs in the sentence ("named" and "did not find") "as for the human" would have been unnecessary.[8] On the other hand, since it is the

---

8. The possibilities here are discussed in Cassuto, *Commentary*, 132–33. Parallel language is used in the human's exclamation in 2:23, "*as for this one (le-zo't)*, it [her name] will be called woman . . ."

human who is providing the names, when he names the woman he seems to be recognizing her as worthy of being named after himself. In either case, God has employed *the test of naming* to determine the failure of His initial attempt to provide a helper.

After noting His lack of success by the names of the animals, God goes on to create the woman and, upon seeing her, the human exclaims, "it [her name] will be called woman (*'iššah*) because from man (*'iš*) she was taken." When the human names the animals, their names bear no relation to the *name* of the man. In ha-*'adam*'s exclamation at seeing and naming the woman *'iššah*, he refers to himself for the first time as *'iš*; the potential for relationship is inherent in the names. It is implicit that God knows that He has succeeded when the human names the woman after himself, giving her the etymologically correct name.[9] The scene ends here, the appropriate helper is the one with the appropriate name. Just as the woman's body derives from that of the man, so does her name derive from his. The whole naming-the-animals scene exists to point to the significance of words in the construction of the story, a conscious process in which words themselves are taken to reflect an intrinsic relationship between objects in the world (human beings and soil, man and woman).

To perceive how important this is to understanding the story in its entirety, we must follow the continuing development of wordplays within it. Although readers of the Hebrew text of Genesis 2–3 may be aware of their presence, not enough attention has been paid to their significance for its overall interpretation.

It is common enough in the book of Genesis to find some detail or episode of a story built around a word (think of the disreputable origin of the Moabites and the Ammonites in Genesis 19 or the birth of Jacob in Genesis 25), although in Genesis 2–3 it is a generic (ha-*'adam*) rather than a personal or place name.[10] Plays on words are not only pervasive in

---

9. God has already used the word *'iššah* in creating the woman (2:22). This couldn't have been easily avoided but may be taken to indicate that He already had in mind the 'correct' answer to the test. On the folk etymology of *'iššah*, see below, pp. 32n24, 33.

10. For a comprehensive list classified by type, see Strus, *Nomen-Omen*. It is inexplicable that in a collection of essays on biblical wordplays (Noegel, *Puns*) there is not a single reference to those in Genesis 2–3. Wordplays not based on names occur elsewhere in the biblical corpus. The majority are found, perhaps surprisingly, in the prophetic literature. Isaiah and Amos seem to have had a particular fondness for them. For more on wordplays in the Hebrew Bible, see Casanowicz, *Paranomasia*; Greenstein, "Wordplay"; Sasson, "Wordplay"; Glück, "Paranomasia"; Guillaume, "Paranomasia"; Bullinger gives

the Garden of Eden story, they are the building blocks in its composition, as if reflecting "a divinely instituted linguistic order."[11]

The dominant wordplay throughout the story is between *ha-ʾadam* (the human being) and *ha-ʾadamah* (the soil).[12] This is explicit from the outset as the story begins with the soil (*ha-ʾadamah*) that has no human (*ʾadam*) to work it. To fill this lack, God forms a human being (whose name throughout is *ha-ʾadam*) from the "dust from the soil" (*ʿapar min-ha-ʾadamah*) moistened by the *ʾed*. Then He plants a garden, places the human there, and brings forth "from the soil" (*min-ha-ʾadamah*) all the trees with edible fruit. (Soon God will also form the animals from the soil, *min-ha-ʾadamah*. As *ʾadamah* is a feminine noun it's tempting to see here the idea of Mother Earth from which all life on earth originates.)[13] After the passage on the geography and mineral resources of the surrounding lands that interrupts the narrative (2:10–14),[14] the story resumes by repeating the placing of the human in the Garden, adding the purpose for his creation, "to work it and to watch over it" (2:15).

---

an almost exhaustive list but also without mentioning Genesis 2–3 (*Figures of Speech*, 307–20).

11. Read, discussing the use of wordplay in early seventeenth-century sermons, when it served as "buried fragments of a prelapsarian linguistic order . . . Its range and subtlety was a constant delight for both preacher and playwright" ("Puns: Serious Wordplay," 87, 94). Stratton traces the role of wordplays in the rhetoric of Genesis 2–3 (*Out of Eden*, 109–68).

12. "This section on the creation of the other living creatures as well as the woman is impregnated by the presence of the name *ʾadam*: v. 18, 19 (2x), 20, (2x), 21, 22 (2x), 23" (Strus, *Nomen-Omen*, 117, translation mine).

13. The idea seems to be reflected in Sir 40:1, where death is characterized as "the return to the mother of all."

14. The geographical description in 2:10–14, later added to the story, represents an attempt to locate Eden in the real world, associating it with known rivers and precious natural resources, in direct conflict with the harsh landscape outside the Garden implied in Genesis 3. The digression is not well integrated into the story. There is a doublet in the passages surrounding it, with a repetition in v. 8 ("there He placed the human being He had formed") and v. 15 ("Yahweh *ʾelohîm* took the human being and set him in the Garden of Eden to work it and watch over it"). The feminine pronominal suffixes in v. 15 ("work *it* and watch over *it*") cannot refer back to the Garden (*ha-gan*, m. sg.) and indicate that these verbs originally followed *ha-ʾadamah* (f. sg.). On the syntax, see Humbert, *Études*, 54–56; on 2:10–14 as a secondary addition, Gispen, "Genesis 2:10–14"; Westermann, *Genesis 1–11*, 215–16; Stordalen, *Echoes*, 270–71, with additional bibliography.

What's in a Name?

Was the Garden made for the human being or vice versa?¹⁵ According to the story, the ʾ*adamah* is missing an ʾ*adam*, necessary to make the ʾ*adamah* productive, and so he is brought into the world to fill this lack (God didn't even bother to make it rain until he was created). Now the ʾ*adam* becomes the problem. Like the ʾ*adamah*, he is lacking something essential to his existence, something that will be of help to him, just as he was to be of help to the ʾ*adamah*. As a result, God introduces the woman into his life, made for him just as he was made for his namesake, the ʾ*adamah*.

Up to this point, the human (*ha-ʾadam*) has been described in terms of the soil (*ha-ʾadamah*), both as his material substance and his purpose. In Genesis 3 it will become the source of his punishment: "Cursed be the soil (*ha-ʾadamah*) on your account" (3:17). The intimate link between the soil and the human justifies the cursing of the one as punishment of the other. This phrase also contains a wordplay. "On your account" (*ba-ʿabûreka*) is a prepositional phrase based on ʿ*bûr* ("produce, yield [of the land]"); the punishment precisely impacts the productivity of the soil (and might be understood as "in your yield").¹⁶

And finally comes the harsh reminder of the human's mortality put in terms of his origin: "until your return to the soil (*ha-ʾadamah*) because from it you were taken" (3:19).¹⁷ To return to his material origin is also his destiny. Life begins and ends in dust.

Both the human and the woman are named from their material source. One might easily say that the narrative in Genesis 2, the creation of both the man and the woman, is generated from these wordplays. To see how this works let's return to the scene of naming the animals that culminates with the naming of the woman (2:18-23). The interpretation of this episode has been singularly unsuccessful, often based on some notion that the human, having been given the right to name the animals, now has authority over them. This, by extension, would imply that when

---

15. "Gen 2:15 suggests that the human was placed in the garden for the purpose of keeping it, that is *for the garden's sake* [italics in the original]" (Callender, *Adam in Myth and History*, 55). For a brief summary of the literature on this question, see Greenstein, "God's Golem," 232-33, who would rather argue for God's sake, to work His private garden (234-35).

16. Josh 5:11, 12.

17. The language here echoes the earlier naming of the woman ("because from man this one was taken," 2:23).

the human names the woman he therefore has authority over her, just as the authority that parents have over their children is made manifest in the act of naming.[18] It seems to me this interpretation is an act of desperation, an attempt to make sense of what appears to be a digression in the story. The arguments about women's secondary subordinate status based on the human's naming her are entirely beside the point; no one argues that the human is secondary and subordinate to the soil from which and for which he was formed and apparently named.[19]

As for the act of naming, the emphasis in Genesis 2 is not on the act but rather on the names themselves. The only information we've been given about the names of the animals is that as a result of the human's naming them it became clear that they didn't fit the bill as helpers.

The process of naming continues for the next in line, the woman. Here the verb is in the passive voice, "it [her name] will be called woman"; this sets it apart from all biblical scenes where parents name children, purportedly asserting parental authority—scenes to which Gen 2:23 is frequently compared. Although usually translated "she will be called," the verb is masculine and refers back to "(her) name," also masculine. The subject of the verb "be called" cannot be the woman.[20] As the human names the animals, the lack of verbal connection to him becomes manifest. The verbal relation, the connection between man and woman (this works almost as well in English), reveals the relationship. It has nothing whatsoever to do with the alleged authority of the namer over the named.

Why didn't God just go ahead and create the woman? One common attempt to resolve this problem is to suppose that only in considering (and rejecting) the animals as potential helpers can the human realize that the woman is actually what he needs. This comes closer to a reasonable interpretation but fails to explain why the human is asked to *name* the animals. The question remains: why does God first create the animals,

---

18. For a well-reasoned (and widely ignored) critique of the notion that naming implies dominance, see Ramsey, "Is Name-Giving," who concludes, "an essence which God had already fashioned is recognized by the man and celebrated in the naming."

19. *Gen. Rab.* 17:4 adds, perhaps to create a basis for his naming of the woman, that Adam was aware of the meaning embedded in his own name: "as for me, it is proper to call me Adam because I have been made from the earth."

20. This use of the passive to describe naming a person occurs elsewhere only in Gen 17:5 and 35:10, where God *renames* Abram and Jacob.

What's in a Name?

and what does naming the animals have to do with the problem of the human's solitary state?

Let's continue to follow the story. After noting that the animals fail to serve the intended purpose, God goes back to the drawing board, puts the human (*ha-ʾadam*) to sleep, removes a rib or some part of his side, and "builds" it into a woman (*ʾiššah*). Upon seeing the woman, the human (*ha-ʾadam*), following the earlier instruction to name, exclaims: "This one, this time, bone from my bones and flesh from my flesh, it [her name] will be called woman (*ʾiššah*) because from man (*me-ʾîš*) this one was taken" (2:23).

The expression "bone from my bones and flesh from my flesh" does not indicate that the human's acceptance of the woman as the appropriate helper depends upon his knowledge that she was made from a part of himself, since he was asleep during the process of her creation. He knows that she was "taken" from him, although how he comes to know this is not obvious; all he knows is that her name is taken from his. Milton, aware of this problem, has Adam "as in a transe" observe by "internal sight" the making of the woman from his own rib.[21]

Rather than providing the cause of the human's positive reception, as is commonly assumed, "bone from my bones and flesh from my flesh" is a metaphorical expression of his recognition of the bond between them, as the use of "flesh and bone" elsewhere in the Hebrew Bible demonstrates.[22] "A relation is affirmed that is independent of changing circumstances. It is a formula of constancy, of abiding loyalty which in the first place has nothing to do with biological derivation, as it is often interpreted."[23] Here "bone from my bones and flesh from my flesh" functions as a double entendre: the human vocalizes an oath of solidarity, while in this instance

---

21. *Paradise Lost* VIII 452–90. "Yahweh Elohim put a deep sleep on the man, according to some early Jewish and Christian commentators an ecstatic state of transformed consciousness" (Blenkinsopp, *Creation, Un-creation*, 70), citing the use of *tardemah* in Gen 15:12 and Isa 29:10.

22. See below, pp. 39, 47, 125, 159n10.

23. Brueggemann, "Same Flesh and Bone," 535. He understands "flesh and bone" as covenant terminology, meaning 'in weakness and in strength' (similar to the marriage vow, 'in sickness and in health'), where the human and the "counterpart helper" are related in "profound loyalty and solidarity of purpose." The animals fail in this role because they "lack the capacity to make oaths and enter into covenants" (539). He, contra this author, takes Gen 2:23b (the wordplay on *ʾîš/ʾiššah*) to be an intrusion into the text and Gen 2:24 to be integral to it (538–40).

31

alone the phrase is also literally true. For him the woman is indeed bone from his bones, flesh from his flesh.

In Genesis 2 both the name of the man (*ha-ʾadam*) and the name of the woman (*ha-ʾiššah*) are based on wordplays. Just as *ha-ʾadam* is formed from *ha-ʾadamah*, *ha-ʾiššah* is made from *ha-ʾîš*. The naming of the woman follows the naming of the animals, and it is by means of the names that the potential helper is rejected or acknowledged. In other words, it was the names of the animals that made it clear that the animals didn't cut it. The emphasis here is on the relationship between the actual creatures and their names.

It is a double entendre shared by the narrator and the audience that the woman is both literally and etymologically made from "man."[24] Within the logic of the narrative the woman must be made from the man because her name (*ʾiššah*) derives from his (*ʾîš*), just as the man must be referred to as "the human being" (*ha-ʾadam*) rather than "the man" (*ha-ʾîš*), because he is made from the soil (*ha-ʾadamah*). The audience alone has privileged knowledge of the analogous verbal relation in material substance between *ha-ʾadam* and *ha-ʾadamah*. The double entendre in the verbal play on both names is meant for us.

This appears to solve the problem of the animal-naming episode without recourse to assumptions about naming as asserting dominance or to the animals as a learning experience for relationship.[25] The scene exists to point out the importance of language to the meaning of the story.

Once we recognize this simple fact, we can reevaluate the way in which the woman was brought into the story in Genesis 2 that has been a crux in legitimizing male domination for millennia, that she was created secondarily, from and for man. Why was the man ("the human" that we intuitively recognize as male) created first? The order within the sequence of wordplays is absolutely necessary: first the human (*ha-ʾadam*) from the soil (*ha-ʾadamah*) and then the woman (*ha-ʾiššah*) from the man (*ha-ʾîš*). The man has to precede her in creation, since her name, the word for *woman*, appears to derive from his (that's why the way of referring to the

---

24. In fact *ʾiššah* is not the feminine form of *ʾîš* but that's irrelevant in terms of folk etymology and the way the sounds of the words function in the story (Wolde, *Words Become Worlds*, 25–26; Meier, "Linguistic Clues," 19–20, 23).

25. This explanation has ancient roots: "He (God) then went and paraded them (the animals) before him (the man) in pairs (male and female). He (the man) said, 'Everything has a partner, but I have none'" (*Gen. Rab.* 17:4).

man had to shift from *ha-ʾadam* to *ha-ʾîš* in the naming of the woman). The verbal relation also involves the material source of each; the human is both named and made from the soil, while the woman is named and made from the man.

Equally important in the context of gender relations, each is the gendered opposite of its material source. In the relation between *ha-ʾîš* and *ha-ʾiššah*, the male is both the material and verbal source of the female. This is inverted in the relation between *ha-ʾadam* and *ha-ʾadamah* where the female-gendered soil provides the material and verbal source of the male.[26] As the ultimate origin of both man and woman, the soil takes priority.

The long-standing view that the secondary creation of the woman as helper and the fact that she is named by the human are intended to reflect her inferior, subordinate status misses the boat completely.[27] The male-first order of creation is necessitated by the verbal relationship, the folk etymology of *woman* from *man*. If one were to suggest that this order could have been reversed, we would have to face the lack of a verbal source for the woman; her "name" depends on his prior existence. Although improbable in the extreme, the man could have been made from the woman (*ha-ʾîš* from *ha-ʾiššah*) but that would leave no material source for *ha-ʾiššah*.

The entire structure of the story of the creation of the man and the woman is based on material and linguistic identities, a structure that takes as its point of departure a human being made from the soil, the verbal relation of *ʾadam* and *ʾadamah*. The Storyteller began with the familiar image of the creation of a human being fashioned from clay, and replaced the expected word *clay* with "dust from the soil" in order to construct an ingenious story structured by wordplays. On the basis of the wordplays alone, the man *must* precede the woman. That she is then made *for* him is not a sign of subordination but rather of the human's inadequacy

---

26. Folk proverbs in the Hebrew Bible "show the fondness for alliteration and assonance which mark colloquial sayings in many languages.... The third 'proverb idiom' to be noted is that of *similarity, analogy, typology*" (Scott, "Folk Proverbs," 418, 421).

27. The view is already legitimated by Paul (1 Cor 11: 7–9), from whom it passes into Christian doctrine. This is a stumbling block in the path to a proper consideration of an interpretation that contradicts the Pauline, which "can only arise where the idea of canonical authority has already been seriously eroded" (Watson, "Recovery," 91). On the impact of the LXX translation on the New Testament, see Loader, *Septuagint, Sexuality*, 27–59, 79–128.

without her (2:18), just as *ha-ʾadamah* was unable to produce cultivated plants without its namesake *ʾadam* (2:5).[28] Likewise, as his namesake, the woman (*ha-ʾiššah*) could not exist without him (*ha-ʾiš*).

The Storyteller began with the making of a single male, and then introduced the woman separately because, as we'll see in the punishments meted out to each, he was interested in the differences he observed in men's and women's lives. The narrative silence on precisely how the woman was meant to help has left room for endless speculation. Clines is undoubtedly correct in concluding that the woman was necessary for procreation,[29] although we may add to his arguments that this emerges directly from the analogy with the reason for the human's creation—to allow the soil to be productive. Ironically, she does help, although not in the way God intended; her decision elevates humankind to its preeminent position in the natural world.[30]

The roots of misinterpretation go back to the period before the fixing of the version of the Garden of Eden story as it now exists. If we look at the addition in Gen 2:24 ("That's why a man leaves his father and mother and sticks with his woman, and they become one flesh"), we can readily see how the author of this verse went astray. Whether referring to sex or marriage, he understood the previous verse (where the human exclaims "This one, this time, bone from my bones and flesh from my flesh, as for this one, it [her name] will be called woman because from man this one was taken") to represent the solitary human's recognition that God got something right in His second attempt to find the human a helpful counterpart.

So far, so good. However, he then took the description of the woman made from the man literally, along the lines of Aristophanes in Plato's

---

28. Initially lacking rainfall and a cultivator, the land is infertile. The man created, "one deficiency is fulfilled: now there *is* a human being, taken and named from the soil, hence (by understatement) well fit to till it" (Stordalen, "Man, Soil, Garden," 15).

29. Clines, "What Does Eve Do to Help?"; Wolde, *Words Become Worlds*, 20–29. Cf. Greenstein, "God's Golem," 236–38; however, that the woman was created to help the human in his physical work had been previously rejected by Augustine, who argued that in such a case another man would have been more useful (*Literal Meaning of Genesis*, IX 5 9).

30. This interpretation was noted by Maimonides ("when he disobeyed, his disobedience procured for him as its necessary consequence the great perfection peculiar to man"), although he rejects it as "theoretical speculation using the first notions that may occur to you" (*Guide of the Perplexed* I 2 214a).

Symposium. According to the author of Gen 2:24 the "sticking with" and "one flesh" represent the man's attempt to reunite a split creature. The author of the gloss misunderstood the meaning of the naming episode (that God knew He had succeeded when the man stated his relation to the woman as a linguistic connection). The relation of the sexes is based, not on the reunion of the man with a body part, but on the words that appear to derive one from the other. An entire scene was added in order to make this point; it's in comparison with the failure to find a connection in the names of the animals that success in creating the woman is expressed. Here we find an additional reason for recognizing Gen 2:24 as a later addition to the text.[31]

To sum up the important point, that the man was made first, and the woman for and from him, shouldn't be taken the wrong way (as it usually is). Yes, the woman was created for procreation (just as, by the way, she had to be included in Genesis 1, where the emphasis throughout is on the sustainability of the entire creation via reproduction). But so too was the man created to work the soil from which he was formed in such a way as to make it productive. There is no implication that these purposes are in any sense demeaning or that those who engage in them are subservient. That will come later, as a result of the punishments.

OTHER WORDPLAYS IN GENESIS 2-3

The length to which the Storyteller has gone to point to the importance of words in his work dramatically illustrates the privileging of verbal relationships in the construction of the story that continues into Genesis 3. There is a second noteworthy wordplay that occurs in two adjacent verses, Gen 2:25 and 3:1, now separated by the late and artificial division into chapters. The story, without this division, would read:

> And they were, both of them, naked (ʿarûmmîm), the human and his woman, and they were not ashamed. Now the snake was judicious (ʿarûm) beyond all the land animals that Yahweh ʾelohîm had made.

As we'll see in detail when discussing the snake, this wordplay pairs ʿarûmmîm ("naked") with ʿarûm ("judicious").[32] Since the snake knows

31. On Gen 2:24, see below, pp. 64n19, 71–75.
32. On the meaning of ʿarûm, see below, pp. 109–11.

35

certain things that the human beings don't, it is more ʿarûm than all the other creatures, including the humans.³³ As a result of eating from the Tree of Knowing Good and Bad, the humans themselves become ʿarûm in the sense attributed to the snake. At the same time, and in consequence, "they *know* that they are naked" (3:7). Which is to say, now that the humans have become ʿarûm they now have the capacity to *know* that they are ʿarûmmîm. If the Storyteller had not wanted his audience to make the connection between naked and knowing, he could equally well have said that they *saw* that they were naked.

The Storyteller is clearly playing on these words, without doubt to the delight of his target audience, which was also led to recognize the need for one to be aware of the other. By taking the story as tragically serious, we have to blindfold ourselves to its language, simultaneously suggestive and playful. On the other hand, it would be foolish to characterize the story in Genesis 2–3 as comic.³⁴ As with Kafka, the subject is serious but presented as an entertaining fable.

In the scene in which the human admits to Yahweh ʾelohîm that he was hiding from Him, the reason he gives is that he was afraid because he was naked (3:10). In the Hebrew text the word for "naked" here is ʿêrom, a frequent variant of ʿarûm. It is probable that this variant was chosen on the basis of its assonance with ʾîraʾ ("I was afraid") to make the verbal play "I was afraid because I was naked (ʾîraʾ kî ʿêrom ʾanokî)."

There is yet another wordplay on ʿarûm. In Gen 3:1 the snake is characterized not simply as ʿarûm but as ʿarûm mi-kol ḥayyat ha-śadeh, "among all the land animals," i.e., smarter or wiser than the others. In punishing the snake, God pronounces it ʾarûr mi-kol-ha-behemah u-mi-kol ḥayyat ha-śadeh, "cursed among all the livestock and among all the land animals" (3:14).³⁵ In this wordplay the peculiar intelligence (ʿarûm) of the snake is paired in almost identical phraseology with a curse (ʾarûr) that causes it to slither—both characteristics not shared with any other type of animal. The contrast implicit in the wordplay and its reflection on the

---

33. Humbert, *Études*, 24.

34. As, e.g., Whedbee, *Comic Vision*, 28–29, 38.

35. On the play on ʿarum/ʾarûr, Cassuto, *Commentary*, 159. "Were it not for the importance of the wordplay, the word *bôš* would normally be used here, as it is in 2.25" (Bechtel, "Rethinking the Interpretation," 91–92); see also her article "Shame," where she goes so far as to translate ʾarûr in 3:14 as "shamed."

What's in a Name?

distinctive dual nature of snakes, their high intelligence and lowly mode of locomotion, would not be lost on an audience of native speakers.[36]

The use of wordplays may extend even to the punishments given in Genesis 3. As Cassuto has observed, words that derive from the root ʿṣb, whose basic meaning is "pain," occur too often in the punishment of the human and the woman to be accidental; these replace words that would have conveyed a more precise meaning.[37]

> **3:16a**To the woman He said, "Be assured that I will increase your suffering/toil (ʿiṣṣabôn) and your conceiving, in pain (ʿeṣeb) you will give birth to children."

> **3:17**To the human He said, "Because you heeded your woman and ate from the tree (ʿeṣ) which I charged you saying you will not eat from it, cursed be the soil on your account. In suffering/toil (ʿiṣṣabôn) you will eat all the days of your life."

The words ʿeṣeb ("pain," 3:16) and ʿiṣṣabôn ("toil, travail," 3:16, 17) contain, as it were, the word for "tree," (ʿeṣ). In addition to the verbal relation based on the sounds of the words, the audience is brought back to their interconnection as cause and effect by the question that God poses before He pronounces the punishments, "From the tree (ʿeṣ) which I commanded you not to eat from it have you eaten?" (3:11); the Storyteller places the stress on "the tree" by giving it initial position in the question. Here the assonance connects the tree directly with the punishments. The verbal relation between ʿeṣ ("tree"), ʿeṣeb ("pain," 3:16) and ʿiṣṣabôn ("toil, travail," 3:16, 17) not only plays on the words as they are connected in the narrative, but also provides a verbal justification for the imposed suffering for having eaten from the tree.[38] As we saw in the pivotal choice of words that describe the creation of the man and the woman, and can-

---

36. A common idiom playing on *aleph-ayin* is found in the expression "dust and dirt" (ʿapar we-ʾeper). Bullinger cites Isa 2:19; Jer: 10:11; Pss. 25:16; 39:12 (*Figures of Speech*, 311, 313, 316). See also Casanowicz, *Paranomasia*, 28.

37. Cassuto, *Commentary*, 165.

38. Cassuto claims to have found another wordplay in God's last words to the snake (Gen 3:15b): "It [the woman's offspring] will crush you (yešûpekah) on the head and you will strike (tešûpennû) it at the heel." Although both verbs are usually translated "bruise" as if from the same root (šwp), the first may be from the verb meaning "crush, trample" (šʾp), certainly more appropriate to the context (*Commentary*, 161). He compares the use of šʾp in Amos 2:7; 8:4, where it is used metaphorically to describe Israelite oppression of the poor and powerless.

not be stressed enough, in the Garden of Eden story words matter, often literally.[39]

PLAYING WITH COMMON IDIOMATIC EXPRESSIONS

2:7Yahweh *'elohîm* formed the human (*ha-'adam*) of dust from the soil (*'apar min-ha-'adamah*).

The way the Storyteller plays with individual words carries over to idiosyncratic play with familiar idioms and images. The relation between *'adam* and *'adamah* in the Garden of Eden story is more than just a play on similar-sounding words. It is based on the widespread depiction of a deity fashioning a human being by modeling it in clay.[40] In order to make the wordplay work, the word used for the material elsewhere in the Bible without exception had to be changed from "clay" (*ḥomer*) to "soil" (*'adamah*).

The playful use of words and images takes a more serious turn with the addition of *dust*, a word that brings the narrative and human life full circle. Toward the end of the story God reminds the human of his lack of divine status, "because dust you are and to dust you will return" (3:19). Here we find a three-fold reference to common images and ideas: the human is made of dust;[41] in burial the body returns to dust as a resting place;[42] and, after death, the body itself turns to dust.[43]

What is common to all these images is a forceful reminder of our mortality. "For He knows our being formed, remembers that we are dust. As for man, his days are like grass, as a flower of the field, so he blossoms, for a wind passes over it and it is no more."[44] When Abraham questions the justice of Yahweh's threat to wipe out the people of Sodom, he begins with a statement of humility, "I have resolved to speak to my lord although

---

39. "Genesis 2–3 as a totality displays an artful narrative anatomy . . . Polyvalent and homonymic words are used in order to create a text where different levels of meaning are played out narratively" (Stordalen, *Echoes*, 199, 217).

40. Isa 29:16; 45:9; 64:8; Job 10:9; 33:6; cf. Lam 4:2. On parallels from the ancient Near East, see Greenstein, "God's Golem," 220–29.

41. Ps 103:14; Qoh 3:20; 12:7.

42. Isa 26:19; Job 17:16; 20:11; 21:26; Ps 7:5; 22:15, 29; 30:9.

43. Pss 90:3; 103:14; 104:29; Job 7:21; 10:9; 30:19; 34:15; Qoh 3:20; 12:7.

44. Ps 103:14–16. Cf. Ps 22:16: "You established/set me in the dust of death (*'apar-môt*)."

I am dust and dirt (ʿapar we-ʾeper)."⁴⁵ In 1 Kgs 16:2, God rebukes Baasha, the king of Israel, "I exalted you out of the dust (min-he-ʿapar) and made you leader over my people Israel," emphasizing his lowly preelection status as a nobody.⁴⁶ When the context aims to emphasize the contrast between divine and human in terms of the relative powerlessness of the human being, "dust" rather than "clay" is the word of choice. By replacing "clay" with "dust from the soil" as the material from which the human is formed, the Storyteller employs both wordplay and proverbial image to underline that contrast. Despite our unique status among creatures, dust is and has always been our origin and ultimate fate.⁴⁷

2:23 Bone from my bones and flesh from my flesh

The clearest adaptation of an idiom is the use of "bone from my bones and flesh from my flesh." As we have seen, this was a means of expressing loyalty or solidarity. This expression can function as a metaphor for the denial of otherness, even as an affirmation of a relationship that transcends the *lack* of blood connection.⁴⁸ "In acknowledging the woman as 'bone of my bones and flesh of my flesh,' the text describes the relations between the man and his woman according to the ideology of kinship (2 Sam 5:1; 19:12–13; 1 Chr 11:1)."⁴⁹ Only in the Storyteller's art can it be literally true that the woman is of the man's flesh and blood.

45. Gen 18:27.

46. "Here also a man is taken from the dust. Only here the language clearly is not to be understood in a primitive or literal sense. Rather it is terminology used to describe his pre-royal status, which apparently means he is a 'nothing' without identity or importance" (Brueggemann, "From Dust to Kingship," 2).

47. See below, pp. 59–61, 87–92. "Several biblical passages describe humankind as dust (ʿpr, ḥmr or dkʾ). This element in human 'physiology' was associated with humiliation and death" (Stordalen, *Echoes*, 234).

48. Although being of the same flesh and blood can indicate literal kinship (Gen 29:14; 37:27; 2 Sam 19:13), it is as often employed metaphorically to express broader relations (Isa 39:7; Neh 5:5), especially in proclaiming an enduring relationship (Jud 9:2; 2 Sam 5:1 = 1 Chr 11:1; 2 Sam 19:12). In Gen 29:10–15 Laban declares to Jacob, "surely you are my bone and my flesh," and "you are my brother," thereby expressing both physical kinship as well as mutual obligation. The family term "brother" may also be used loosely (Gen 29:4; 2 Sam 1:26; 1 Kgs 9:12–13; 20:33–34; Amos 1:9; Ps 133:1) and was commonly done by rulers throughout the ancient Near East to express political affiliation and relatively equivalent status.

49. Yee, "Gender," 183.

3:16b You are drawn back to your man (*lit.*, to your man is your return), and he will rule over you.

We'll consider this verse in detail in the next chapter. It's worth looking at from different vantage points as "he will rule over you" has long been understood to ordain male domination as a divine directive and to justify patriarchal institutions that keep women in the place God Himself had relegated them.

The translation above will strike the reader as strange, since virtually every modern version renders the Hebrew word *tešûqah* as "desire," which now has the unfortunate connotation of sexual desire. "It may simply be that conceptually the term 'desire' (in the sense of being naturally drawn toward or *back to* something) was useful in older English but has since become problematic on account of its usage and connotations in a highly sexualized Western society."[50]

However, the basic meaning of *tešûqah* as it was used and understood in the ancient world was "return" and, as we will see, this meaning is particularly apt in the context of Genesis 3. It's possible that *tešûqah* had a wider range of meaning, one that would have included a sense of being pulled back toward someone or something.

> It seems more likely that ancients understood *tešûqah* to be close in meaning to *tešûbah* ['return'], though perhaps there was a nuance involved whereby with *tešûqah* there is a strong movement toward, perhaps of an impelling nature, returning someone (or thing) to where he or she (or it) belonged, perhaps for refuge or to one's origins, or even for destruction or in the sense that the returning is final. One might suggest that the movement is to an appropriate or natural place, almost as if part of the genetic makeup of the one (or thing) returning.[51]

If we continue to render *tešûqah* as "desire" it should be taken to indicate a strong innate proclivity devoid of sexual innuendo, even, like magnetic force, equally based in both the subject and the object of the attraction.

Here we consider Gen 3:16b as two interconnected parts, as yet another idiomatic expression that the writer has modified to fit the story. It appears to be a variation of an expression that also occurs in the story of

---

50. Lohr, "Sexual Desire?" 245 (italics original). In all probability the translation of *tešûqah* as "desire" is due to the influence of Song 7:11.

51. Ibid.

Cain and Abel, in God's warning to Cain, "At the doorway sin is a lurking thing; toward you is its desire [*lit.*, return], but you shall rule over it."[52] Here the lurking thing returns to Cain, apparently based on some mythological notion that externalizes and personifies the temptation to sin as a "lurking thing" waiting to attack its prey; its desire is really Cain's desire. God warns Cain to control (*lit.*, rule) his inclination to sin, an exhortation that appears to have fallen on deaf ears as Cain goes on to murder his brother.

The similar language and sentence structure makes one wonder whether there might be a *tertium quid*, some proverbial saying that related power and desire (in the sense discussed above) on which both Gen 3:16b and 4:7b were based. The similarities are striking but no one has come up with a satisfying explanation of the relationship between them, a task made more difficult by the obscure imagery in Gen 4:7a that luckily doesn't concern us here. The relation of these two passages poses a real conundrum and I'd just let it go at that if it didn't concern the biblical passage most often cited to justify male domination. It may be possible to attack the question a little bit at a time, so here goes yet another try.

If both Gen 3:16b and Gen 4:7b reflect a common idiomatic expression, if they are variations of a stock adage, there are two possibilities for its original sense. It may have been a saying intended to encourage efforts at self-control, something to the effect that desire will return to you (as if from outside the self), but you will be able to keep it in check. This is generally the way Gen 4:7b has been understood.

On the other hand, it may have been used as a warning (you will be repeatedly impelled towards something, and it will control you [if you don't do something about it]). At first glance this seems a somewhat better fit for Gen 3:16b as it appears that the woman's impulse to return to the man will result in her subjection to him. To get a better idea of what's going on here, let's look more closely at the two verses, simplifying the grammar for greater clarity. Each is composed of two parts:

> 4:7b(a) It (the temptation to sin) will return to you (Cain) (b) and you will control it.

---

52. Gen 4:7. On this verse, see Hendel, *Text*, 45–46; Westermann, *Genesis 1–11*, 298–301; Cassuto, *Commentary*, 208–13, who remarks, "This is one of the most difficult and obscure Biblical sentences . . . In modern times the expositors have found the text so hard to elucidate that some, like Gunkel and Jacob, have actually abandoned hope of understanding it."

3:16b(a) You will be impelled to return to your man (b) and he will control you.

According to Gen 4:7b, Cain will in the end control an inclination to sin (although he doesn't). Sin is personified as some sort of "lurking thing," and the image in this verse is that this "lurking thing" (whatever it is) is waiting at the door to attack Cain.[53] Because in and of itself neither sin nor "the lurking thing" can be controlled, the phrase seems to be a roundabout way of saying that the impulse to sin is internal to Cain.[54] He has some proclivity that he is importuned to control. If we remove the externalizing lurking thing and sin, we're left with a theoretical: "Inclination (to sin) returns to you, but you will control it."

In Gen 3:16b, the impulse is expressly internal, here to the woman; it is "your desire." Both 3:16b and 4:7 have a chiastic structure. In each the subject of the first part (the one that returns: "the lurking thing" in 4:7b, the woman in 3:16b) becomes the object of the second part (what is controlled). The object of attraction in the first part of the saying (Cain in 4:7b; the man in 3:16b) becomes the subject in the second part (the one that will "rule"). In both verses, the object (Cain in 4:7b, the man in 3:16b) triumphs: it will "rule." In both, the one that returns ("the lurking thing" in 4:7b; the woman in 3:16b) will fail in its aim; instead of attaining its goal it is subjugated to its object.

If the supposition is correct that there is some sort of proverbial saying that underlies both verses, it refers to a recurrent desire that will control ("rule") or be controlled. Both passages agree that this desire acts against the interests of the person who is the main subject in the narrative (Cain, the woman), but by internalizing the source of desire in Gen 3:16b (as compared to externalizing it as "a lurking thing" in 4:7b) a reversal of meaning takes place. This has the effect of recasting the expected exhortation to resist into a prediction of failure. The saying in its original

---

53. The pronouns in this verse ("*its* return," "control *it*") are masculine singular, while "sin" is feminine, so the pronouns must correspond to the "lurking thing" (*robeṣ*) (m. sg.), to which we should compare the "lurker" (*rābiṣu*) in Babylonian demonology (*CAD* R 20a–23b).

54. "We can understand why the serpent is said to speak and think; in reality it is not he that thinks and speaks but the woman does so in her heart" (Cassuto, *Commentary*, 142–43). Blenkinsopp considers the snake as an externalization of the woman's desire; see below, p. 118. This line of thought no doubt relies on identifying the "lurking thing" in Gen 4:7 as the externalization of Cain's experience of the temptation to sin.

form assumes that this recurrent impulse can be mastered; its aim is empowerment. In Gen 3:16b the opposite occurs. Cain had a choice, the woman does not. If indeed as it appears the Storyteller used a variation on a familiar saying to explain the origin of male domination, he gave it an ironic twist.

In one interpretation of 3:16b, the woman will desire to control her man but will lose that struggle.[55] Following immediately upon the punishment of the snake, it's natural to hear one as parallel to the other, to carry over the newly instituted hostile relations of humans and snakes (3:15b) to a new tension in the relations between man and woman (3:16b).[56] This interpretation has the virtue of connecting the two parts of 3:16b (the woman's desire and her eventual subjugation).

However, reading in this way, the prediction in 3:16b bears no clear connection to the woman's punishment; in this respect it would differ from the remarks made at the end of the punishment of the snake and the human. Considering Gen 3:16 in its parallels with the punishment of the human yields a suggestive reading of 3:16b. In the case of the ʾ*adam*, the ʾ*adamah* can be cursed "on his account" because of their intimate relationship *based in words*. It's implicit that the woman's punishment derives from the intimate relationship between man and woman (both in words and in physical intimacy). Just as the human is punished in terms of his work with the ʾ*adamah*, to which his life becomes subject, so the woman is punished in her work (with the man, so to speak): pregnancy and childbearing. Just as the human will return to dust, his material origin, so too will the woman return to the man, her material origin. She will return despite the pain of the increased pregnancies that she will suffer as a result of the punishment itself, pregnancies that her return makes possible. The upshot is that, like the man, she will also return to her material source (the man) and be subject to him.[57]

---

55. Ironically, the idea that Gen 3:16b is the prediction of a power struggle that the man will ultimately win was taken up both by Sarah Grimké, a nineteenth-century protofeminist ("Original Equality"), and by Susan Foh, a twentieth-century Christian evangelical for whom 3:16b provides the proof-text that patriarchy is divinely ordained ("Head of the Woman").

56. The prediction of human conflict appears in the Qurʾan at the expulsion from the Garden: (literally, "We said, Go forth, some of you enemies of others" (Surah 2:36; 7:24; 20:123).

57. See below, pp. 63-64. "Read in this way, both texts in Genesis 3 speak of return and subservience: the man, to the earth, for which he must toil; and the woman, to the

The Storyteller and the Garden of Eden

This completes the structure that the Storyteller used to build his tale of human origins with a systematic parallelism between the human and the woman and their interconnectedness, all founded on word plays. Each is first described in terms of material source, the human (*ha-ʾadam*) from the soil (*ha-ʾadamah*), the woman (*ha-ʾiššah*) from the man (*ha-ʾîš*). There can be no doubt that the springboard of the Garden of Eden story was the Storyteller's observation of the assonance of these words, from which he equated material and verbal origin. At that point he reflected on our fundamental tasks, tending the earth and reproduction, associating the former with the human and the latter with the woman as the very purpose for which they were created. This is explicit for the human (Gen 2:5, 15; 3:23) and implicit for the woman as she is punished in her work just as the human is punished in his. In the final piece of the word play, material origin becomes destiny as the human returns to the soil and the woman to the man, both now subject to their respective material origin as a consequence of the punishments.

As we'll see in discussing the punishments in the next chapter, the Storyteller doesn't view this as a happy state of affairs for women.[58] Phrased as a consequence of her punishment, women's subordination is an unfortunate condition; the story contains an implicit critique of patriarchy. It should be noted that there is no hint here of woman's inherent inferiority, of male domination inscribed in the natural hierarchy of all beings as this idea develops in Western philosophical thought.[59] Despite this obvious fact, belief in intrinsic male superiority based on concepts of natural order appear in allegorical readings of the Garden of Eden story early in first century C.E.[60] That Genesis 2–3 asserts that God at the outset created a gender hierarchy continues to be read into Genesis 2–3 to this day, usually based on the manner of the woman's creation (the man first, the woman from and for him). This, as discussed above, was necessitated

---

man, who will rule over her" (Loader, "Beginnings of Sexuality," 304). "It would seem that *tešûqah* (in Gen 3:16) is operating in conjunction with *tašûb* (in Gen 3:19) to form a type of *inclusio*" (Lohr, "Sexual Desire?" 246).

58. "It is noteworthy that to the writer this is not the ideal relation of the sexes, cf. 2:18, 23" (Skinner, *Genesis*, 83); according to Humbert, the author of 3:16b viewed it "like a curse" (*Études*, 187).

59. This idea of natural order derives, often explicitly, from Aristotle (see, e.g. *Politics* 1 1254b); Thomas Aquinas, *Summa Theologica* Part I Question 92 Article 1 Reply to Objection 2.

60. See within, pp. 11, 108n9.

by the way in which the story was built on wordplays and favors neither the man nor the woman.

The Tree of Life (Gen 2:9; 3:22–24)

Another transformation of a preexisting image involves the Tree of Life, one of the two trees that play such a large role in the story of the Garden of Eden. Both are planted in the Garden apparently at the same time ("And Yahweh *'elohim* caused to sprout from the soil every tree desirable in appearance and good for eating and the Tree of Life in the center of the Garden and the Tree of Knowing Good and Bad").

The syntax is awkward; the relation of the two trees, their proximity to one another, is confused by the phrase "in the center of the Garden" that separates them. Although there are other examples in the Hebrew Bible where two objects are separated by a phrase that applies to both, the least we can say is that this syntactical oddity points to a notional otherness. We only learn that the Tree of Knowing Good and Bad is also "in the center of the Garden" when the woman later identifies it in this way ("but of the fruit of the tree that is in the center of the Garden, God said . . ." 3:3). By having the woman refer to the Tree of Knowing in this way rather than by its name, the Storyteller subtly reminds his audience of the existence of the Tree of Life that earlier had been more explicitly identified as the one in the center of the Garden.[61]

Both trees are necessary to the narrative. Each is forbidden, the one at the outset, the other at the conclusion ("And Yahweh *'elohim* said, 'See, the human has become like one of us, in knowing good and bad, and now, lest he send forth his hand and take *also* from the Tree of Life and eat and live in perpetuity . . .'"). The word "also" makes it clear that God is barring the way to the Tree of Life *because* they had already eaten from the *other* tree.[62] It is only because the humans have already eaten from the Tree of Knowing that the Tree of Life is denied to them. This is the principal purpose of the narrative, to explain how we lost the possibility of some form of immortality, but gained instead the faculty, exceptional in the animal kingdom, of knowing good and bad.

---

61. Mettinger, *Eden Narrative*, 21–22.

62. "Also" is missing in some ancient versions, leading to the supposition that it was "an explicating plus" added later (Hendel, *Text*, 45).

The Storyteller and the Garden of Eden

The Tree of Life was not an invention of the Storyteller. It is one of the few images in the Garden of Eden story that appear elsewhere in the Hebrew Bible.[63] Found only in Proverbs, it never refers to an actual physical tree but rather is employed metaphorically in various contexts: it is "the fruit of the just" (11:30); "a wish fulfilled" (13:12); "a healing word" (15:4).

As part of the Wisdom literature, Proverbs privileges knowledge, but only the wisdom that flows from following Yahweh's teaching (*tôrah*). Its attitude toward wisdom is ambivalent, as it also warns against "being wise (*ḥakam*) in your own eyes," a possible effect of the Tree of Knowing, whence forbidden by God (Prov 3:5-7).[64] While the Garden of Eden story has a Tree of Knowing and a Tree of Life, in Proverbs 3 wisdom (*ḥokmah*) is the Tree of Life whose fruits yield understanding, peace, success, health, and long life, all "more precious than rubies" (3:7, 13-20). In the Garden of Eden story, the Storyteller has taken this metaphorical tree literally and juxtaposed it to a Tree of Knowing Good and Bad, both apparently similar to the other trees in the Garden.

The metaphorical Tree of Life in biblical imagery may itself be a transformation of the common idea that eating or drinking a substance can convey a certain attribute, especially prolonging life, a perennially popular type of magical thinking. Because food and drink are necessary to sustain life, the belief that some are more efficacious in this regard than others is not altogether improbable. The universality of such beliefs makes the search for ancient Near Eastern parallels unnecessary.[65] That in this case it's a tree rather than a plant (as in the *Epic of Gilgamesh*) is particularly appropriate in the context in which trees have been provided for food. Moreover, the connection of trees with immortality has some basis in observation. Trees live much longer than all other living things,[66]

---

63. On the Tree of Life in Israelite Wisdom literature, Stordalen, *Echoes*, 288-94, 372-77, 459-60, with bibliography. In the New Testament the Tree of Life is mentioned in Rev 2:7; 22:2, 14, 19. In Rev 2:7, repeated in 22:14, 19, it remains in the Garden of God and will be accessible to the righteous, while in Rev 22:2 there are two such trees whose leaves "are for the healing of nations."

64. The danger of wisdom is also expressed in Jer 8:8-9, its subservience to Yahweh, in Deut 4:6.

65. According to Sjöberg, "there is no evidence that there was a Tree of Life in Mesopotamian myth or cult" ("Eve and the Chameleon," 221).

66. As such they can serve as a permanent landmark (Gen 12:6; 13:18; 14:13; 18:1,4; Deut 11:30; Josh 19:33; Judg 4:11; 9:6; 1 Sam 10:3; 14:2; 22:6; 31:13; 1 Chr 10:12).

themselves approaching immortality ("for as the days of the tree are the days of my people").[67]

Whatever the prehistory of the idea of such a tree, the Tree of Life was an image that the Storyteller had at hand and could turn into a physical tree in the Garden. Our Storyteller, true to form, has placed the Tree of Life among the other trees in Eden as a concrete entity with edible fruit, just as he transformed the metaphorical expression "bone from my bones" into a literal physical description of the creation of the woman. According to the story, if the humans had not been expelled from the Garden (a proposition impossible based on the explanatory function of the narrative) and had retained access to the Tree of Life, we would have had some means for prolonging life and vigor. In other words, the Storyteller made the Tree of Life true to its name.

Knowing Good and Bad

Ignorance is the curse of God,
Knowledge the wing wherewith we fly to heaven.

—SHAKESPEARE *HENRY VI PART 2*

In the Garden narrative the Tree of Life held open the possibility of not dying, the closest humans could have come to the immortality characteristic of the divine. According to the story, there was a second possible way of becoming "like gods," represented as the effect of the fruit of a Tree of Knowing. It seems that the Storyteller could have left it at that, yet he has further specified it as the Tree of Knowing *Good and Bad*. Here too he seems to be calling into service a familiar phrase, 'knowing good and bad.'[68]

What the Storyteller intended to convey by this phrase is best understood when we consider it as an idiomatic expression in the ordinary language of the biblical period. Two examples drawn from spoken language

---

67. Isa 65:22.

68. Clark ("Legal Background," 267) suggests that J (presumed author of Gen 2–3) had begun simply with the Tree of Knowing as a better counter to the Tree of Life, and added "of good and evil" in order to make a point, now lost on us. According to Humbert, "c'est donc, en bref, l'arbre du Savoir ... Il s'agit d'une connaissance universelle et efficace qui rend expérimenté, avisé, capable d'agir, donc d'un 'Savoir' impliquant à la fois connaissance, discernement et, notamment, pouvoir" ("Faute d'Adam," 229).

should clarify its meaning. Barzillai, an aged ally of David, employs this phrase to describe his failing powers, "I am this day eighty years old. Can I discern [*literally*, know] between good and bad? Can your servant taste what I eat or what I drink? Can I hear any more the voice of singing men and singing women?"[69] The other end of the age spectrum is illustrated in the scene in which God tells Moses who will be allowed to enter the promised land, "Your children who now do not know good and bad—they will go there and I will give it to them and they will possess it."[70] Here knowing good and bad indicates reaching the age of reason.[71]

In these examples, it's evident that the ability to know good and bad belongs neither to the very old nor to the very young. It's an idiomatic description of fully functioning human intelligence. The Storyteller took this idiomatic expression and imputed it to the effect of a tree, a tree of his invention that he set alongside the familiar Tree of Life. The two trees together give graphic representation to what he considered two key aspects of humanity, intelligence and mortality. The Garden of Eden story is a narrative that describes how in choosing one we lost the possibility of putting off the other, how we ended up as we are, uniquely intelligent but humbled by our fragile hold on existence.

3:4 Your eyes will be opened ... 3:7 The eyes of both of them were opened.

While we're all concerned with the meaning of "knowing good and bad," no one seems to care much about the other effect, that the humans' "eyes were opened," assuming that the two effects were synonymous, that having one's eyes opened and knowing good and bad are two ways of saying the same thing. But the grammar of the text separates them as distinct entities.[72]

---

69. 2 Sam 19:36.

70. Deut 1:39; cf. Isa 7:13–15, where children eventually grow to "know" to "reject evil and choose good," perhaps an explication of the idiom in moral terms.

71. Buchanan, "Old Testament Meaning."

72. In 3:5 the repetition of *waw* differentiates the two effects (literally, "*and* your eyes will be opened *and* you will become like gods..."), BDB 253a. The same may be said of 3:7 ("and the eyes of both of them were opened and they knew they were naked"), although there the initial "and" may be taken as normal biblical style.

This is such a familiar image that it requires some effort to recognize it as a metaphor, used in the same way in ancient Israel as we use it now.[73] The basic meaning seems to be 'to see something you didn't see before,' 'to get it.'[74] In the latter sense it has nothing to do with physical vision, the literal act of seeing with the eyes.

In the language of Israelite religion, when someone has a vision beyond this world, it is said that Yahweh "opened his eyes,"[75] just as Yahweh Himself "sees" beyond the abilities of human sight.[76] By extension, it's also possible for Yahweh to "open someone's eyes" so that their eyes physically see something they hadn't noticed before.[77]

Here the idea of having one's eyes opened is an effect, not of Yahweh's power to open eyes, but of having eaten from the Tree of Knowing Good and Bad. It seems to be a further way of describing what it is to know good and bad. This made them "like gods" so that now they could, like Yahweh Himself, see more than is visible to the naked eye, see (in a figurative sense) more than any other creature. When the eyes of the two are opened they not only *know* they are naked, but also see it in a new way. It is another case of the Storyteller taking a common metaphor for knowing or understanding, and applying it both in its original figurative *and* in a physical sense in order to convey to the audience a vivid impression of this critical moment in the story.

At times the audience of a biblical text can take a passage literally, at times figuratively. Here we are called on to do both, and more. When the Tree of Knowing was planted among the others in the Garden, all the trees were described as "desirable in appearance (*neḥmad le-marʾeh*)," as we would say they looked good enough to eat (*ṭôb le-maʾakol*), and indeed they were. The woman paraphrases "desirable in appearance" as she considers whether or not to eat; she finds the Tree "attractive to the eyes"

---

73. Gen 21:19; Num 22:31; 24:4, 16.

74. Ps 119:18; Isa 42:6–7. In this sense the expression may be used to mean 'be aware or mindful of' (Jer 32:19), especially in entreaties to God: 1 Kgs 8:29, 52; 2 Kgs 19:16; Isa 37:17; 2 Chr 6: 20, 40; 7:15; Neh 1:6; Dan 9:18.

75. Num 22:31; 24:4, 16; 2 Kgs 6:17 (although the phrase is literal, the removal of physical blindness, in the sequel, 6:18–20). Also in the New Testament, Acts 26:17–18.

76. Jer 32:19; Job 28:24; 10:4. On what God sees versus what we see, Pidoux, "Encore les Deux Arbres," 41–43.

77. Gen 21:19 (Hagar and the well). This single exception makes one wonder whether or not the well had been there all along. Sasson ("Mother," 214) argues that the use of the verb *paqaḥ* rather than *pataḥ* "always implies enhanced consciousness."

(*taʾawah-hûʾ la-ʿênayim*). The Storyteller could have had her simply reiterate the original description (*neḥmad le-marʾeh*), as he has her do with "good to eat," but instead he substitutes a phrase that refers specifically to her eyes, eyes which soon will be opened to see something she hadn't seen before. She will physically see as she had, but what she sees will now be invested with meaning. This helps us, the audience, subtly refine what the Storyteller intended by "knowing good and bad."

2:4a These are the generations of the heavens and the earth when they were created [*lit.*, in their being created].
2:4b When [*lit.*, on the day] Yahweh *ʾelohîm* made earth and heavens

There seem to be two introductions to the Garden of Eden story here.[78] The first, Gen 2:4a ("these are the generations . . .") occurs as a formulaic structural element in Genesis, in some instances serving as the introduction to a genealogy, a list of someone's descendants,[79] in others as the preface to a narrative about a particular individual.[80] Here in Gen 2:4a it picks up on the first words of the story, taking as its point of departure the phrase "earth and heavens" in the following verse.

Elsewhere the formula "these are the generations of" invariably refers to progeny, either in a genealogical list or a narrative. It occurs uniquely in Gen 2:4a to refer to cosmic location (the above and the below, so to speak) rather than to individuals and so would be an immediate attention-getter. As it is used in Gen 2:4a "the generations of the heavens and the earth" makes no literal sense unless it is understood to be rooted in the details of the narrative: the soil (*ha-ʾadamah*) on the surface of the earth (*ha-ʾareṣ*) that brings forth the trees, the human being, and the animals. These are the offspring of the earth. The formulaic reference to offspring, whether part of the original story or added in the redaction, points to and anticipates the narrative's description of the creation of the trees, *ʾadam*, and the other animals from the *ʾadamah*.[81]

---

78. On Gen 2:4, see Carr, *Reading the Fractures*, 73–75; Blenkinsopp, "P and J," 7–8; Stordalen, "Gen 2,4"; Hess, "Gen 1–2."

79. Gen 5:1; 10:1; 11:10, 27; 25:12; 36:1, 9; also Num 3:1; Ruth 4:18; 1 Chr 1:29.

80. Gen 6:9 (Noah); 25:19 (Isaac); 37:2 (Joseph).

81. If 2:4a had been added as a transitional device by the redactor, it would provide a

At the same time (and in some contradiction) these offspring of the soil are themselves clearly divided into their respective realms, the earth or the heavens: "Yahweh ʾelohîm formed from the soil (ha-ʾadamah) every land animal and every bird of the heavens" (2:19). As we'll see, the story of the Garden of Eden revolves around the distinction between the earth and the heavens and the proper inhabitants of each. To the attentive listener, beginning the story this way indicates from its very first (rather singular) words that this will be its primary subject.

We should note that the word used for "the earth" in 2:4a and 2:4b is not ha-ʾadamah but ha-ʾareṣ. This follows the standard biblical convention of referring to the universe as the heavens and the earth (ha-šamayîm we-ha-ʾareṣ).[82] In the second part of Gen 2:4 ("When Yahweh ʾelohîm made earth and heavens") the order is inverted, giving precedence to the earth.[83] By inverting the expected order, the Storyteller makes it clear to his audience that it's the earth and its inhabitants that interest him.

Just as he used other idioms, like "bone from my bones" and a Tree of Life, here the Storyteller took a familiar expression that referred to God as the creator of the universe ("the heavens and the earth") and gave it a little twist in the very opening words of his story. By using this expression in the "these are the generations" formula, he provides a template for reading: "according to its native introduction the Story of Eden is not a creation story, but a story of what became of heaven and earth some time after their creation."[84]

From beginning to end, the Garden of Eden story plays with everyday language and imagery, even the name and idea of Eden itself.[85] It may also be that, as some have argued, an earlier creation myth having nothing to do with a garden or Eden was adapted by the Storyteller for his own purposes.[86] Whatever might have been the traditional elements that

---

concrete example of his methods in reshaping the materials at his disposal.

82. With and without the article, the combination "(the) heavens and (the) earth" occurs with some frequency, especially in blessings, vows, and praise of God as creator.

83. This order occurs elsewhere only in Ps 148:13.

84. Stordalen, "Gen 2,4," 175.

85. "We can assume with good reason that the story of Eden preserved in Genesis 2 and 3 is a refined version of an earlier and grosser account which was rich in mythological symbolism . . . These rejected elements, though removed from the story in Genesis, were current in the language of ancient Israel." (Neiman, "Eden," 110). For an examination of the imagery of Eden, see Stordalen, *Echoes*.

86. This is most ably argued by Humbert, *Études*, 48–81.

he brought into play, they were employed as background for the plot of a story whose main characters are defined on multiple levels by the words used to name them.[87]

How the Storyteller uses language has to play an indispensable role in interpretation, especially when it's evident that words have been chosen with extreme care and are themselves in some sense the very substance of the story. As we've seen, the construction of the narrative takes its point of departure from the wordplay on ʾadam and ʾadamah; from this it proceeds to ʾîš and ʾiššah. The rest of the story is built on this substructure and cannot be properly understood without it.

As *readers* (especially silent readers) we approach literature visually, we see words rather than hear them, and as a result we process them in a different way than when they come to us as sound. From a cultural point of view our literacy is not the same as that of people in the ancient world for whom stories were primarily heard. For us, a story is composed of images and characters. Wordplay on the written page doesn't really work for us, as is obvious when we compare hearing versus reading poetry or jokes.[88]

When I taught on the Navajo reservation, the students were required to recite the Pledge of Allegiance each morning. I was too young to fully appreciate it at the time, but the Navajo children recited the Pledge in their own way, with one pun after another. The only one I recall now is "one naked individual" for "one nation indivisible." Even though they spoke English as a second language, they were inveterate punsters.

Their relation to language was quite different from ours. Navajo was never a written language and great honor was accorded to those who spoke it well. The children told me that our instructor in Navajo, a missionary who had spent decades on the reservation and had written our textbook, *Navajo Made Easier*, spoke it like a five-year-old.

As I reflect on that experience, it seems clear that wordplay is most particularly an aspect of spoken rather that written language, playing a

---

87. "The author has not drawn his narrative from a single source ... Their [the sources, images, and ideas] present position and function in the narrative is due entirely to the creative imagination of the writer, and they indicate his capacity to assemble scattered strands from many sources into a compactly unified narrative" (McKenzie, "Literary Characteristics," 171).

88. Poetry is primarily oral. On poetic aspects of Genesis 2–3, see Wallace, *Eden Narrative*, 38–41; and on considerations of ancient literature as originally oral compositions, see Cooper, "Babbling On"; as meant to be heard, see within, pp. 7, 149–50.

much larger role for non-literate peoples than it does for us. The etiological narrative now found in Genesis 2–3 was constructed on the basis of a sequence of wordplays. Euphony, of which wordplay is a sub-type, is characteristic of oral performance. That there is euphony and parallelism points to an originally oral composition, one that was supposed to be heard rather than read silently. It is little wonder that we've missed the clues embedded but not concealed in the words of the story, clues that shape its mood as well as its meaning.

The intention of wordplay is to focus and delight the mind.[89] Recognizing a play on words is a pleasurable experience no matter the context.[90] Playing on words and assonance is characteristic of other biblical texts, but none uses them as systematically as does the Storyteller. Unlike an occasional wordplay, the prevalence of wordplays and adaptations of conventional images and expressions in the story of the Garden of Eden has profound implications for interpretation. As we've seen, nothing in the text is extraneous. Words are not wasted; on the contrary they have been chosen quite deliberately. Here words and ideas play off one another. They invite us into the construction of the story and into the mind of the Storyteller. "A responsible and proper articulation of the words in their linguistic patterns and in their precise formulations will reveal to us the texture and fabric of the writer's thought, not only what it is that he thinks, but as he thinks it."[91]

The pleasure of the text is as recoverable in biblical writings as in any great literature. "A close study of these writings in the original discovers

---

89. According to Cassuto (*Commentary*, 212–13), biblical narrative prose developed from oral epic poetry and continued some of its stylistic devices such as repetition of familiar phrases that served to, as he put it, "enchant" the audience. This may be true of familiar phrases, but the use of wordplays and puns by our Storyteller, as well as by the biblical prophets, is also calibrated to enrich meaning.

90. "Writers put together words in a certain pleasing order partly because the order pleases but also, very often, because the order helps them refine meanings, make meanings more memorable, more satisfyingly complex, so that what is well wrought in language can more powerfully engage the world of events, values, human and divine ends" (Alter, "Introduction," 15). The process by which the brain deals with ambiguity in language is extraordinarily complex, and it has been suggested that success in resolving the challenge results in pleasing surprise. On the technical side, see Coulson and Severens, "Hemispheric Asymmetry"; for a popular summary, see Pollack, *Pun Also Rises*, 31–53.

91. Muilenberg, "Form Criticism," 7. It remains an open question whether the association of words and ideas that we find in the story reflects a belief in the ontological significance of the words in and of themselves.

again and again, on every level from word choice and sentence structure to the deployment of large units of composition, a delight in the manifold exercise of literary craftsmanship."[92]

Now that we have a better idea of the story in terms of its language and imagery, of how sensitive the Storyteller was to the smallest detail, we can turn our attention to broader questions of meaning. Here we begin on more familiar ground, looking at the story in its explanatory function. As we recognize the precision in the Storyteller's use of language, we're encouraged to find it as well in the articulation of his views on the human condition, his description of who we are in terms of how we got to be this way.

---

92. Alter, "Introduction," 15.

FOUR

Crime and Punishment in Eden

O, that a man might know
The end of this day's business ere it come!
—SHAKESPEARE, *JULIUS CAESAR*

A CREATION STORY EXPLAINS how the universe as we know it came into existence. The creation narrative in the first chapter of Genesis is the parade example. An origin story, on the other hand, has a more restricted aim, to explain the existence of particular details of our reality, details that vary according to the purpose of the author. Some may be whimsical, others quite serious. Rudyard Kipling's *Just So Stories* explain phenomena ranging from the rough, wrinkled skin of the rhinoceros to the alphabet. As stories they get and hold the attention of children and adults alike because they are about us and the world we inhabit, although this is often implicit in the telling. The primordial history in Genesis 1–11 contains several origin stories. The most obvious is the one we know as the Tower of Babel, a story that focuses on the multiplicity of languages and peoples, explaining this diversity as a divine plan to reduce people's ability to act collectively.

From the Greek *aítios* meaning "cause," the word *etiology* is used to describe both creation and origin stories and it's easy to see that the story of the Garden of Eden is etiological, containing explanations for, among other things, the existence of weeds and labor pains and the peculiar locomotion of snakes.[1] These are presented as punishments for violation of the divine prohibition against eating from the Tree of Knowing Good and Bad.

After violating the prohibition the humans and the snake are punished, but the punishments that they receive bear no apparent relation to their crime. The common assumption is that God is reacting to *an act of disobedience*. The humans have acted autonomously, rebelling against God's will, and are punished for the *sin* of disobedience. This assumption has several difficulties, chief among them in failing to relate this offense to the punishments. There is a virtual conspiracy of silence on this apparent inconsistency in the logic of the story; the few who even consider the problem just throw up their hands.[2]

On the other hand, some have looked at the story in terms of divine justice.[3] There's the issue of proportionality: were the punishments for eating a piece of fruit just? Here the argument in favor claims that the crime was not the act of eating *per se* but disobeying a direct command from God.[4] The underlying assumption is that the punishments address the act of disobedience, itself predicated on a valorization of human autonomy over divine authority. No matter how trivial the command, disobedience is a sin, and when someone is a sinner, well, there's no end to what s/he might do. To this line of thought the particular circumstances of the narrative are irrelevant, it was all just a test, it could have been the violation of any command that triggered the punishments.

Further we might ask in what sense these punishments can be viewed as constructive. What exactly is their purpose? If the problem is disobedi-

---

1. Prov 30:18–19 refers to the mysterious movement of snakes.

2. E.g., "In each of the judgments which God pronounced in Gen 3:14–19 and 4:11–12, the nature of the curse has no essential relationship to the nature of the sin committed" (Busenitz, "Woman's Desire," 206). "If they ever did so, the punishments no longer fit the crime" (Bailey, "Initiation," 150). For a summary of partial explanations, see Stratton, *Out of Eden*, 141–42. Miller finds "correspondences" to the crime for the snake and the man, but not for the woman (*Genesis 1–11*, 28–31) and Clines recognizes the connection of the punishments of the man and woman to their work, the purpose of their being ("Noah's Flood," 135), although both fail to determine God's goal in imposing them. Arnold (*Genesis*, 68–71) correctly explains that their intention was to humble.

3. Cassuto, *Commentary*, 161–62.

4. Mettinger sees this as a recapitulation of the theme of the Deuteronomistic History. "*The Deuteronomistic notion of law is here repristinated to the divine commandment, addressed* in illo tempore *to the first human couple in the garden of Eden*" (*Eden Narrative*, 56; italics original).

ence, how do, say, labor pains make obedience to God more likely? If the punishments are arbitrary, their purpose can only be to inspire fear of God's wrath; that would lead us to question divine justice and open up a new theological dilemma. Yet the punishments inflicted on the characters don't appear to have any relationship to the problem of the human proclivity to disobedience. The lack of logical connection makes unlikely the commonly held view that the punishments are solely for disobedience. If this had been the case, they would have been anomalous, unconstructive, and fundamentally irrational.

For an example of unconstructive punishment, consider Augustine's addition to the biblical etiologies, that humans lost control over sexual arousal. Augustine observed that the desire for sex arrives on its own and is often difficult or impossible to suppress, while at times the body itself fails to engage. "In short, to say all in a word, what but disobedience was the punishment of disobedience in that sin? For what else is man's misery but his own disobedience to himself, so that in consequence of his not being willing to do what he could do, he now wills to do what he cannot?"[5]

According to Augustine, the sin of our first parents was an act of the will; disobedience was willful. If the will sinned by rebelling against God, then the will must be punished. The punishment resulted in the experience, apparently acutely felt by Augustine himself, of uncontrollable sexual desire. If one of the punishments involved a weakening of the will in all of Adam's descendants, reflecting Augustine's analysis of this fundamental human inability to control its sexual proclivities, this would prove a singularly unconstructive penalty. If, as Augustine assumes, perhaps correctly, that the decision to disobey God's command resulted from an act of the will, what would have been the divine purpose in weakening the will further? Despite the illogicality of a punishment that makes recidivism more rather than less likely, Augustine's liberty to invent an etiology unconnected to the text at least shows an interest in finding some connection between what he supposed to be the punishment and what he assumed to be the crime, the willful act of disobedience itself.[6]

---

5. Augustine, *City of God* XIV 15.

6. We can compare a more modern attempt to find a correspondence between crime and punishment by Clines, for whom the crime is an attempt to be independent from God and the punishment, equally unconstructive, is further estrangement from God (Clines, "Noah's Flood," 135).

If we are to credit its author with a well-crafted story, we must dig deeper for the rationale behind the punishments. If we view them simply as attempts by the Storyteller to explain some of life's difficulties without looking for what they have in common and how *precisely* they relate to the prior act of disobedience, we implicitly assume he has not really thought the narrative through. It's ironic that those who claim to take the biblical text seriously refuse to consider it as a serious text, carefully constructed with a consistent internal logic.

It would be at least as satisfying to understand the connection between what the humans did and God's reaction as it was to explain the naming-the-animals episode in Genesis 2. In the broadest possible terms, the argument in the following pages goes as follows: by eating from the forbidden tree, the human beings created a problem for God and the punishments He imposes represent His attempt to resolve it.[7] The history of interpretation has gone astray in failing to identify that problem and in consequence failing to make sense of the punishments. Indeed, determining the logical relation of crime to punishment will be key to understanding the choice of etiologies in Genesis 3 and to interpreting the story in its entirety.

ETIOLOGIES AS PUNISHMENTS: GENESIS 3:14–19

In this passage, the snake changes its form of locomotion, the human is condemned to struggle for subsistence, and the woman is made subject to the ordeals of childbirth. It is usually assumed that these punishments are simply penalties for sin, in particular for the sin of disobeying God's explicit command to refrain from eating from the Tree of Knowing Good and Bad. This assumption makes a significant part of the story superfluous. It obscures the effect of having eaten from that particular tree (Gen 3:7) and ignores God's admission that by eating the pair thereby attained a characteristic of the divine (3:22).

What, one might well ask, was God thinking? What effect did He imagine the punishments would have? Looked at as a whole, the punish-

---

7. "The new characteristic acquired by man through eating the fruit poses a problem for Yahweh God . . . That the man might try to eat the fruit [from the other tree] can be taken as a difficulty primarily because Yahweh God takes action to avert the possibility. There is no notion of punishment here since the man has not had a chance to do anything" (Culley, "Action Sequences," 29).

Crime and Punishment in Eden

ments in the third chapter of Genesis go beyond simply inflicting pain or making life more difficult. They have a clear goal. Let's take a look at them in detail, beginning with the first punishment meted out, that of the snake.

> 3:14–15Because you did this, cursed are you among all the livestock and among all the wild animals. On your belly you will move and dust you will eat all the days of your life. Enmity I will establish between you and the woman and between your offspring and her offspring. It [her offspring] will crush your head and you will strike it [her offspring] at the heel.

In the first part of its punishment the snake goes from being "judicious (ʿarûm) among every (kind of) land animal that Yahweh ʾelohîm had made" (3:1) to "cursed (ʾarûr) among every (kind of) livestock and every (kind of) land animal" (3:14). Its punishment consists in a new form of locomotion, going about on its belly.[8] Slithering on the ground undercuts the snake's once-superior status in the animal world. In many species including ours even a momentary act of prostration serves as a signal of submission, self-humbling as a gesture of lower status. The phrase "cursed are you among . . ." in 3:14 mimics the description of the snake in 3:1, with a wordplay on "cursed" (ʾarûr) and "judicious" (ʿarûm). The juxtaposition of these phrases underlines the reversal of the snake's status among animal species.

This is precisely what God rubs in by pointing out to the snake that, as a consequence of its transformation, "dust you will eat all the days of your life" (3:14). Eating or licking dust is apparently a common way to describe humiliation.[9] If we assume that the Storyteller constructed the narrative with care, it's difficult to overlook the straightforward parallel he invites us to draw between this and the concluding statement in the human's punishment, "for dust you are and to dust you will return" (3:19b). Both reiterate the word *dust*, a term of scorn that was deliberately added to the description of the creation of the human.[10]

---

8. The snake's unique form of movement was considered one of the most remarkable aspects of creation (Prov 30:18–19).

9. The enemies of Israel will "lick dust like a snake" (Mic 7:17); "with their faces to the earth they will bow down to you and lick the dust of your feet" (Isa 49:23); "its enemies will lick dust" (Ps 72:9).

10. Because of its abundance, dust can imply worthlessness. Because it is walked on or trampled underfoot, it can indicate low status, but also, like sand and stars, it can be

These concluding remarks about "eating dust" and "turning to dust" seem gratuitous and mean-spirited. However each points to a kind of inferior station. The snake is explicitly compared to its fellow creatures; among them it is the only one that will crawl and eat dust. In the case of the human being, our mortality is implicitly compared to divine immortality. We don't want to be reminded that we're going to die; returning to dust casts a shadow over all sense of the worthiness of human endeavor.

Indeed the punishment of the snake provides the clues that the Storyteller has left us for interpreting the punishments of the humans. The second part of the snake's punishment doesn't concern the snake alone. The hostility between snakes and human beings that is established by the punishment of the snake is life threatening to both, a kind of permanent state of war between the species.[11] It should be noted that such a situation makes sense only for mortal beings whose lives are thereby directly put at risk, a significant point when we consider whether the punishments include the loss of immortality. The snake's punishment serves to frame the ensuing punishments of the man and woman in terms of increased danger to their lives, punishments that are based on their mortality.

The story presumes the existence of gender roles. It is in these roles that the man and woman are penalized. In the punishment of the man, "the soil is cursed on your account." Man, viewed as worker of the soil, the task for which he was created (2:5, 15; 3:23), will have to overcome new obstacles in order to survive. His food supply is much reduced in quality, so that what he now eats will reflect his disobedience in eating something prohibited. "Because you have heeded your woman and eaten from the tree about which I commanded you" (3:17a) reiterates the prohibition and the act of disobedience. It is followed by "you will eat cultivated plants" (3:18b)[12] and then, lest the point be lost, by "in the sweat of your face you will eat food" (3:19). The connection between the human (ha-'adam) and the soil (ha-'adamah) is repeated in the curse on the soil

---

used as a metaphor when a biblical writer wanted to evoke an enormous uncountable quantity of something desirable, like descendants (Hillers, "Dust," with examples from the Bible and other areas of the ancient Near East).

11. Snakes were a common source of danger in ancient Israel (Num 21:6–9; Deut 8:15; Isa 30:6; Jer 8:17; Amos 5:19; Qoh 10:8).

12. Until then he had been provided with food from the trees of the Garden (2:17). The punishment anticipates the expulsion when these are no longer accessible. One might take this as an indication that the story of disobedience and punishment was once independent of the theme of Eden and expulsion.

Crime and Punishment in Eden

(3:17b) and in his return to dust (3:19b). Threats to the food supply signal the new possibility of famine and starvation. "The economic problem, the struggle for subsistence, always has been hitherto the primary, most pressing problem of the human race."[13] Although the human being had been warned that eating would cause death ("when you eat from it be assured that you will die"), as a result of the curse on the earth he instead faces a more precarious existence.

Parallel to this, the woman's survival is threatened by the dangers newly inherent in procreation; even if she survive childbirth (and the rate of maternal death in childbirth was vastly higher in the past than it is today), her procreative labor will be riddled with pain. For both the man and the woman, life is now filled with suffering; the same word for suffering/toil (ʿiṣṣabôn) is used for each of them. The man and the woman are punished in the tasks for which they were created, the man to work the land and provide food, the woman to bear children, tasks that henceforward will be a painful struggle. These tasks had as their basic purpose to sustain human life in the present and the future. From now on, in various ways, human survival will be less secure.

This is the reality that the Storyteller sets out to explain. His question appears to be, why is life so tough? He answers the question he has posed by attributing the situation to divine decree. The explanatory function of the narrative is clear, but its meaning has been widely misunderstood.

The punishments of all the characters address their mortality. We can consider whether the narrative intends to explain mortality itself only with a fuller consideration of the story. However, we have to keep in mind the impact of the punishments, that they underscore the fact that human beings are mortal, that we must struggle to survive, that we are now burdened by difficulties that make survival more problematical. These punishments can be appropriate only if the "crime" for which they were punished is somehow related to mortality itself. What is the point of making our hold on existence more tenuous?

To answer this we must examine these verses more closely. In the punishments God addresses the characters in turn and each of His statements consists of two parts. First comes the specific punishment, then a

---

13. Keynes, "Economic Possibilities," 210. The stress on eating throughout recalls the creation story in Genesis 1 with its focus on the survival of the various species via reproduction (Gen 1:11–12, 22, 27–28) and food supply (1:29–30). Walsh takes eating as the dominant motif in the story ("Genesis 2:4b—3:24").

statement on its indirect effect. The snake will not only crawl, it will eat dust; not only will it become an enemy of humankind, it will attack and be attacked. The woman will suffer in painful multiple pregnancies, and she will be subject to male domination. The human being will not only have to work much harder, but the quality of his food will decline, and he is told that he is, after all, just dust.

Not part of the punishment strictly speaking, this remark serves to remind him of his mortality, now underlined by increased threats to his survival. If he has become godlike in one respect (3:22), he still lacks the greatest attribute of divinity, immortality. He is reminded of this not only in the punishment, which as it were enlarges upon his mortality, but also in this parting shot about his ultimate fate, that he will return to dust.

Most challenging to present-day readers is the way in which the Storyteller treats the female character. Made from the man, she ends up subject to him, just as the man becomes subject to the recalcitrant soil of his own material origin.[14] The woman, whose punishment is tied to her role as mother, is now "ruled" by the man responsible for her pregnancies, "You are drawn back to your man, and he will rule over you." This line alone has caused many women (and some men) to declare the Bible (and the God it represents) hopelessly patriarchal, to close the book and never open it again. Whether this is a fair assessment remains to be seen as we look at this verse in context.

Various attempts by modern scholars to "depatriarchalize" Genesis 2–3 have not proven successful.[15] This results from their reading the narrative within the context of "the Fall," as a story about sin and punishment. According to "the Fall" the woman commits the first sin and then also leads the man to sin. When the punishments are understood to include the loss of human immortality, the burden of guilt placed on the woman increases exponentially. When we remove the template of "the Fall" from our reading, all these implications disappear with it.

A new perspective on the role of the woman opens up when we consider the punishments more closely. The question properly posed is

---

14. "Working the land is a burden in Genesis 3, one that comes to an end only when the land reabsorbs the farmer at death. The land wins. The earth (*'ādāmâ*) triumphs over the earthling (*'ādām*)" (Levenson, *Resurrection*, 32).

15. For surveys of feminist interpretations, Abraham, *Eve*; Kimelman, "Seduction of Eve"; Milne, "Eve and Adam"; Milne, "Patriarchal Stamp of Scripture"; Lanser, "(Feminist) Criticism in the Garden."

the connection between Gen 3:16 and the "crime" of the woman. The Storyteller has structured the woman's punishment in exactly the same way as the punishments of the snake and the human. In each case there is the punishment itself followed immediately by a description of its effect. The snake, cursed, will now crawl on its belly; the effect is that it will eat dust. It is also made hostile to humans and vice versa; in consequence each will try to attack the other. For the man, the soil is cursed; it will now bring forth weeds and thorny plants. As a result, food production will be more difficult ("by the sweat of your face you will eat food"). As for the woman, she is punished with suffering in her role in childbearing, parallel to the man's suffering in his gender-specific role, and, as a result, she will be "ruled" by her husband. Here the writer had to choose one hardship for each of the characters, and the choices he made are not unsympathetic to their plight. These hardships are in fact what the Storyteller set out to explain: why snakes crawl and attack humans, why food production is so difficult, why women suffer in childbirth. They are all, needless to say, depicted as punishments decreed by God.

What light does this shed on Gen 3:16? In what sense can we understand the relation between "you are drawn back to your man, and he will rule over you" and the punishment of harder labor and multiple difficult pregnancies? The linchpin lies in the first half of 3:16b. Whether *tešûqah*, usually translated as "desire," actually means "return," the result in either case is the same, as her desire would cause her to return to him despite the pregnancies that ensue.[16] The woman's return to her man will exacerbate the punishment. The consequence of her return will be more debilitating pregnancies, which, coupled with increased work, will reduce her to greater dependence upon and, finally, subordination to her husband.[17] If the Storyteller intended to relate male domination to the preceding punishment, he may have concluded, as has often been done, that "biology is destiny," that multiple pregnancies make male domination inevitable.[18]

How can we apply what we have learned from the story itself, from the parallels to the concluding statements made to the snake and the man? In the case of the snake there are two punishments with their respective comments on what the snake's life will be like. Crawling results in the

---

16. For a detailed discussion of *tešûqah*, see above, pp. 40-44.

17. On the relation of Gen 3:16 to the roles and status of women in ancient Israel, see Meyers, *Discovering Eve*, especially 95-121, assuming an early date for the story.

18. On male domination in the story, see Yee, "Gender," 185-87.

humiliation of eating dust ("you will eat dust all the days of your life"). Enmity results in danger for snakes and for humans ("they will crush you on the head and you will strike them at the heel").

For the human, we have a single punishment, the soil is cursed ("on your account"). As a result, we must now submit to painstaking labor to produce food from the ground ("by the sweat of your face . . ."). We will have poorer quality food ("you will eat plants of the field" rather than fruit from the trees in the Garden). The remarks directed at the human conclude with a reminder of mortality ("to dust you will return").

In the case of the woman, there are two punishments: increased labor (just as for the man) and pregnancies, and pain in childbearing. Her continued return will increase the severity of these punishments and the upshot will be the man's position of dominance.

In all three cases of the remarks subsequent to the specific punishments, God is *describing* what life will now be like for each of the characters. This may or may not imply a change from the preexisting situation. The human will return to the soil not because of any preceding event but "because from it you were taken" (3:19). The woman's inclination (assumed to be part of her nature) will cause her to return to the man, her material source, just as he will return to the soil, his material source.[19]

We have to keep in mind that these conditions (snakes crawling, people struggling for subsistence, women suffering in childbirth under male domination) were the starting-point of the story, the difficult circumstances of everyday life as the Storyteller observed them. He doesn't intend to *justify* these conditions but merely to describe them by way of providing an explanation for how they originated.

It should be apparent that we should not look for something positive in Gen 3:16. Commentators have often attempted to interpret the woman's punishment as promise or consolation. According to Luther, it is "happy and joyful" (*laeta et hilaris*), as she is given "the hope of eternal

---

19. "In fact, this second story [Gen 3] ends up, on the one hand, with the ʾiššâ who compulsorily returns to ʾîš (ʾel-ʾîšēk tĕšûqātēk) and, so to speak, is reabsorbed by him (hûʾ yimšol-bāk) (Gen 3:16, correlated to Gen 2:18-23), and, on the other hand, with ʾādām who compulsorily returns to and is reabsorbed by the earth (šûbĕkā ʾel-hāʾădāmâ, ʾel-ʿāpār tāšûb) (Gen 3:17-19, correlated to Gen 2:4b-8)" (Tosato, "On Gen 2:24," 392). "It is the final reuniting of each which the artificial etymology depicts in each case: man reuniting with the earth (ʾădāmâ) in death and man reuniting with the woman (ʾiššâ) to create life" (Meier, "Linguistic Clues," 21).

Crime and Punishment in Eden

life and the honor of motherhood."[20] However, in structural terms, the woman's increased pregnancies and concomitant suffering parallel the curse on the snake and the curse on the soil.[21] This view of motherhood is in direct contradiction to the normative biblical view of procreation as an unalloyed good (even in the case of Rachel, for whom it proves fatal).[22] In general, "the reward most often bestowed on biblical women is motherhood."[23] On the contrary, in Gen 3:16 the woman is punished as a mother and there is nothing positive in the analogues with the snake and the human.

Much earlier, before the story was fixed in the form in which we now have it, someone decided that spin in a positive direction was necessary and added the verse in which the human names the woman Eve, "because she became the mother of all life" (3:20). Similarly in the verse that connects the story of the Garden of Eden with that of Cain and Abel (4:1), Eve names Cain and provides the name with an etymology in which she declares herself a creator on par with Yahweh Himself ("She said, I have made a man as has Yahweh").[24] These verses put motherhood on a pedestal that is clearly out of line with the intent of the punishment of the woman that highlights the suffering of women precisely in their role as mothers.[25]

---

20. Martin Luther, *Lectures on Genesis 1–5*, on Gen 3:16. Similarly, Cassuto, *Commentary*, 163.

21. "In the punishment over the woman the concept of procreation is introduced into the story—ironically not in the conventional perspective of a blessing (Ps 127:3–5; 128:3–4), but as a curse" (Stordalen, *Echoes*, 248). Similarly the view of agricultural work as hard labor is unusual (Skinner, *Genesis*, 84).

22. Gen 35:16–19. Childbearing (of boys) confers status. Compare the problem of the barren wife in Gen 11:30; 17:15–19; 18:9–15 (Sarah); 24:60; 25:21 (Rebekah); 29:30–35; 30:1–24 (Rachel and Leah); 1 Sam 1:1–19 (Hannah); also Gen 20:17–18 (Abimelech's wife and female servants); Judg 13 (the mother of Samson); see Bal, "Rhetoric of Sexuality," 349. The custom of levirate marriage also demonstrates the critical problem of the childless man, even deceased; in socioeconomic terms, a son is an heir, a means of maintaining property rights. Theologically, paternity is "the only form of immortality available in a culture without a belief in the afterlife" (Caird, *Language*, 141).

23. Shectman, *Women in the Pentateuch*, 44.

24. The verb here, usually translated "acquired," should be understood as "made," as in Gen 14:19, 22, particularly in the light of its direct object, "a man."

25. For further discussion of Gen 3:20 a gloss, see below, pp. 94–96, 127–29. On its relation to Gen 4:1, see above, p. 3n5. On "mother of all the living" as an honorary title, see Kikawada, "Two Notes on Eve."

If this is the Storyteller's take on maternity, what does he make of male domination? Taken in isolation, "he will rule over you" appears to ordain patriarchy as women's punishment for the disobedience of the first woman; it reads as a divine decree. The way it is phrased gives the impression that this outcome is perfectly okay with God. We have to work out from the story itself why this should be so.

This involves looking at the events in the story from God's point of view. First of all, it's important to see that He holds the woman responsible. This is apparent from the questioning of each. God begins by asking the man whether he had eaten from the forbidden tree, then He asks the woman the broader question, "What is this you have done?" "The expression carries with it a sense of finality, of an action taken which can never be undone."[26] From God's point of view the man's disobedience is due to his following the lead of the woman. His accusation "because you heeded your woman and ate . . ." points directly to the woman and subsumes the man's own act of disobedience to hers.

Many readers have sought to find justice in what they take to be the divine decree of male "rule" as the woman's punishment for her role in the man's violating the divine prohibition, as if he had no personal responsibility of his own, as indeed he claims when he tries to pass the blame on to her. If we accept his excuse, and focus on the first part of God's accusation, we overlook the fact that it was *his* decision to eat, that *he* shouldn't have disobeyed, no matter the circumstances.

In such arguments there is always the sense that the woman had stepped out of line by instigating the man to act against God's express command. The line that she crossed is one inscribed in nature. This presumes the Western philosophical tradition in which women are considered to be inherently inferior to men. They are viewed as less rational, more curious (compare Pandora), more gullible (Eve, "deceived" by the snake is the parade example) and by definition benefit from male control.[27] Male domination is understood to be an essential part of a well-ordered society. This presumes that men were created with natural authority, so that the violation began not with the disobedience but with the man's submission

---

26. Savran, "Beastly Speech," 49.

27. From Aristotle on, reason is held to be the male quality par excellence. Aristotle's view of women as inferior by nature was adopted by the Jewish philosopher Philo and passed from him to Origen and Christian thought; for Aquinas, Aristotle was "the Philosopher." On the tradition of reason identified as male, see Lloyd, *Man of Reason*.

to a woman ("because you heeded your woman . . ."). "He will rule over you" would set things to right again; it would reestablish the status quo ante as God had intended it to be.

In terms of the story itself the problem with this line of reasoning is that it's at odds with the transformational impact of the punishments and ignores their structure. We've seen that "he will rule over you" is *not* one of the punishments, rather it is one of the summary remarks on what a woman's life will be like as a result of the newly instituted condition involving multiple difficult pregnancies. Only in her new post-punishment condition will biology become destiny. And, instead of viewing male domination as part and parcel of a social hierarchy intended by God from the outset, the Storyteller implies that it was only *after* the critical moment when the woman chose to eat the fruit that male "rule" becomes particularly suitable *from God's point of view*. We'll have to examine the punishments more closely in order to better understand what God saw as the purpose that male domination serves in the new situation brought about by the disobedience.

This leads us to the argument regarding divine justice that is based, more appropriately, on the woman's larger role in violating the prohibition. The differential treatment of the woman in the punishments simply reflects the Storyteller's perception of female subordination in his society. In the terms set by the story, he accounts for it by according her greater responsibility for bringing about a state of affairs opposed to God's wishes.

By giving the woman the more active role (leading many commentators to note the passive role of the man in the critical scene, whereas male passivity in patriarchal society is typically condemned), by representing her thought process as she decides what to do while omitting that of the man, the Storyteller leads his audience to focus on the female character. Having just presented her in the most endearing light, through the eyes of the man seeing her for the first time, he now turns the spotlight on her alone, leaving the man present but effectively in the dark. Whatever the consequences of disobeying, there is no doubt that in the story the primary responsibility has been assigned to her.

Aquinas observed that the punishment of the woman exceeded that of the man, although he drew from this the unfortunate conclusion that her "sin" must therefore have been greater.[28] Indeed in the accusation

---

28. Thomas Aquinas, *Summa Theologica* II /2 Question 163 Article 4, presuming the sin of disobedience as the issue in the story.

directed at the man, "because you heeded your woman" (3:17a), God Himself seems to accept the half of the man's defense in which he shifts the blame to the woman ("*she* gave to me from the tree and I ate"), ignoring the other half ("the woman whom *You* gave to be with me") in which he holds God responsible for providing him with the woman in the first place. The man's self-serving attempt to evade responsibility by ultimately blaming God hardly makes a case for intrinsic male superiority.

According to the story the woman acts independently and is made responsible for the consequences of her act (for which God Himself holds her to account). However she is only responsible for her actions and their immediate effects and *not* for what happens afterwards, namely God's reaction, for which He has His own reasons.

This leads us to put some fundamental questions to the text. What precisely does God hold the woman responsible for and how does this relate to her subordination to the man? And, more generally, what happens in the course of events that makes these particular punishments appropriate? What does God intend to accomplish by them? When we recognize the purpose of the punishments we'll be able to see how perfectly suitable they are to what the characters did, and the story will become much more coherent.

In order to find an answer to these questions we turn again to Gen 3:14–19. We've seen that what the punishments have in common is that they are humbling. The snake's superiority to its fellow creatures is counterbalanced by an undignified way of moving about. Human beings will now struggle in order to find sustenance from the "plants of the field (cultivated plants)" rather than from the fruit of the trees in the Garden.[29] Women will suffer in their particular task of mothering. There is something demeaning for each of the characters.

The concluding remarks that follow each of the punishments emphasize this purpose. The humbling of the snake is the most apparent; henceforward it will eat dust. The man is reminded of his mortality in the cruelest possible terms, his return to dust. His life, now a struggle to survive, will come to naught. He is also reminded of his lowly origin: "what, after all, could be more humbling than to be told that one was made out of dust?"[30] "The irony (and the punishment) is that in the in-

---

29. On humbling by way of food as a divine tactic, Deut 8:1–3.
30. Hayter, "The New Eve," 99.

terim between his emergence from the dust and his return thereto, he is to be a slave to the ground, toiling for his bread."[31] For the woman, "just where the woman finds her fulfillment in life, her honor and her joy, namely in her relationship to her husband and as mother of her children, there too she finds that it is not pure bliss, but pain, burden, humiliation and subordination."[32]

In effect, male domination will reduce the status of the woman. It is, in the view of the Storyteller, the manner in which women across the board suffer humiliation. He examined his social world to find the particular way in which women were humiliated (parallel to the snake's eating dust) and identified it as their subordinate social status. In terms of the etiological function of the narrative, he accounts for it by according her greater responsibility for bringing about a state of affairs opposed to God's wishes. The woman is more culpable as she not only was the first to violate the prohibition but also instigated the man to disobey.

Some have argued that male domination is simply a disordered social relationship between the sexes where both suffer. In contemporary thought, in male-dominated ('macho') societies men (and boys) are required to suppress their feelings and so become emotional cripples. But this isn't what the Storyteller had in mind. The woman, in her relation to the man, in her being in the world, is humiliated; he is not. It's absurd to maintain that women's subjection is somehow equivalent to men's power over them. She is unquestionably left in a more wretched position than the man and God's final words to the woman (the last time that He addresses her) point to this inevitability.

What did the characters do to merit such humiliation? God Himself explains His motive: "The human has become as one of us, knowing good and bad, now lest he reach out his hand and *also* take from the Tree of Life and live in perpetuity" (3:22). In other words, the humans, having eaten from the Tree of Knowing Good and Bad, have gained a quasi-divine quality, and God makes it clear that He is driving them out in order to prevent their attaining yet another.

According to the story, God singles out the woman for greater humiliation because of her prominent role in raising human beings a rung

---

31. Levenson, *Resurrection*, 32.

32. Westermann, *Genesis 1-11*, 263. In his commentary on Gen 3:16, Luther notes that "the female sex has been greatly humbled and afflicted" (*Lectures on Genesis 1-5*, 200).

in godlikeness, because she was responsible for our making inroads on the distinction between divine and human. The Storyteller chose the woman for this role in order to account for women's inferior social status. The existence of male domination, which the Storyteller viewed as a negative condition in women's lives, required that the story be framed in such a way that a woman had to be the primary actor.

"He will rule over you." Patriarchy, the subordination of the wife to her husband's authority, is the social reality that the Storyteller tackles in this one phrase. It is not often enough observed that he recognized male domination as a social practice and framed it in the context of the negative corollaries of the other punishments, structurally parallel to eating dust (3:14), murderous aggression (snake and human, 3:15), and the struggle to provide subsistence from a now intractable soil (3:19). In terms of the situation of each character subsequent to the punishments, the snake will eat dust, the man will eat the "plants of the field," and the woman, as we might say, will eat crow.

It's altogether remarkable that the Storyteller even notices the existence of male domination, feels obligated to explain it, and moreover places it in such negative company. The culture of biblical Israel was patriarchal through and through, and the Storyteller is surprisingly critical of it. We must keep in mind that male domination did not actually come into existence with this statement; it was already an established social reality that the Storyteller viewed as worthy of explanation. The story no more intends to legitimate patriarchy than to endorse poisonous snakebite.

It is beyond doubt that the Storyteller assumes that male domination is not a happy state of affairs for women. Nor, as we have seen, is it imposed as a punishment (strictly speaking, the woman's punishment is limited to physical affliction). In the two-part structure of the three verdicts, "he will rule over you" falls within the remarks that follow the punishments as characterizations of how life will be from now on. There is nothing positive in any of this.

As the Storyteller attempted to provide an explanation for the male-dominated society in which he lived, he showed his sympathy for women's plight by choosing to give a woman credit for the one quality that he identified as the source of human preeminence. It was not the act of disobedience itself but the *result* of that act that occasioned the punishments. "The result of the eating was a permanent alteration of human consciousness,"³³ a transformation of the nature of what it is to be human that, according to the story, made us "like gods." The woman was made to suffer more (both in terms of physical pain and the indignity of male domination) not because she was more gullible or rebellious or proud, but simply because she was the one who managed to subvert God's determination to keep us in the place in which He had created us.³⁴ From God's point of view she's more culpable, from our point of view, she's a hero, risking death that we might attain a "godlike" status.³⁵ Whether the social consequences she suffers are just or not is left to the audience to decide, but it's clear where the Storyteller stands.

THE OUTLIER ETIOLOGY

2:24That's why a man (*'îš*) leaves his father and his mother and sticks with his woman (*'ištô*) and they become one flesh.

Here we find the one etiology that stands outside the climactic scene of eating and the ensuing divine response in which all the other etiologies are found. This alone should raise some suspicion about its relation to the rest of the story. This "statement of fact" follows upon and draws a conclusion from the man's exclamation upon seeing the woman for the first time. While the latter expresses his immediate reaction, Gen 2:24 generalizes and projects the man's feelings into some sort of relationship, marital or sexual or both.

It is generally assumed that the verse intends to provide an etiology for marriage. In contemporary arguments on the definition of marriage and the concomitant legal battles against gay marriage Genesis 2:24 remains a biblical proof-text. More recently the notion has gained traction that what is described here refers to sexual desire and its consummation in "one flesh" and has nothing to do with marriage as a social institution.³⁶

---

33. Williams describes the fruit as a "mind-altering substance" ("Genesis 3," 276).

34. Whether this is understood as a state of childlike obedience (Humbert, *Études*) or without the complicating possibilities of culture (Pfeiffer, "Wisdom and Vision").

35. "A certain degree of ambiguity is created with regard to the act of eating the fruit. It is a wrong which brings an advantage and a gain which brings a disadvantage" (Culley, "Action Sequences," 31); see also Jobling, *Sense of Biblical Narrative*, 26.

36. "How can one explain the attraction between the sexes that is strong enough to tear a man away from father and mother? . . . The point of this entire episode is to affirm

Both views are represented in the New Testament. On the one hand, Jesus cites this verse in an argument against divorce,[37] and Paul uses it as a metaphor for the relationship between Christ (as the husband) and the Church (as the wife).[38] On the other hand, elsewhere Paul uses the image of "one flesh" to describe both spiritual union with God and Christ as well as sex with a prostitute.[39] Whether "one flesh" refers to mutuality in marriage or to the sexual act (or the child born as a result), all we can say with certainty at this point is that the verse is expressly explanatory ("That's why . . ."), based on the preceding creation of the woman and the man's acceptance of her as the missing "helper."

Some readers have observed that there are problems with Gen 2:24 as part of the narrative itself. Because of the abrupt shift of voice, it does not fit well into its immediate context. Who's speaking here? Is it one of the characters in the story or the narrator we've had all along? If Gen 2:24 continues the man's speech, it is incompatible with the poetic style of his exclamation in v. 23. If it's a statement by the narrator, it certainly doesn't suit his style either. If it's a disembodied voice independent of the narrator, it violates the simple structure of the story where we have only the characters and the narrator.

Furthermore, Gen 2:24 stands outside the situational logic of the story. It contradicts the reason given for the woman's creation in the first place, that the man is alone. It is a broad generalization that doesn't apply in any way to the characters in the story who have neither father nor mother. In v. 18, the problem is defined as the solitary human, while v. 24 involves the opposite, separation within the community of the family.[40]

---

human sexuality" (Tucker, "Creation and Fall," 116). Among those who see this verse as explaining sexual desire, von Rad, *Genesis*, 84–85; Trible, *Rhetoric*, 94–105. Tosato evaluates various interpretations of Gen 2:24 with additional bibliography ("On Gen 2:24," especially 398–409). On the entire history of reading sexuality in Genesis 2–3, see Turner, *One Flesh*.

37. Mark 10:1–12; Matt 19:3–12. For an illuminating examination of the use of Gen 2:24 in these passages, see Daube, *New Testament and Rabbinic Judaism*, 71–85 (also, in greater detail, Loader, *Septuagint, Sexuality*, 79–127). Divorce (except in cases of adultery) was prohibited for centuries in Christian countries based on the application of "one flesh" to the marriage bond in the Gospels.

38. Eph 5:21–33. "In Eph 5:32–33 the readers are instructed that the metaphorical application (*mysterion*) of Gen 2:24 to Christ and the Church does not cancel the literal obligation of mutual love between husband and wife" (Caird, *Language*, 186).

39. 1 Cor 6:12–20.

40. For this and further observations on the contrast between Gen 2:24 and its con-

There's yet more evidence that this verse is a later addition by a different writer. Referring only to future generations, it takes the reader outside the entire context in which the story takes place and to which it is otherwise strictly limited. In Genesis 3 it is only by the audience's inference that the punishments will fall on all men and all women. The one exception is the newly decreed enmity between the descendants of the snake and of the woman but in that case it is not a disembodied narrative voice but rather God who speaks about a permanent condition (3:15). In all the other punishments the Storyteller has let the audience *infer* that the penalties will apply to subsequent generations, that the story is in fact an etiology for their own situation. With the single exception of the relationship between snakes and humans, there is nothing in the narrative that points directly to this conclusion.

The strongest argument for this verse as an intrusion into the text depends on sensitivity to the Storyteller's methods. All the etiologies flow from within the narrative and attention is never overtly drawn to their explanatory function. It is extremely improbable that the Storyteller would suddenly make this function explicit by employing the expression (ʿ*al-ken*) "that's why."[41] "The initial ʿ*al-ken* ('therefore') in fact certifies beyond any doubt that he intends here *to explain* something, presenting it as a consequence of what has been narrated in the previous verses."[42] It is precisely the *obvious intention* in Gen 2:24 that sets it apart from the rest of the story. The verse is not only intrusive but actually jarring to one tuned to the narrative voice and the subtlety of the Storyteller's art. "Even a mediocre sensitivity to artistic literary composition should be sufficient, at this point, to recognize Gen 2:24 as a foreign body, and therefore to label it as a gloss."[43]

---

text, see above, pp. 34–35; Tosato, "On Genesis 2:24," 391–94; cf. Alter, "Sacred History," 146–47, 149; Wolde, "Facing the Earth," 35–36.

41. "Hebrew has two conjunctions that are often confused: ʿ*al ken* links explanation and fact, 'that is why . . .'; and *laken* introduces a conclusion, 'therefore.'" Translating ʿ*al-ken* as 'therefore' mistakenly gives the impression of a command (Louw, *Transformations*, 141).

42. Tosato, "On Genesis 2:24," 398.

43. Ibid., 392. "In the rich narrative in which it is embedded the verse sounds trite, like a Mincus *pas de deux* in a Tchaikovsky ballet" (Lawton, "Genesis 2:24," 97). Alter notes the contrast between the "one flesh" in 2:24 and the stress on "the two of them, the human and his woman" in the verse immediately following, although he views the verse as possibly "part of a proverbial statement adopted verbatim by the writer" ("Sacred

In this verse we have a new narrator, one who draws conclusions and thereby attracts attention to himself. Up to this point, the narrator is essentially invisible as we are drawn into the events of the story. This new narrator breaks our attention to plot and spells out what we are to conclude. "The narrative will be more vivid, dramatic, gripping and realistic the less the narrator's existence is felt, the less aware we are of the fact that someone is mediating between us and the events, and the less we feel that someone is selecting and interpreting them for us."[44] Whoever introduced this verse just at the poetic highpoint of the story was completely oblivious to the subtle aspects of narrative art.

If we look more closely at this verse we can see that it does indeed contain an *interpretation* of the story, one that shows how the story was understood at a very early stage, before the fixing of the text as we now have it. Its author was apparently aware of a myth of the origin of the sexes similar to the one we find in Plato's *Symposium*.[45] In the myth put forward there by Aristophanes the first human beings had composite double bodies (either man/woman, woman/woman, or man/man). Through belief in their own powers they attacked the gods, who then determined to weaken them by dividing each one in half. The composite rebel human was split into two beings, so that forever after each attempted to *reunite* with its missing half, longing to "fuse with the beloved, to become one from two." The original myth was meant to provide an explanation for the origin of erotic love expressed as a yearning to reunite the separate parts of what had been a single being.[46] It isn't quite suitable to the creation of woman

---

History," 149). "It is clear then that v. 24 is but an addition to the narrative which is complete without it" (Westermann, *Genesis 1–11*, 233).

44. Bar-Efrat, *Narrative Art*, 31.

45. Plato, *Symposium* 189c–193d. The idea of an original androgynous human is also found in the Talmud and early rabbinic midrash; e.g. *Gen. Rab.* 8:1; b. ʿ*Erub.* 18a; b. *Ber.* 61a; b. *Nid.* 31b. "The myth of the primal androgyne was widespread in late antiquity, particularly among platonists in the Jewish (and eventually, Christian) traditions" (Boyarin, *Carnal Israel*, 36; also 17–18; 35–37; 42–46; 80 n.6). "Exactly how the myth reached the Rabbis we need not here decide. Probably it came from Plato, though we must bear in mind that Plato himself had it no doubt from the Orient. It does not give the impression of a native Greek product; and, quite possibly, by putting it in the mouth of Aristophanes, Plato means to suggest that he does not want it taken too seriously" (Daube, *New Testament and Rabbinic Judaism*, 73).

46. In a similar vein, Bechtel argues: "The ʾiššâ is originally a unity with the ʾîš. In her creation or birth the ʾiššâ is separated from the ʾîš. This attempts to account for the powerful physical and psychological draw between the sexes" ("Rethinking the

Crime and Punishment in Eden

in Genesis 2, a process in which the woman is not made from a split human being but rather is "built up" from a body part. It's ironic that Gen 2:24 is often cited as a biblical mandate for heterosexual monogamous marriage[47] although it started out as a mythological explanation for the kind of blind erotic desire that constitutes one of marriage's most formidable obstacles.[48]

ETIOLOGY AT THE NARRATIVE CENTER

2:25 And the two of them were naked, the human and his woman, but were not ashamed ... 3:7 And the eyes of both of them were opened and they knew that they were naked, and they sewed together fig leaves and made coverings for themselves.

This etiology lies at the epicenter of the story, the violation of the prohibition and its immediate effects. God had warned the man that eating from the Tree of Knowing Good and Bad would result in death (2:16–17). On the other hand, the snake denied that they would die, but claimed rather that God knew that having obtained this faculty of knowing their eyes would be opened and they would become like gods (3:4–5). Strictly in terms of the narrative, the snake proved to be correct, they did not die and "their eyes were opened." However, the immediate effect of eating was that "they *knew* that they were naked and sewed fig leaves together and made coverings for themselves" (3:7).

At this turning point in the story the Storyteller made a choice about how to represent the new faculty for knowing good and bad. He had to highlight just one aspect of the human condition to epitomize the effect of eating from the forbidden tree. Thus far in the story tension has been

---

Interpretation," 95–96). However, she admits that, for the woman, "linguistically, the unity/separation does not work here" because "'iššah" does not separate out of "'iš". Nor, we might add, does it work for *ha-'adam*, who certainly isn't in any hurry to reunite with the *'adamah* from which he had been separated.

47. "'And he will cleave to his wife'—and not to the wife of his fellow, nor to a male nor to a beast" (*Gen. Rab.* 18:2).

48. "Men who of that kindred section which was once called androgynous [i.e. men who are missing a female half] are lovers of women; most adulterers are generally of this type, and also adulterous women who love men and are adulteresses are of this type" (Plato, *Symposium* 191d–e).

built up: Under the threat of death, what would the humans choose to do? And if they disobeyed, what would be the consequence?

We can imagine the thought process, the reflection on what is peculiarly human, that led to the choice of self-consciousness about nudity and clothing. At this key moment in the narrative we come closest to the mind of the Storyteller. His observation that what distinguishes humans from the other animals is that we are the only species that is clothed is both profound and ironic. The irony lies in the fact that this quasi-divine characteristic resonates in us as self-consciousness, and results in a need to cover our bodies, in particular our reproductive organs. Of all the peculiarly human characteristics, this is, at least at first glance, so trivial as to be almost funny; as special as we are, the joke's on us. Why should we deny to the people of ancient Israel the universally human sense of humor?

From the Storyteller's point of view we have, generally speaking, been improved, not worsened, by the transformation effected by eating the forbidden fruit. This he expresses by describing it as approaching divinity (Gen 3:22). Whatever it is that we might have lost, it is more than offset by what we have gained. To suggest, as he does, that our need to be clothed is due to our godlikeness subverts the notion of a catastrophic loss of innocence, an innocence characterized by being "naked and not ashamed" (Gen 2:25).[49] Before eating from the Tree of Knowing Good and Bad, the humans were, like children and all the other animals, unselfconscious about their nakedness.[50] They come to know something they hadn't been aware of earlier, something we think of as characteristic of adults. Everyone agrees that if they hadn't eaten, we wouldn't be us.

It's unclear whether cultural attitudes toward nudity are at base sexual; certainly interpreters have read sexuality into the story at almost every point. However, other passages in the Hebrew Bible demonstrate that exposure of the naked body was viewed as shameful.[51] At the conclu-

49. Humbert sees the human's joy at finding a sexual partner in 2:23 "diametrically opposed" to the innocence of the pair in 2:25, for him an indication that two stories have been merged here (*Études*, 64–65).

50. Blenkinsopp notes that in the *Epic of Gilgamesh* the clothing of Enkidu is "a necessary preparation for the passage from animality to humanity . . . The motif also speaks to the transition from one phase of existence, life with the animals where to be naked was appropriate and natural, to another which is about to open out to the couple" (*Creation, Un-creation*, 69, 72).

51. "Nakedness in the Old Testament usually refers to the loss of human and social

sion of the story of the Flood we find the scene of the drunken Noah[52] and, in a text from real life, Yahweh commands Isaiah to go about without clothing to symbolize the coming plight of Egyptian and Ethiopian prisoners of war who would be paraded naked after the Assyrian victory.[53] Humiliation remains one of the greatest human fears; for good reason it is synonymous with mortification (with its root in death). Ironically it seems that it's the possession of the godlike faculty for knowing that makes the experience of humiliation possible.

THE TREE OF KNOWING GOOD AND BAD

At the center of the narrative as well as at the center of the Garden stands the Tree of Knowing Good and Bad. Planted there by God, the tree has the transformative power to change the nature of what it is to be human. The faculty of knowing good and bad imparted by eating the forbidden fruit is what makes us such exceptional creatures, "like gods." Among the etiologies in the story of the Garden of Eden this faculty also holds central place; the story revolves around how we came to acquire it and God's response when we did.

What is so distinctive about human beings? "Humans uniquely inhabit 'the cognitive niche': we gain most of our advantages from intelligence."[54] "Knowledge has been the lever which has raised man to a higher state, from the moment when Jehovah proclaimed that man, by increasing his knowledge, has become more assimilated to the Divine. In all ages, through all the varied experience of individuals and nations,

---

dignity . . . The only passage where nakedness clearly has to do with sexuality, specifically sexual arousal, is II Sam 11:2 (David and Bathsheba)" (Bailey, "Initiation," 145). Nakedness as loss of dignity is abundantly illustrated in Exod 20:26; Deut 28:48; 2 Sam 6:20; 10:4–5; Isa 47:2–3; 58:7; Ezek 16:36–39; 23:10, 18; 29; Amos 2:16; Mic 1:11; Nah 3:5; Hab 2:15; Lam 1:8; 4:21; Job 22:6; 2 Chr 28:14–16.

52. Gen 9:20–27.

53. Isa 20:1–6; also 2 Sam 10:1–5; 2 Chr 28:15 (and perhaps as a metaphor for shame, Isa 47:2–3; Nah 3:5–7); compare the treatment of prisoners at Abu Ghraib. This is a form of psychological warfare, "a means of status manipulation" (Bechtel, "Shame as a Sanction," 63–70). See also Satlow, "Jewish Constructions of Nakedness," esp. 436–38, 447–51. Attitudes toward nakedness vary cross-culturally (Oduyoye, *Sons of the Gods*, 46), but not in ancient Israel where it was considered humiliating to be seen unclothed.

54. Boyd, *Origin of Stories*, 14.

The Storyteller and the Garden of Eden

knowledge has been the power which has civilized, elevated and dignified humanity."[55]

Why then was eating from the Tree of Knowing prohibited? Some have argued that the particular tree is irrelevant. For example, Westermann throws up his hands at explaining the prohibition, considering it like a taboo; "it is part of the taboo that there is no rational basis for it."[56] This ignores the particular effects of eating from the tree. On the contrary, according to the story "the fruit has an automatic, almost magical effect."[57]

It is not just any tree that happens to be restricted, as would have been the case if the theme of the story had been the failure to obey God.[58] The etiological function of the story makes the presence of *this* tree *and* the disobedience imperative; the story presents its characters (and its audience) with an illusion of choice. The fruit must be eaten just as the Garden of Eden must be circumscribed in order for the humans to be cast out. There had to be a Tree of Knowing Good and Bad and a Garden no longer accessible because these define what and where we are.

All attempts to define what it is to know good and bad must distinguish the before and after, but, because the Storyteller has no interest in what might have been had the pair not chosen to eat the fruit of this forbidden tree nor in specifying precisely what sort of knowledge the pair possessed before or after the event, no explanations really make complete sense.[59] If this knowledge is restricted to the moral sense, one wonders what human life would have been like without it.[60] Ditto for practical and

---

55. Grimké, *Letters*, 109 (composed in the 1850s).
56. Westermann, *Genesis 1–11*, 224.
57. Naidoff, "Man to Work the Soil," 8.
58. As in the version of the story in the Qurʾan, where there is only one tree (Surah 2:35; 7:19). In one verse Satan/Iblis refers to it as "the tree of eternity and a power that does not decline with age" (Surah 20:120). This tree is similar to the Tree of Life in Genesis and to the "plant that makes old men young" in the *Epic of Gilgamesh*; however in the Qurʾan it is described in this way by Satan/Iblis in order to entice the humans to disobey, as the effects of eating that Satan claims prove not to exist.
59. Various explanations of the knowledge of good and bad are discussed in Westermann, *Genesis 1–11*, 242–45. "Only a handful of words like 'good' and 'bad' are so totally evaluative as to have no descriptive element whatever" (Caird, *Language*, 26).
60. For a different critique of knowing good and bad as the moral sense, see Humbert, *Études*, 101–13. Maimonides understands the knowledge gained as moral, yet views this as relativistic knowledge and as a fall from the purely philosophical knowledge endowed at creation (*Guide of the Perplexed* I.5), a particularly dangerous idea when applied to politics.

sexual knowledge. As for knowledge of everything, who could argue that we ever attained that?[61] Rather "knowing good and bad" is an idiomatic expression that refers to fully functioning adult intelligence.[62] It is not knowledge of anything in particular but a mental power that we can exercise (or not). Whatever it is that differentiates us from other creatures, it includes a kind of spirituality that engenders both a unique relationship with the divine (and the elaborate social institutions we call religion), all of which may be summed up in the few words of the story, that "their eyes were opened." We are the sole creatures to "know God."

We should not accept the traditional view that, whatever the faculty of knowing good and bad might be, it can't be a good thing if God had forbidden it.[63] Wisdom can be dangerous, but is never discouraged by God *per se*. In other biblical texts, being wise can lead to a sense of autonomy, away from reliance on God.[64] In some biblical narratives and prophetic texts, a person characterized as wise acts in a way condemned by the narrator or by God.[65] The theological message there and elsewhere (including the entire book of Job) emphasizes the proper subjection of the wise to the will of God, the ultimate incapacity of even the wise to know that will, and the transcendent power of God to subvert even the best of human intentions.

This is rather different from the portrayal of "knowing good and bad" in the Garden of Eden story. There, because human intellectual capacity is not something that God wants us to have, it finds expression as a violation of a divine command. Nevertheless, in the story the key description of this capability is that it makes us "like gods." The plural "gods" puts us with respect to this one faculty on a par with or (at least relative to other creatures) comparable to divine beings, but not with Yahweh Himself.

---

61. But some do anyway; e.g., von Rad, *Genesis*, 78–79; Wallace, *Eden Narrative*, 128; Oden, although he refines this as "cultural knowledge" ("Divine Aspirations," 212–13). These authors understand the fruit in terms of the acquisition of content rather than as a *faculty* for knowing.

62. See above, pp. 47–48.

63. For Milton, the knowledge is cast in purely negative terms as the recognition of "Good lost, and Evil got" (*Paradise Lost* IX.1072; XI.87), both the awareness of moral failure and an inkling of original sin.

64. "Do not be wise (*ḥakam*) in your own eyes, fear Yahweh" (Prov 3:7); also Isa 5:21; 29:13–14; Jer 9:23; Hos 14:10; Prov 1:7.

65. 2 Sam 13:3 (Jonadab) and 16:23 (Ahithophel). See Blenkinsopp, *Pentateuch*, 66–67.

The Storyteller and the Garden of Eden

In the first chapter of Genesis human beings are created godlike. Being created in the image of God endows us with sovereignty over the rest of creation (1:26–28). No such clarity in the meaning of "like gods" exists in the Garden of Eden story. Comparisons normally proceed from the known to the unknown, but not here. The audience is assumed to have a sense of human uniqueness and is relied upon to interpret the expression "like gods" correctly. The way in which the Storyteller describes the consequences of becoming "like gods" thus becomes an opportunity for us to reflect on that uniqueness.[66]

Unlike the portrayal of human dominance in Genesis 1, the Storyteller takes a more nuanced view of human capacities; the godlikeness that differentiates humans from all other species has a paradoxical impact on human existence. We are, on the one hand, exceptional in our capacity for knowing, yet hamstrung by the consciousness it engenders. It may be that his awareness that this faculty is not an unadulterated good led him to attribute it to an act of disobedience.[67]

Insofar as the Garden of Eden story is about crime and punishment, we have now identified the crime and discovered the intent of the punishments. The crime was not disobedience but rather breaching the boundary that God had established between human and divine. The purpose of His punishments was to reinforce the boundary by reducing the humans' status in their own realm, in particular by bedeviling them in the very work for which they were created, so that they end up subservient to the materials of their origin, the man to the soil, the woman to the man. God's goal was to counterbalance the ascendance of human beings to a status "little lower than a god."

---

66. Stordalen, *Echoes*, 240–41.

67. Stordalen, *Echoes*, 247; cf. Qoh 1:16–18. "Sleep on/ Blest pair; and O yet happiest if ye seek/ No happier state, and know to know no more" (Milton, *Paradise Lost* IV 773–75).

FIVE

Mortal or Immortal?

The life that you seek you will never find. When the gods created man they allotted to him death, life they kept for themselves.

—*Epic of Gilgamesh* (Sippar iii)

Does the Garden of Eden story explain why we die? This is perhaps the most important question we can put to the text. Death certainly comes up in the story: God threatens the humans with death, and the story ends with a permanent barrier to our access to the Tree of Life. In a story that clearly sets out to explain the most trying aspects of human existence, it seems that it would be natural that it tackle the big one.

Indeed it's often assumed that the Garden of Eden story explains the origin of mortality— that nothing would have ever died if the first human beings had not disobeyed God by eating from the Tree of Knowing Good and Bad. According to the story, it was the woman who was the first to disobey and then inveigled the man ("she gave also to her man with her and he ate"). If one of the results was the loss of immortality, the implication that a woman in particular bears responsibility for bringing death into the world makes a thorough investigation of this assumption imperative.

The idea that death resulted from the sin of our first parents dates from early Christianity if not earlier and is based on two assumptions: that human beings were originally immortal and that the snake's intention toward them was malevolent. Both of these assumptions take us to the heart of the interpretive matrix of the story and each requires examination on its own terms.

Let's first consider whether the first human beings were immortal when they were created. It is difficult to approach this with an open mind. The idea that human beings were originally immortal appears infrequently in early Judaism, where, however, it never quite took hold.[1] The belief that through their disobedience the first human beings were punished by the loss of the immortality with which they were originally endowed was first articulated in the New Testament, and thus became embedded in the center of Christian theology. Among Christians the idea begins, as far as one can discern, with Paul: "It was through one man that sin came into the world, and, through sin, death, and so death spread to all men in that all have sinned" (Rom 5:12), although for Paul, death, at least in some cases, meant rather permanent alienation from God.[2] However, as we consider the threat of death in the Garden of Eden story, the plain meaning is physical death, what would be ordinarily understood by both the audience and by the human to whom the threat is directed. This would be true whether the threat involved the loss of immortality or a more immediate demise.

THE DIVINE THREAT

2:16–17Yahweh ʾ*elohîm* enjoined the human, saying "From every tree of the Garden be assured that you will eat, but from the Tree of Knowing Good and Bad you will not eat from it, because when [*literally, on the day*] you eat from it be assured that you will die."

The principal arguments for the loss of immortality as punishment rest on the divine threat in Gen 2:16–17 and the statement at the end of the human's punishment in Gen 3:19 reminding him that, after a life in which he will struggle for subsistence, he will return to dust.

---

1. Sir 25:24; Wis 2:23; *2 Bar.* 56:6; as well as early midrash, *Gen. Rab.* 21:5; *Num. Rab.* 10:2; *Ex. Rab.* 30:3; 38:2; *Deut. Rab.* 9:8; *Qoh. Rab.* 7:13; *b. Šabb.* 55b.

2. For this meaning of death, see Ezekiel 18. Also, "For since death came through a human being, the resurrection of the dead has also come through a human being; for as all die in Adam, so in Christ all will be made alive" (1 Cor 15:21–22). On the meanings of death in Paul, see Malina, "Some Observations."

Mortal or Immortal?

However, in the prohibition God seems to be threatening the human that he will die as soon as ("on the day") he eats from the Tree of Knowing Good and Bad. The perennial problem faced by interpreters of Gen 2:16–17 is that when the man and woman do eat from the forbidden tree they don't die, instead they are punished in ways that affect their life but don't end it, at least not immediately.

It appears that, when God asserted that eating would result in death yet they ate and didn't die, God's threat was empty. To get around this it has been argued that He didn't mean physical death (the threat didn't really mean what it seemed to mean),[3] or that He changed His mind,[4] even that He had lied.[5] These are conclusions that, however, stand outside a narrative that has its own logic.

If God commanded the human to avoid eating from a particular tree, assuring him that death would ensue, we can only conclude that God intended to deter him from eating, that He did not want him to do it, and that He threatened him with the one consequence that mortals fear most in order to keep him from doing so. "To understand why a speaker says what he does is not the same as understanding what he is saying."[6] And, in fact (according to the story) the humans don't die. However, God eventually expels them from the Garden in order to deny them access to the Tree of Life (3:22); although this is not the explicit meaning of the threat, it does affect mortality.

The most prevalent solution to the problem assumes that God meant (literally) what He said. If God threatened that death would result from eating from the tree, and they did eat, since they didn't die right away they must have been condemned to death. They had been stripped of their im-

---

3. For a summary of such arguments, see Westermann, *Genesis 1–11*, 224–25, 266–67. He adds his own way out of the theological dilemma posed by the unrealized threat: "This is not in fact a threat of death, but rather the clear expression of the limit which is the necessary accompaniment of the freedom entrusted to humanity in the command" (224). He omits those who argue that "death" in 3:19 is not to be taken literally, but rather refers to spiritual death, following Paul.

4. This is Westermann's (self-contradictory) solution: "After the man and the woman had eaten from the tree, a new situation arises in which God acts differently from the way he had indicated ... God's acts and words are open to misinterpretation and the serpent makes use of this" (*Genesis 1–11*, 225).

5. See Albert, "Zu Gen 3: 17–19." For God as deceiver, see 1 Kgs 22:19–23; Jer 4:10; 20:7; Ezek 4:9; also 2 Thess 2:11; on these passages, see Roberts, "Does God Lie?" 127–31.

6. Caird distinguishes three types of meaning: of a word, of a sentence (context), and of the speaker's intention (*Language*, 37–61).

mortality and would have to die eventually. The defense of God's truthfulness seems to depend on the claim that we were created immortal.

To determine whether we can understand the threat in this way, let's look at it more closely. First we should focus on its commonsense meaning. If someone tells you that he's certain that if you eat something you'll die, how would *you* understand it? The obvious inference is that the substance is poisonous; according to ordinary usage the statement is not in any way ambiguous. If it turned out not to be poisonous, you would conclude that you had been misinformed. If only in this particular case the threat from eating is not meant literally but refers to a change in status from immortal to mortal, how could the human have correctly understood a warning that seems to refer to ingesting a toxic substance? That is, even if God were telling the truth and the result would be loss of original immortality, His words would be disingenuous since they convey quite a different impression, and one that on the face of it seems to be addressed to a mortal.

Moreover, if the prohibition is purely a test of obedience (with disobedience resulting in the very consequential loss of immortality), then any immediate effects of eating from the forbidden tree should be small potatoes. This is clearly not the case, since the dramatic turning point of the story focuses precisely on these effects, that their eyes were opened and that they knew that they were naked. When interpreters hold that not only was the forbidden fruit a test of obedience whose failure necessitated the loss of immortality, but also that the disobedience entailed some immediate, real (in the story) and imagined (not in the story) effects of eating from the tree itself (such as the rupture in the relationship with the deity, loss of innocence, the discovery of sexuality, the loss of control of sexuality, the introduction of death into the entire natural world, and so on), it's obvious that such interpreters are trying to have it every possible way. Imagined effects tend to dominate the discussion, while the punishments and their relation to the new godlike status of the human beings are relegated to only marginal interest. The supposed loss of immortality would be so momentous for humanity that it would dwarf in importance the effects of eating (attaining godlike status and the awareness of nakedness) and the divine response (the specific punishments of each of the characters) that are actually the focus of the story.

Put theologically, God, after warning the human that eating would entail death, had a legitimate right to employ capital punishment when they did eat. Yet the divine threat doesn't convey the impression that by it God puts the human on notice that He retains the right to apply the death penalty some time in the distant future. If anything, the threat in Gen 2:17 gives the impression that they will die immediately or very soon after, "*on the day* you eat from it be assured that you will die."

Now it can be argued that since they don't die "on the day" they eat from it, as God's warning is literally translated, therefore the threatened effect did not come to pass. However, this objection needs refinement. In biblical Hebrew, "on the day" does not refer to a literal day, but is an idiom meaning "when." Solomon makes exactly the same threat to Shimei, an old enemy of his father David: "*on the day* you go out and pass over the brook Kidron assuredly know that assuredly you will die."[7]

Both Gen 2:17 and 1 Kgs 2:37 employ the identical expression, literally "dying you will die." The verbal form in biblical Hebrew combines the finite verb with its corresponding infinitive absolute, and occurs only in quoted speech and legal pronouncements. It expresses the speaker's confidence that the event indicated by the verb will come to pass.[8] The sense in Gen 2:17 and 1 Kgs 2:37 is that the speaker is certain that death will occur, not immediately but as soon as possible within the context. In both verses "assuredly you will die" may be construed as a death sentence, which would allow the possibility that Gen 2:17 threatened the loss of immortality.

Similar threats (divine or otherwise) can be expressed without a specified time and convey a sense of immediacy.[9] This is the case in legal contexts or royal commands (both conveying strong conviction) where, without any indication of time, the expression "dying he/they will die" or "dying he/they will be put to death" implies a sentence of *imminent* capital punishment.[10]

---

7. 1 Kgs 2:37, repeated in 1 Kgs 2:42, on each occasion using the cognate infinitive absolute twice. For other occasions where "on the day" must be taken in context, see Exod 10:28; Num 3:1; 30: 6, 8, 9, 13; Josh 6:10; Isa 11:16; Ruth 4:5.

8. "In this way BH speakers/narrators *express their conviction of the verity of their statements regarding an action* " (Van der Merwe et al., *Reference Grammar*, 158; italics original); Kim, *Tautological Infinitive*, 13–17, 92–95, 133–34.

9. Gen 20:7; 1 Sam 14:44; 2 Kgs 1:6, 16–17; Ezek 3:18; 33:8–16; cf. Exod 19:12–13.

10. Exod 21:12, 15–17; 22:18; 31:14, 15; Lev 20:9–16, 27; Num 35:17, 18, 31; cf. Judg 21:5; 1 Sam 22:16–18; Jer 26:8–16.

Likewise the temporal expression "on the day" does not necessarily refer to a particular day but rather to a time proximate to the act in question (whether it be crossing the Kidron or eating the forbidden fruit).[11] Translations of the literal "on the day" as "when" or "if" leave the time frame too open ended. Thus such interpretations as "you must die (someday)" or "you are doomed to die (someday)" express the idea of the loss of immortality but are actually unjustified renderings of biblical language.[12] If "on the day" should not be taken literally to mean "on that very day," it also can't refer to an indefinite time in the future.

Here we face the objection that the humans do indeed die "on the day" in the sense that they immediately lose the immortality with which they were originally endowed. In other words, if we assume that the first humans were immortal until they ate from the Tree of Knowing, then either as a direct effect of eating or as a punishment (God following through on His threat) we suddenly became mortals subject to death. This is indeed a possible way to understand the threat, although it's not what it seems to imply.

Can this possibility survive a study of the threat when we look at it in context? To begin, there's the larger context of the Hebrew Bible in its entirety. Although this suffers from being an argument from silence, it is remarkable that, despite the pervasive theme of sin and punishment, there is not a single allusion to a loss of immortality. No prophet bothers to bring it up when threatening all sorts of catastrophic divine punishments.

Nonetheless, in good part due to the way Paul integrated the Garden of Eden story into his interpretation of the life of Jesus (or at least the way Paul was interpreted), Christians have long believed that Adam and Eve bear responsibility for why we die.[13] Christian artistic depictions of the Garden of Eden bear an implicit reference to Christ's redemption and are often paired with an image of the crucifixion or the lamentation. The death and resurrection of Jesus is believed to (re)open the path to eternal

---

11. Robbins, "Day"; Whybray, "Immorality of God," 91; cf. Humbert, *Études*, 138–41, for whom the expression "on the day" may have a temporal or conditional meaning but excludes the notion of immediacy.

12. Westermann dismisses this interpretation categorically, "The meanings 'you will become mortal' or 'you will die sometime later' are quite impossible. The majority of exegetes have rejected this explanation" (*Genesis 1–11*, 225).

13. "Paul is thoroughly uninterested in the speculative question of physical death" (Malina, "Some Observations," 33). On the key role of Adam and Eve in Christian doctrine, see Spong, *New Christianity*, 121–25; Spong, *Christianity Must Change*, 83–99.

life, a substitute for an original immortality lost by the sins of Adam and Eve.

Now let's look at the evidence to the contrary in the story itself—evidence that demonstrates that human beings were created mortal and would eventually die. First of all, the human is formed, just as the other animals, from perishable material and is therefore, like other creatures, bound to pass away. The difference most remarked on between the creation of the human and that of the animals in Genesis 2 is the addition, in the case of the human being, that its form is animated by God blowing into its nostrils a "breath of life" (*nišmat ḥayyîm*). We have to examine both aspects of how the human came into existence, the material (dust from the soil) and the manner in which the material was animated (breath of life).

Since the story seems to privilege human beings by mentioning how the form was brought to life, let's start there. In the Hebrew Bible breathing is understood to be characteristic of all animal life. In Gen 7:21–22, as the floodwaters rise, "They perished, everything of flesh that moves about the earth among the birds and livestock and animals and all the creeping things that creep on the earth and every human being (*kol ha-ʾadam*). All that had a breath of the wind of life (*nišmat-rûaḥ ḥayyîm*) in its nostrils of all that was on dry land died."

Here the same expression ("breath of the wind of life") is used for all animals, including human beings.[14] The chief difference between the two is the way that this breath enters the human in Genesis 2 where the storyteller uses the anthropomorphic image of God's breath ("Yahweh ʾelohîm formed the human of dust from the soil and *breathed into his nostrils a breath of life*"). The idea that this process conveyed immortality assumes that the human now uniquely possesses divine breath, and that this makes him immortal.

However, breathing implies the possibility of not or no longer breathing. "A human being (*ʾadam*) is like a breath (*hebel*), his days like a passing shadow."[15] Just as God bestows a breath to bring a creature to life, He may equally take it away. "You remove their breath (*rûaḥ*), they

---

14. Both animals and humans have "one breath (*rûaḥ*) and there is no superiority of *ha-ʾadam* among the animals, for all is a breath (*hebel*). All are going to one place, all are from the dust and all return to the dust" (Qoh 3:19–20). The word *hebel*, literally "a breath," comes to indicate the evanescent, and thus the insignificance of whatever is characterized as *hebel*, often translated as "vanity."

15. Ps 144:4.

die and to their dust they return. You send forth your breath, they are created."[16] The breath is ephemeral, as is life itself. "Remember my life is a breath (*rûaḥ*)."[17] "Cease regarding the human (*ha-ʾadam*) who has breath (*nešamah*) in his nostrils, for at what is he is esteemed?"[18] Just as in Gen 7:21–22, these passages reflect the belief that life ends when a person ceases to breathe, that breathing was identified as the distinctive sign of being alive. The breath of life *is* life, as long as it lasts. "My breath (*nišmatî*) is still in me, and the breath (*rûaḥ*) of God in my nostrils."[19] In this passage the "breath of God" is not sufficient to convey immortality. Whatever the source of breath, even the "breath of God," it's a marker of mortality.

In addition to the transitory nature of breathing, the very manner in which the human being is formed indicates its tenuous hold on life. The connection with the soil (*ha-ʾadamah*) goes beyond the soil providing the material for the human (*ha-ʾadam*).[20] Forming a human being from clay is the metaphor, common in mythology and in the Hebrew Bible, of a potter bringing into existence a pot, a fragile ceramic object. The metaphor contains an implied threat: just as the potter can create it, he can easily destroy it.[21] By employing the metaphor of the potter, the writer indicates right at the beginning of the story that the human being so formed is a fragile creature as also are all his works. The metaphor emphasizes the distinction between the immortal potter and the mortal clay object He fashions.[22] As God the potter can break the pot He has made, He can also remove the breath.[23] Both breath and clay imply impermanence.

Let's consider in more detail the material from which the human being is made, "the dust from the soil." The word "dust" (*ʿapar*) appears on three occasions in the story. In Genesis 2:7, "Yahweh *ʾelohîm* formed

16. Ps 104:29–30; also Job 34:14–15.

17. Job 7:7.

18. Isa 2:22.

19. Job 27:3. Compare Ezek 37:1–14 where, whether the breath comes from the winds or from Yahweh, there is no hint that those who receive it will become immortal.

20. This has been explored at length in Stordalen, "Man, Soil, Garden"; Naidoff, "Man to Work the Soil."

21. Ps 2:9 ("like a formed vessel [i.e., a clay pot], You will shatter them"); Jer 18:1–10; Job 10:8–9; Isa 41:25.

22. Isa 29:16; 45:9; 64:8; cf. Job 33:6; Lam 4:2.

23. "Who doesn't know that in all these, that the hand of Yahweh has done this, that in His hand is the life (*nepeš*) of every living being (*kol-ḥâi*) and the breath (*rûaḥ*) of every man of flesh (*kol-baśar-ʾîš*)" (Job 12:9–10).

the human (*ha-ʾadam*) of dust (*ʿapar*) from the soil (*ha-ʾadamah*)." Then, pointing out to the snake the consequence of its debased manner of locomotion, God says "dust (*ʿapar*) you will eat all the days of your life" (3:14). And lastly God concludes the man's punishment by noting, "by the sweat of your brow you will eat food, until your return to the soil (*ha-ʾadamah*), because from it you were taken, because dust (*ʿapar*) you are and to dust (*ʿapar*) you will return" (3:19).[24] In Gen 3:14 and 3:19 God sums up for the snake and the human being the pitiable circumstances of their existence. For the snake "eating dust" is a new condition, the result of its punishment. Not so for the human being who returns to dust "because" this is the material from which he was made.[25]

Modern translations mistranslate "until your return (to the soil)" as "until you return (to the soil)." The difference is subtle but significant: "until your return" has a sense of inevitability, of something natural and expected, while "until you return" can be and has been understood as a gentle reminder of a death sentence.

Also missing from most translations is the repetition of *because* in Gen 3:19: "*because* you were taken from it, *because* dust you are and to dust you will return." Both these conditions are independent of the events and punishments of the narrative in Genesis 3. To say that the human is dust is to say that he is worthless, as close to nothing as you can get, and this is implicit from the moment and manner of his creation.

Although most comparisons of the forming of the human in Gen 2:7 and the forming of the animals in Gen 2:19 typically focus on the addition of divine breath for the human, no attention has been paid to the addition of dust.[26] In 2:19, "God formed from the soil (*min-ha-ʾadamah*)

---

24. Vawter observes "*Until you return to the ground, from which you were taken* corresponds with *all the days of your life* of v. 14" (*On Genesis*, 85). Also Skinner, *Genesis*, 84–85; Humbert sees both 3:17c ("all the days of your life") and 3:19 (whose chiastic structure he describes) in terms of the temporal duration of the increased labors to which the man is condemned (*Études*, 143–45).

25. "Interestingly, the text never says that the *ʾādām* returning to the *ʾadāmâ* (death) is bad. Death is presented neutrally, not as punishment, but as part of the natural cycle of unity and separation of life" (Bechtel, "Rethinking the Interpretation," 109).

26. Orthographically different but semantically equivalent, the verb 'to form' is written with two *yodhs* (*wyyṣr*) in reference to the man and with a single *yodh* (*wyṣr*) in the case of the animals. The notion that every detail in the received text, no matter how small, is significant provides the basis for the rabbinic explanation for the existence of evil; in the case of the human being, the two *yodhs* represent the two "inclinations" (*yeṣer*), one good and one bad, an idea that differs from the notion of original sin in that

every animal of the field and every bird of the sky." This demonstrates that the idea of fashioning living things from the soil could have been perfectly well expressed without the addition of "dust."

In all other biblical texts, humans are made not from "the soil" (*ha-ʾadamah*) or from "the dust from the soil" (*ha-ʿapar min-ha-ʾadamah*) but rather from clay (*homer*).[27] In Gen 2:7 the unique choice of the words "dust from the soil" is conditioned by the use to which they will be put in the rest of the story. The theme of human frailty finds expression in those biblical passages that make reference to humans as being made from clay; in the Garden of Eden story this is reinforced by replacing *clay* with "the dust from the soil." On one level, it's a distinction without a difference: "Do remember that as clay (*homer*) you made me and to dust (*ʿapar*) you will return me."[28] Here there is a sense, conveyed by the choice of words, that there is greater nobility in being made from clay than there is in returning to dust, despite the fact that the two materials are essentially the same. It is our future death that concerns us (dust), not our origins (clay). Vladimir Nabokov's memoir begins, "The cradle rocks above an abyss, and common sense tells us that our existence is but a brief crack of light between two eternities of darkness. Although they are identical twins, man, as a rule, views the prenatal abyss with more calm than the one he is heading for."[29] Combining Job and Nabokov we might conclude that it is the dust we will become in the future that is more disquieting than the clay of our origin. To say (as the narrator does at the beginning of the story and God confirms at the end) that the human was made from dust already foreshadows his death.

In both Gen 3:14 ("dust you will eat") and 3:19 ("because dust you are") the word *dust* occupies the stressed position in the phrase. Here we find the reason that the Storyteller chose to describe the forming of the first human from "the dust from the soil" rather than the expected "clay." The addition of "dust" looks forward to this declaration in Gen 3:19 that just rubs in the punishment: the man's now unremitting labor to produce sustenance from the soil embitters his return to it. Here, in God's sum-

---

both inclinations are embedded in humans by God at the creation; on this see Tennant, *Sources*, 160–76; Porter, "Yeçer Hara"; Cohen, "Original Sin"; Urbach, *Sages* I:471–83.

27. Job 33:6; Isa 29:16; 41:25; 45:9; 64:7; Jer 18:1–6. In these texts we find the explicit metaphor of God as potter.

28. Job 10:9.

29. Nabokov, *Speak, Memory*, 9.

mary of the conditions of human life, He brings home the point of the story-as-wordplay: that at the end of a now much harsher existence, the human being (*ha-ʾadam*) will return to the soil (*ha-ʾadamah*) as both his original material and his resting-place.

There are thus two differences in the creation of the animals and that of the humans in Genesis 2. First, the animals are simply made from the soil, while the human is made from the dust of the soil. The second difference is that, in the case of the human, there is the additional statement that God "blew into his nostrils a breath (*rûaḥ*) of life and he became a living being (*nepeš ḥayyah*)" (2:7). Every living, breathing creature is a *nepeš ḥayyah*.[30] The breath of life simply serves to animate the clay figure. When He formed the animals from the soil, their bodies also had to be animated, although the story doesn't bother to say so explicitly. "Adam is fashioned of mud, and God breathes into him the breath of life; he thus becomes an animate being, like any other animal. The passage is obviously dualistic: there are two ingredients in man, the mud and the breath. Or, alternatively, one can make it monistic: then the 'breath' is not 'part' of man but something that comes into him and goes out again; the only element that really *is* man is the mud or dust. 'Dust you are, and to dust you will return' (Gen 3:19) is the obvious continuation of this line of thinking."[31]

The ability to breathe is only of limited duration. For all animals, the distinction between the living and the dead is the presence or absence of breath. The inbreathing by God in Gen 2:7 is often taken to imply the addition of an immortal soul or spirit (two notions foreign to the writers of the Hebrew Bible).[32] "It is not at all permissible either to read into the sentence [Gen 2:7] that something of the divine was given to humans at creation or to explain *rûaḥ* from the Greek or contemporary idea of spirit."[33]

It is equally if not more reasonable to suppose that, by mentioning breath in the case of the human being, the implication of mortality was emphasized as it is to find something elevating in it. It's hardly surprising

---

30. See Gen 1:30, where each creature on earth, even creepy, crawly ones, has a *nepeš ḥayyah* "in it."

31. Barr, *Garden of Eden*, 37.

32. Barr explains the development of these ideas based in part on ambiguous passages such as Qoh 12:7 (*Garden of Eden*, 21–56).

33. Westermann, *Genesis 1–11*, 207.

that when considering how the description of the creation of the human being differs from that of the animals, commentators tend to give theological significance to the addition of a "breath of life" while ignoring the less flattering addition of "dust."

That the human is made of fragile material, that the narrator emphasizes the lowly nature of this material by adding the term *dust* and repeating it in the context of the snake as a term of particular contempt, and that breathing, whether divinely imparted or not, is characteristic of all creatures while they remain alive, all point to the conclusion that we were created as mortals and would eventually die. To this we might add that if the loss of immortality were intended here, it is not how the divine threat would have been understood in ordinary language. It appears rather to be a threat directed at mortals, that by eating they face imminent death.

The argument for creational immortality requires making a series of unsubstantiated assumptions while ignoring the evidence of the story itself. If we begin by assuming that human beings were endowed with immortality, we have to pile on additional assumptions: that the material with which the human was formed doesn't matter; that the metaphor of the potter and the pot is irrelevant; that the language of the threat doesn't mean what it seems to mean.

While we can conclude that there is nothing in the way the humans were created that implies they were originally immortal, we should examine the rest of the story to see if that conclusion is indeed warranted. Assuming original immortality naturally leads to questions about the nature of these immortal human beings and how they might have otherwise differed from us. Would they have procreated? If so, this leads to further difficulties (sexual passion and eventual overpopulation among them).[34] The existence of the passions related to sex was viewed as problematic for the presumed state of innocence of the first couple, a problem solved by Augustine, who posited a passion-free sexuality rather different from that with which we are now familiar.[35] It's often the case that one incorrect assumption forces us down a path of endless speculation.

In the first chapter of Genesis, sexual reproduction is not only assumed, it is the first commandment, "Be fruitful and multiply," directed

---

34. Overpopulation was on the minds of the fathers of the early church; see Herlihy, *Medieval Households*, 23–25.

35. Augustine, *Literal Meaning of Genesis*, IX 3 6; XI 42 59.

at both humans (v. 28) and animals (v. 22).³⁶ That chapter has as its main focus the sustainability of God's creation, specifying the means by which all life regenerates (including plants from seeds, trees from seeds in their fruit). It is for this reason that in Gen 1:27 both men and women were created simultaneously.

The first explicit mention of sexual reproduction in the Garden of Eden story is found in the woman's punishment, that her pregnancies would be greatly increased.³⁷ The phrasing here clearly implies that there would have been *fewer* pregnancies before the punishment was imposed. That there was *any* procreation before the punishment contradicts the very common notion that once having lost immortality the species had to reproduce sexually in order to survive, and that the knowing they got from the Tree of Knowing was about sex. For example, "the person ʾ*adam* will die as a result of his being exiled from Eden, but the class ʾ*adam* will multiply as result of the knowledge gained."³⁸

If our awareness of sexuality depended on eating from fruit that had been forbidden, what of the other creatures? Wasn't reproduction part of their nature as they were created? And, since the basic theme of the Garden of Eden story involves how we became so *different* from the other species by eating from the Tree of Knowing, would we have started out uniquely unable to procreate? Weren't we created with the physical apparatus that made sexual reproduction possible, and if so, what purpose would it have served had we not disobeyed the prohibition? Aquinas confronted this question directly and concluded that human sexuality (which for him should serve only for reproduction, no one I am aware of argues that it was created originally only for pleasure) was part of the plan in

---

36. Cassuto, assuming the couple to be immortal as long as they remained in Eden eating from the Tree of Life, concludes that there was "no need, of course, for them to propagate their species or to spread about the earth and fill it." He sees this as a "serious discrepancy" and a "far graver contradiction" with the command to reproduce in Gen 1:28 (*Commentary* 161–62).

37. Humbert finds human sexuality implied in Gen 2:23: "Nulle ignorance et nul ingénuité . . . chez cet homme si certain de son unité charnelle avec la femme et de leur convenance réciproque qu'il exprime sa jubilation amoureuse en termes d'une si vigoreuse sensualité. Nul blame sur l'union de ces deux êtres à qui leur sûr instinct révèle d'emblée la loi de leur nature" (*Études*, 179).

38. Stordalen, *Echoes*, 248. This view is expressed by Sasson, "Tower of Babel," 453, and many others. It is so commonly held that Stordalen repeats it despite denying original immortality.

creation. The idea that sexual reproduction only came into existence after the disobedience violates the Thomistic rule that everything God created, including the sex organs, had a "natural use."[39] This principle could also be applied to a well-constructed narrative. Despite Milton's sexually active angels in *Paradise Lost*,[40] reproductively active immortal beings are problematic. Human biology points to an original mortal state.

When the story was understood as the origin of human mortality, the issue of reproduction became urgent. This reading of the story developed before the text as we now have it reached its final form and led to two additions to the story, the naming of the woman and the clothing of both, "the human named his woman Eve (*ḥawwah*) because she became the mother of all life (*ḥâi*), and Yahweh 'elohîm made for the human and for his woman garments of skin and clothed them" (Gen 3:20-21).

For those who claim that loss of immortality was one of the punishments, these verses seem to address the situation of newly mortal beings who now need to procreate to survive and require defenses against the weather.[41] And this is likely to be what whoever added these verses had in mind (which implies that the notion that the humans lost immortality occurred before the text took its final form).

Genesis 3:20 apparently endeavors to reframe the status of the woman (and by extension all women) by indicating her positive role in human survival, now at risk. "This is at once the benison of fertility and the assurance of the continued existence of the species, a promise that begins to be realized immediately [in the births of Cain and Abel, Gen 4:1-2]."[42] The attempt by the author of Gen 3:20 to reestablish the value of women in terms of maternity ignores the fact that it was precisely in the process of childbearing that the woman was punished.[43] He ascribes

---

39. Thomas Aquinas, *Summa Theologica* I Question 98 Article 2.

40. Milton, *Paradise Lost* VIII, 614-32, where there is no indication of reproduction, just pleasure.

41. For the many interpreters who read 3:21 in this way, and an alternative suggestion, see Oden, *Bible without Theology*, 94-105.

42. Cassuto, *Commentary*, 163.

43. That Gen 3:20 was meant to compensate for the punishment in 3:16 was argued by Westermann: "The pains of pregnancy and birth in no way diminish the dignity of womanhood and motherhood, as 3:20 expressly confirms" (*Genesis 1-11*, 262). See also Williams, "Relationship."

Mortal or Immortal?

to the general approbation of motherhood in the Hebrew Bible, in stark contrast to the author of Genesis 3.[44]

The naming of the woman here has long been recognized as a gloss, an addition to the text that is out of synch with its context.[45] We are asked to accept that, immediately after describing the punishments that will burden women in their role as mothers, the same storyteller did a complete about-face by praising the woman (the one that he has just blamed for everything that has occurred), rather hyperbolically, as the "mother of all life."

Yet these verses must be read in just this way; for example, "the man's giving the woman a second name evokes the memory of the first name which was given at the climax of the search for a helpmate. It is an affirmative action which, in the context of the man's earlier accusation of the woman, reestablishes a positive relationship between them," just as 3:21, "also reestablishes Yahweh in the role of sender of good gifts to the people," taking away "the shame of nakedness" and giving them "a measure of dignity."[46] If this is the thrust of Gen 3:20–21, these verses stand in direct contradiction to the narrative up to this point in which the whole point of the punishments is to deny dignity, while they also interrupt the story which without these verses continues on to the act of expelling the humans from the Garden.

Genesis 3:20 follows the sequence of punishments that ends with a reiteration of human mortality, "because dust you are and to dust you will return." In terms of this context it is perhaps inevitable that maternity (procreation) will be read as a substitute for immortality, supporting the claim of original immortality and of its loss as a consequence of disobedience.[47] When we bracket out Gen 3:20 as a later addition another argument in favor of creational immortality bites the dust.

---

44. On the representation of motherhood in the Hebrew Bible, see Fuchs, "Literary Characterization of Mothers."

45. Skinner, *Genesis*, 85–87. For detailed arguments on Gen 3:20 as a later addition, see within, pp. 65, 127–29.

46. Boomershine, "Structure," 119, 125–26. "What seems to account for all these anomalies [in Gen 3:20–21] and to recompense for them is the author's intent to demonstrate God's continued solicitude for his creatures despite all" (Vawter, *On Genesis*, 87).

47. E.g., Mettinger refers to procreation as "vicarious immortality" (*Eden Narrative*, 26).

The added verses in Gen 3:20–21 serve to recast both the woman and the deity in a more favorable light. Unfortunately, when they were inserted in the middle of God's response to what the man and woman had done they effectively separated the punishments from the expulsion and obscured the link between them. By bracketing out these verses, we can more easily see that the explanation God gives for expelling the human pair from the Garden of Eden also applies to the reason for the punishments in vv. 16–19.

As we've seen, the purpose of the punishments was to reduce the humans' stature in the world by hobbling their ability to perform the tasks for which they had been created. They could no longer easily find sustenance from the land nor reproduce without pain. Their relationship to their material and linguistic source (man to soil, woman to man) is now disrupted either by the punishment directly (the curse on the soil) or as an aftereffect (male domination).

The punishments also had the effect of accentuating and exacerbating their mortality, the remaining absolute distinction between the human and divine realms, while the expulsion eliminates the possibility that they might become even more like gods by eating from the Tree of Life and thereby extending their lifespan. It is not because they disobeyed a divine command but rather because "they have become like one of us" (3:22) that God both denies them access to the Tree of Life and, by means of the punishments, compensates for their new godlike status. In different ways, both the punishments and the expulsion serve the same purpose, God's determination that the humans He created remain inferior mortal beings.

Thus far we've considered the unlikelihood that human beings were originally immortal, taking into account the manner and matter of their creation and the question of their sexual and reproductive status. By the end of the story, the human characters are decidedly mortal, because of the punishments and the expulsion one might say more mortal than ever. "While the death penalty is not executed, the human couple exiled from the garden no longer have access to the Tree of Life. Their mortality becomes critical, and the issue of death achieves new significance."[48] Yet

---

48. Stordalen, *Echoes*, 247.

this does not speak to the question whether they started out as mortal or immortal.[49]

There is one more point to consider, one that seems to me decisive. If we begin by assuming that the first humans were created as immortal beings, it was only in the course of events that God transformed them into mortals subject to death, which we remain to this day. Whether this transformation occurred directly as an effect of eating from the Tree of Knowing Good and Bad or was imposed as punishment for it we really don't care. This makes for a good etiological story, one that accounts for the most troubling aspect of our existence. Unfortunately it makes no sense in the context of Genesis 2–3.

It is precisely here, within the internal logic of the narrative, that we find the most compelling argument against the idea of original immortality. To see this clearly we have to work backward from the end of the story. In Gen 3:22, God explains why He is removing the humans from the Garden. He doesn't cite their disobedience but rather speaks to the fact that they have "become like one of us," that they have acquired something that makes them "like gods." The plural of divinity ("like *one of us*") makes it clear that we have to do with a characteristic of divinity in general. Having determined that the humans had moved a step toward divinity God acts to prevent them from moving any further in that direction ("lest he send forth his hand and *also* take from the Tree of Life and eat and live in perpetuity").

In Gen 3:22 God describes Himself as acting to preserve the absolute distinction that remains between the divine and the human. It seems unreasonable in the extreme to suppose that from the start He would have endowed the lowly human made from dust with the prime attribute of divinity. Even the hyperbolic description of the elevated status of human beings in Ps 82:6–7 can't get around it: "I said you are gods and the children of ʿelyôn all of you, but as a human being (*ke-ʾadam*) you will die and like each of the rulers you will fall."

When we consider God's reaction to the human attainment of what is arguably the lesser quality of godlikeness called "knowing good and bad," the notion that He would have created human beings as immortal as Himself defies the logic of the entire story. If at the time of their initial

---

49. For the early history of this discussion, see Schmid, "Loss of Immortality?," 58–78.

creation humans had been endowed with immortality, they would have possessed the one quality that practically defines God, that He cannot die.

In an act of disobedience, the human beings became "like gods." Here the operative word is *like*, which means "similar but not identical to." They do not become gods. Had they been immortal at their creation, there would have been little reason for God to fret about their becoming like gods by "knowing good and bad," certainly a minor attribute of divinity when compared with immortality. If created immortal, the boundary between human and God would have been indistinct at the outset.

It is not only God who states clearly why He acts. His interest in maintaining the boundary is also known to and stated explicitly by the snake in explaining the prohibition (which doesn't make it any less the case): "*because God knows* that when you eat from it your eyes will be opened and you will be like gods, knowing good and bad" (3:5). Indeed God does know and acts precisely in consequence of that knowledge: "See, the human has become like one of us, in knowing good and bad, and *now*, lest he send forth his hand and take also from the Tree of Life."[50] "The new situation to be avoided is *not* the eating of the Tree of Life, but the eating from the tree *after* having taken from the Tree of Knowledge."[51]

This brings us back to the threat of death in 2:16–17. God's purpose here is clear. It is intended to deter the mortal human from eating the fruit of the Tree of Knowing Good and Bad. Since the humans do eat, do attain this faculty of knowing, and do achieve an attribute of godlikeness, they must be removed from the Garden due to the possibility of becoming yet more godlike by eating from the Tree of Life. The line dividing human and divine is ordained from the beginning, and the humans are punished for crossing it.

Genesis 2–3 is not the only biblical text in which God comes down hard when He fears that humans are getting bigger than their britches. It can be compared to God's reaction to human potential in the story of the Tower of Babel, now found at the very end of the primeval history (Gen 11: 1–9). The problem of transgressing the boundary is also explicit in the first of the list of reasons given for Yahweh's decision to wipe out humanity by the flood: the offspring that resulted from the miscegenation of the

---

50. The stress here falls on the words *and now* (we-ʿattah).
51. Stordalen, *Echoes*, 231 (italics original).

"sons of God" and the "daughters of men" (*bᵉnôt ha-ʾadam*) had blurred the line of demarcation separating human and divine (Gen 6:1–4).

We might not find this characterization of God to our liking, but that cannot blind us to its presence in the text. It subverts the supposition of an original intimacy in the relationship between God and human that is presumed to be lost in the act of disobedience (note the double assumption: God is like such and such; the divine-human relationship is like such and such; if only the humans had left the tree alone, how different would this relationship have been!). No one seems to wonder what human beings might have been like had they not partaken of the forbidden fruit, what godlike quality we now have that we would then have lacked. Through disobedience we became "like gods." That is the most original aspect of the story, and we owe it all to the woman.

THE TREE OF LIFE

3:22 Yahweh *ʾelohîm* said, "See, the human being has become like one of us, in knowing good and bad, and now, lest he send forth his hand and take also from the Tree of Life and eat and live in perpetuity (*le-ʿolam*) ..."[52]

If God had been concerned with keeping the humans from attaining any aspect of divinity, why would He have planted a Tree of Life in the Garden in the first place? Of course in view of its etiological function, the story simply explains why such a tree is now inaccessible to us, but why is it there at all? And what is the Tree of Life anyway and what does eating its fruit confer? To answer these questions we have to look at it in the context of the narrative.

The Tree of Life is mentioned only at the beginning and the end of the story (Gen 2:9 and 3:22), a fact that has led some to speculate that two traditions have been merged to form the narrative that we now have, one for each tree. However that may be, the Tree of Life contributes to no small extent to the etiological function of the existing story in which eating from one of the trees means we are not allowed to eat from the other.

---

52. The ellipsis here may indicate an unimaginable situation. Bullinger classifies it as an instance of aposiopesis, sudden silence: "It is the sudden breaking off of what is being said (or written), so that the mind may be the more impressed by what is too wonderful, or solemn, or awful for words" (*Figures of Speech*, 151).

The Storyteller and the Garden of Eden

God's response to our achievement is to deny us a means to forestall death. "The brief reference to the Tree of Life in Gen 2:9, 3:22–24 agrees with that in the Gilgamesh Epic that eternal life is inaccessible. Humans have nothing that can save them from death."[53]

The information that the text provides indicates that the Tree of Life was planted by God "in the center of the Garden" (Gen 2:9) and that eating from it would either defer or do away with death (3:22). Its fruits were available to the first humans, who would have been free to eat from it. It also functions as the basis for their expulsion, which denies them access to it. Having become more godlike through their disobedience, God felt it necessary to constrain the humans from further breaching the boundary between human and divine. This is the limit of the information that the text provides.

What would have been the effect of eating from the Tree of Life? The notion that eating its fruit provided permanent immortality (where it is not possible to die) assumes that it would have to be consumed just once. This is indeed a possible meaning of *ḥâi le-ʿolam* (and how Gen 3:22 is usually translated, "live forever"). However, for those who assume that humans were originally immortal, the Tree of Life would have had no original purpose; if created immortal, eating from the Tree of Life would have had no effect.

Recognizing this difficulty, one has to postulate an omniscient deity who foresaw the loss of original immortality and provided a remedy in advance (one that He immediately put out of reach by the expulsion). According to this argument, God had provided the Tree of Life in case the humans would need it in the future, having lost the immortality with which they were created. The problem here is that, by expelling the two from the Garden, God denies them the opportunity to eat from the Tree of Life at the very time they come to need it. One would then have to argue that God changed His mind about the purpose of the Tree of Life, another assumption required by a theory that reduces to absurdity. The very presence of the Tree of Life, whether conferring permanent immortality (where dying is not possible) or simply prolonging life, is another argument against the concept of creational immortality.[54]

---

53. Westermann, *Genesis 1–11*, 214.

54. To get around these objections Humbert postulates that the Tree of Life was intended as a reward for obedience and thus must have been hidden until God decided to reveal it (*Études*, 129, 143–51). However, if this were the case, the tree could have

Mortal or Immortal?

Which then is it? Can we determine whether the Tree of Life was a one-time deal, conferring permanent immortality (the kind the gods have) or did one have to eat from it periodically in order to stay alive? According to the story, if the humans ate from the tree they would *ḥāi le-ʿolam*. *ḥāi* is the present tense of the verb "to live." So the question boils down to the meaning of *le-ʿolam*. It consists of the preposition *le* that means "to" and the noun *ʿôlam*. The basic meaning of *ʿôlam* is a really long time, either in the past[55] or in the future.[56] The length of time depends on the context; in Exod 21:6, *le-ʿolam* refers to a lifetime: "he [the slave] shall serve him [his master] *le-ʿolam*," i.e., for life. On the other hand, *le-ʿôlam* occurs often in the context of God's promise to preserve the nation of Israel and the Davidic dynasty.

So, does *le-ʿolam* in Gen 3:22 mean "forever"[57] or "a really long time" (longer than the expected life span of a mortal)?[58] In terms of its context, as the sequel demonstrates, God had no intention of allowing humans *the* essential attribute of divinity, which makes it extremely unlikely that eating from the Tree of Life would have conferred the true immortality possessed by divine beings, that, after once eating, they would live forever. For the same reason that God wouldn't have created humans immortal (they would be too much like Himself), He wouldn't have provided them with a means for attaining it.

It follows from the broader context that the pastoral existence of life in the Garden would have been prolonged by occasional eating from the Tree of Life, although the humans would have remained mortal, as they

remained hidden, and the expulsion would have been unnecessary.

55. E.g., Deut 32:7; Josh 24:2; Isa 44:7; 63:9; 64:3. For further citations, see BDB 761b–63a.

56. Especially of an "everlasting name" (*šem ʿôlam*) inscribed in the memory of a people (Isa 56:5; 63:12; cf. Exod 3:15, parallel to *le-dor dor*, "for generations"). As a very long time, 1 En. 10:10: "And they will all petition you, for they hope for eternal life, and that each of them will live for five hundred years" (Knibb, *Ethiopic Enoch* II 88–89).

57. Only in Dan 12:2 does *ḥāi ʿolam* mean "everlasting life" (not, however, in this life but the next). This is a very late text and the first and only passage in the Hebrew Bible to clearly refer to the idea of the resurrection of the dead, judgment, and eternal life in the World-to-Come as it developed in rabbinic thought; see Levenson, *Resurrection*, especially 181–200.

58. In Gen 6:3 mortality (*not* living *le-ʿolam*) characterizes everything made of flesh. Stordalen suggests that the Tree of Life would allow the humans to complete a normal lifespan, a biblical ideal (*Echoes*, 292). On *ʿôlam* in Genesis, see Jenni, "Das Wort ʿôlām," 10–12.

had been created. It is perfectly clear that the Tree of Life is present in the story to explain why it is *not* part of our, the real, world; it continues to exist but is no longer accessible. By gaining the faculty of knowing good and bad that makes us "like gods," we have been denied the possibility of living *le-ʿolam*.[59]

Little has been said, here or elsewhere, about the meaning of *life* in the expression "Tree of Life." Other biblical texts amply demonstrate that the notion of life was then rather different from what it is today.[60] Illness makes one less alive; being alive has its degrees. We see the same basic meaning in the English *revive*, literally "return to life," not from the dead but rather as restoration of strength. In Judg 15:19, when Samson was weakened by thirst, "God split the hollow place that is in Lehi, and water came out from it, and he drank and his breath returned, and he lived." In this sense of "life" the Tree of Life would have been restorative and always available for occasional consumption.

The Tree of Life, like the Fountain of Youth, reflects the perennial desire for a magical source of rejuvenation.[61] In the mythology of all peoples, we find extraordinary plants and waters that both extend the lifespan and restore youthful vitality. In the epigraph to T. S. Eliot's *Wasteland*, quoting Petronius's *Satyricon*, the sibyl, an oracular prophetess at Cumae, who had given her favors to Apollo in exchange for a life of as many years as in a handful of sand (but who had forgotten to ask for perpetual youth), when asked what she wants now, replies, "I want to die." The moral is that long life without renewed vitality is not worth living.

From the ancient to the modern world, the search has been for a source of rejuvenation rather than immortality, the latter generally understood as some kind of survival *after* death either as immortality of the soul, resurrection, or reincarnation.[62] Closest to the biblical text, the *Epic of Gilgamesh* contains an episode in which a snake steals from Gilgamesh the plant called "An Old Man is Grown Young" (*šību iṣṣaḥir* LÚ).[63] Why a snake and not some other creature? Perhaps because, by shedding its

---

59. This is Barr's conclusion, based on somewhat different evidence (*Garden of Eden*, 4–20, 57–61).

60. Pidoux, "Encore les Deux Arbres," 38–39.

61. For an extensive discussion, see Ries, "Immortality."

62. On the distinction between immortality of the soul and resurrection, see Barr, *Garden of Eden*, 94–114.

63. *Epic of Gilgamesh*, XI 281.

skin, as it does immediately upon eating the plant, the snake seems young again; it has "the appearance of immortality."[64] It is quite possible that the Storyteller also chose the snake as interlocutor in the Garden of Eden for the very reason that it appears to possess the ability to rejuvenate so coveted by humans.

Although the question of original immortality or original mortality seems to be framed as an either/or, there is a middle ground. It appears that, by placing the Tree of Life in the Garden, God would have been willing to allow human beings some kind of immortality, although not the one that characterizes divinity, in which it is not possible to die.

On this point Augustine makes the very useful distinction between the idea that the first humans were immortal in the sense that it wasn't possible for them to die (the kind of immortality associated with God) and the idea that they were *potentially* immortal in the very restricted sense that under certain circumstances it was possible for them not to die. "It is one thing to be unable to die [*non posse mori*], as is the case with certain immortal beings so created by God; but it is another thing to be able not to die [*posse non mori*] in the sense in which the first man was created immortal. This immortality was given to him from the tree of life, not from a natural constitution."[65] The story of the Garden of Eden seems to envision the latter, as the expulsion removes from them the possibility of rejuvenation as long as they had access to the Tree of Life. This constitutes immortality *in a sense*.

Once outside the Garden of Eden the means of prolonging life is no longer available to us. "The death penalty of 2:17 is not carried out. But what *is* effectuated—cursing the ground and expelling the humans—has a thematic bearing on the original penalty."[66] In this very restricted sense, the divine threat is not entirely empty; the first humans were able to put off death while they had access to the Tree of Life. That possibility is now lost.

As an etiology, the logic of the Garden narrative begins from the current state of human mortality where a Tree of Life, a means of prolonging life and vitality, is *not* available to us, and the story works backward to explain why. In other words, according to the explanatory logic

---

64. Sharon, "Doom of Paradise," 65.
65. Augustine, *Literal Meaning of Genesis* VI 25 36.
66. Stordalen, *Echoes*, 292 n223.

of the story, the Tree of Life is put into the Garden only to be denied to us. According to the *etiological function* of the story, the prohibited tree is the Tree of Life, the one that the narrative sets out to describe as now inaccessible. How it might have functioned had the humans not been expelled is of no interest. We were created mortal with the possibility of prolonging life and becoming in this respect somewhat more like gods, but having achieved, through disobedience, another quality of godlikeness, the Tree of Life is now forever out of reach. It's not too much to say that the whole point of the story is to provide an occasion to reflect on our exceptional status among creatures although, like them, limited by our mortality.

SIX

The Snake

Three spoke the truth and perished from the world and these were the snake, the spies, and Doeg the Edomite.

—Midrash quoted in Nachmanides,
Commentary on the Torah, on Genesis 2:9

THE MOST MYSTERIOUS FIGURE in the Garden of Eden story is the snake, and the "Fall" story depends almost entirely on some assumptions about what it is and why it does what it does. Clarifying how it is actually portrayed takes us a long way toward better understanding the story.

After describing the creation of the woman and the shameless nakedness of the first humans, the narrator abruptly changes the subject and introduces a snake that will play a pivotal role as the story unfolds.[1] The critical act in the narrative occurs when the humans eat from the Tree of Knowing Good and Bad, and the snake is the vehicle that moves the story along to get to that moment.

In general we can say that the snake is one of the characters in the story, interacting with the other characters, including God, who addresses it directly ("Yahweh *'elohîm* said to the snake . . ."). It is treated in the same manner as the humans in the punishments, which is to say it receives similar etiological attention, one that in its case speaks to its

---

1. In the sentence structure of biblical Hebrew, the initial position of the subject (here the snake) signals a shift of subject or emphasis.

current form of locomotion and the dangers it presents and with which it is now confronted.

What are we to make of the fact that the story includes an animal that talks, reasons, and has some sort of privileged knowledge about God?[2] The presence of an animal with human attributes is characteristic of fable, where it is often "used to make a general statement about human nature"[3] and if ever there was a story about human nature, the story of the Garden of Eden is it.

The snake's role in the story is to provide the occasion for the woman to consider the Tree of Knowing Good and Bad by challenging the truthfulness of the divine threat and clarifying its purpose. God's claim that eating from the Tree of Knowing Good and Bad will result in death is directly contradicted by the snake (who negates the very language God used in the prohibition): "*Be assured that you will not die*, because God knows that when you eat from it your eyes will be opened and you will be like gods, knowing good and bad." Here we find the first point of dramatic tension in the story. The audience is left wondering which statement is correct, although it is predisposed to believe what God says and to suspect that it's the snake that speaks falsely.

Based on the assumption that the theme of the story is "the fall," the snake becomes the villain, the enemy of humankind, the agent of human catastrophe. Further, it's usually assumed that God doesn't lie, and therefore, because the snake disputes the truth of God's death threat, it must be the one who is lying. Then, since the snake interacts with the female character, the natural inference is that it was the woman's gullibility, her acceptance of the snake's assertion that brought about the fall. All this is already apparent in the New Testament, from which it became a cornerstone of Christian interpretation, summed up neatly in 1 Tim 2:14: "Adam wasn't deceived, but the woman, deceived, came into transgression."

Before considering the snake as it actually appears in the story we have to clear up a common misconception about its identity. The snake is among the animals created by God in His first attempt to find a helper

---

2. The only other passage in the Hebrew Bible that involves such an animal is Balaam's donkey, who sees what humans cannot and to whom God gives the power of speech temporarily (Numbers 22). In that episode, God "opened Balaam's eyes" so that he might see Yahweh's messenger whom the donkey had seen all along. On talking animals in the Bible, see Savran, "Beastly Speech."

3. Caird, *Language*, 160.

for the human (2:19; 3:1). The punishments are directed at and limited to the three characters (the human, the woman, and the snake). No one else is involved.

However, in the history of interpretation the snake doesn't stay a snake for long. In the one allusion to the snake in the Garden of Eden in the New Testament it's still a snake, although a malevolent one.[4] However, toward the end of the first millennium BCE we find a explosion of interest in angels and demons, and the figure of Satan, so prominent in the book of Job, was reconfigured into a rebel against God, the leader of a host of fallen angels.[5] It seems that sometime during this period Satan came to be identified with the snake in the Garden of Eden and the interpretation of the story took a more sinister turn.

The earliest known version of the Garden of Eden story that explicitly identifies the snake with Satan is *The Life of Adam and Eve*.[6] The story it tells was apparently in wide circulation beyond the first half of the first millennium, as details of *The Life* appear also in the version of the Garden of Eden story in the Qurʾan.[7] Given the importance of the figure of Satan in Christianity and Islam, one might easily qualify *The Life of Adam and Eve* as the least known, most influential text in the world.

In the Latin *Life of Adam and Eve*, in the scene in which Satan explains to Adam and Eve why he brought about their disobedience, there is no snake at all; it has been replaced by Satan. Originally an angel, he explains how it came about that he refused God's command to bow down before the newly created Adam. For his rebellion against God (due to pride, which thereby becomes the sin *par excellence*), he was expelled from heaven and came to earth, determined to seek revenge. *The Life* supplied a crucial element lacking in Genesis 2–3, an explicit motive for the alleged villain.[8]

---

4. " I fear that somehow, as the snake deceived Eve in its villainy, your thoughts may depart from exclusive [and purest devotion] to Christ" (2 Cor 11:3).

5. On the development of the figure of Satan, see Pagels, *Adam, Eve*; Pagels, *Origin of Satan*; Day, *Adversary in Heaven*; Forsyth, *Old Enemy*.

6. The Latin version is known as the *Vita Adae et Eva*. The relevant passage in the *Vita* is 12:1–17:3. For the full text of all versions, see Anderson and Stone, *Synopsis*; online: www2.iath.virginia.edu/anderson/vita/vita.html.

7. Sura 2:30–39; 7:20–28; 15:27–44; 20:116–124.

8. Apparently the version in *The Life* originated from a solution to the missing motive by combining the multiplicity of heavenly beings in Gen 1:26 ("Let *us* make") and 3:22 ("like one of *us*"), with the motif of a fallen angel, borrowed, in good midrashic fashion,

The Storyteller and the Garden of Eden

When we factor in the belief that the Garden of Eden story was an actual episode at the dawn of human history, the figure of Satan finds a real jumping-off point for the search for the origin of evil. Understood in this way, the events in the Garden of Eden had to have actually occurred. As the Christian idea of original sin developed, Adam's sin was understood to have affected all his descendants, which is to say all of us. And if Satan was present in the Garden of Eden, he's still around, tempting everyone to sin.

Together with the judgment on all women, for whom Eve was taken as prototype, the idea of Satan as provocateur in the Garden of Eden has echoed through the religious imagination ever since. The repercussions of this interpretation of Genesis 3 have fallen heavily on women in the Christian West, reaching their zenith during the witch craze of the fourteenth through nineteenth centuries. Over the course of centuries the notion of special, even sexual, relations between women and demons continued and expanded upon ancient traditions about the nature of the relationship between the snake (especially the snake as Satan) and the woman in the Garden of Eden.[9]

By identifying the snake with a fallen angel, a malevolent motive becomes firmly established in the history of interpretation, and Satan enters the popular imagination as the source of evil in the world. Having obtained his initial goal, the expulsion of the humans from Eden, Satan didn't stop there. He not only attacked the original humans but remains the perpetual enemy of both God and His special creation. Thus the snake-as-Satan has become thoroughly embedded in Christian discourse and in Christian self-understanding.[10]

---

from an interpretation of Isa 14:12–14 (where it is used as a metaphor to describe the fall from power of a king of Babylon). On this development, see Evans, *Paradise Lost*, 38–39.

9. In early Judaism we see a tendency toward this kind of speculation in *Gen. Rab.* 18:6; 20:4; *b. Soṭah* 9b; *Tg. Ps.-J.* Gen 4:1; 5:2–3. The intimate connection between the woman and the snake also underlies Philo's allegorical interpretation when he identifies the woman as sense-perception and the snake as the pleasures experienced by the senses that distract man-as-mind from the contemplation of God. On Philo and his impact on early church fathers, see Boyarin, *Carnal Israel*, 37–41, 78–83.

10. Similarly in Islam, where Satan plays an important role. In the Qur'an, as in the *Life of Adam and Eve*, Satan (also named Iblis) entirely replaces the snake. Unlike the snake in Genesis 3 and Satan in *The Life*, who interact only with the woman, in the Qur'an Satan directly addresses Adam alone (Surah 20:120) or both Adam and his unnamed wife (Surah 7:20).

The Snake

This is the primary obstacle to a thorough rereading of Genesis 2–3. The suggestion that the snake might not be the enemy of humankind, that it actually told the truth, results in profound cognitive dissonance. Not only does this idea challenge the dominant interpretation, it comes up against an entrenched belief system where Satan is a central player. As a result, the burden of proof is increased so that the bits and pieces of argument that together make possible a radical reinterpretation come up against a stone wall of resistance. Once one entertains the possibility that another interpretation is possible, an entire belief system is threatened. If the snake is not a villain, much less Satan, if Adam and Eve do not sin, if there is not even an Adam and Eve in the story, we really must go back to the drawing board and take another look at the whole story and the snake's role in it.

Despite these enormous obstacles to reinterpretation, let's consider the text itself. We may begin by noting that the snake is *made* hostile to mankind as part of its punishment, only *after* the scene between the snake and the woman. This is the first explicit clue in the text as to how the Storyteller wants his story to be understood. If the snake is not hostile at the outset, then its actions are open to interpretation. Did it rather act in furtherance of humankind? If so, what then is the story about? Let's continue to look at what other information the text provides.

GENESIS 3:1

The snake (*naḥaš*) was ʿ*arûm* beyond every (kind of) land animal that Yahweh ʾ*elohîm* had made.

The Storyteller begins this scene by telling his audience something about the snake's character. "There are not many instances of direct characterization by the narrator in biblical narratives. What is evident is that the trait noted by the narrator is always extremely important in the development of the plot."[11] Here the narrator informs us that the snake is the most ʿ*arûm* of all the animal species. If this kind of characterization is "extremely important in the development of the plot," it is crucial in interpreting this story in particular as it occurs at the beginning of the critical scene, the turning point in the narrative. Because, to a large extent, the

---

11. Bar-Efrat, *Narrative Art*, 53.

interpretation of the story of the Garden of Eden hangs on the meaning of this one word, we'll have to exert some patient effort to try to ascertain what the Storyteller meant to convey by choosing it.

The word ʿarûm has been variously translated as "subtle,"[12] "cunning,"[13] "shrewd,"[14] and "crafty."[15] Clearly, these translations predispose the reader to an unfavorable assessment of the character of the snake, reflecting the conventional view of its evil nature, and frame its role in the story as villainous. We should also note the usual translation of the Hebrew word naḥaš as "serpent" rather than as "snake." Using an archaic term that substitutes the alien for the commonplace puts an even more subtle spin on the animal's character. Who uses the word *serpent* anymore? Reading the Bible in translation leaves us at the mercy of the views of the translator.

The way in which we approach the story hangs on how we understand this one word. How do we go about figuring out the meaning of a word in the Hebrew Bible? The primary way to determine meaning is by looking at other occurrences of the word first in the Bible itself, then in cognate Semitic languages (which in this case aren't helpful). Unfortunately, the word ʿarûm is rather uncommon. It's used in Proverbs of someone who is contrasted to a fool.[16] In these cases it must be translated by such positive terms as "prudent" or "wise."[17] It's very difficult to find an equivalent in English. "Clever" is too negative, "prudent" doesn't quite fit the context and in current use is overly limited to the practical, while "wise" implies a special gift rather than a faculty available to an entire species. I've settled on "judicious" in the translation, but it should be taken in the *OED*'s sense

---

12. KJV, ASV, JPS 1917, RSV, NJB.

13. NKJV, NAB, REB, TEV.

14. NJPS.

15. ESV, NASB, NEB, NIV and TNIV, NRSV.

16. Prov 12:16, 23; 13:16; 14:8 (ḥokmat ʿarûm, "wisdom of a prudent person"); 15, 18; 22:3; 27:12; cf. Job 5:12–13; 15:5.

17. Unlike the adjective ʿarûm that we find in Gen 3:1 and the substantive based on it ('an ʿarûm [person]'), the verb ʿrm may be used to mean "be prudent" as opposed to "act foolishly" (Prov 15:5), as well as to characterize the behavior of an enemy ("to plot or strategize"), but that the latter is negative depends on one's point of view (1 Sam 23:22; Ps 83:4; the nominal form in Exod 21:14). So too ḥakam can indicate someone who knows how to get things done, without any moral connotation (Ackermann, "Knowing Good and Evil," 56). See also Blenkinsopp, *Creation, Un-creation*, 72–73.

of "forming correct opinions or notions; sound in discernment; wisely critical."[18]

In several instances we find a general statement to the effect that God is able to frustrate the plans of those characterized as ʿarûm, those who rely on their own reasoning ability rather than on God.[19] But this is not to say that there is anything wrong with being ʿarûm in and of itself. It is basically a good thing to be ʿarûm, except when it leads someone to fail to take God into account, precisely what happens in the Garden of Eden story. If this is what the Storyteller had in mind, the man and woman in Gen 2:25 are ʿarûmmîm in more ways than one.

While there appears to be nothing particularly negative in the way the snake is characterized, what about the choice of a snake as interlocutor? Modern readers tend to view snakes in a negative light; the English idiom "snake in the grass" reinforces the stereotype. This makes it difficult for us to consider the snake as anything but dangerous, devious, and ultimately malevolent.

This was not the case in biblical Israel, and contemporary readers should take care not to project their own attitudes onto the peoples of the ancient world. In Numbers 21, after God punishes the Israelites for their complaints about the quality of life in the wilderness by sending venomous snakes,[20] Moses is instructed by Yahweh to "make a fiery snake (not naḥaš as in Genesis 3, but śarap), and set it on a standard: and it shall happen, that everyone who is bitten, when he sees it, shall live." This story provides an origin for the Nehushtan (a word related to naḥaš), a bronze statue of a snake in the temple in Jerusalem to which sacrifices were dedicated and which was destroyed by Hezekiah in his reforms in the late eighth century (2 Kgs 18:4).

The incident in the wilderness in Numbers 21 is cited in the New Testament, where the snake "exalted" by Moses is compared to Jesus as a source of "eternal life" (John 3:14–15). This seems to indicate that even into the period of the writing of the New Testament, the symbolism of

---

18. OED, 2nd ed., s.v. "judicious."

19. Job 5:12–13 where ʿarûm also characterizes those who are wise (ḥakam). In Job 15:1–5 Eliphaz warns Job that the wise person, speaking the language of the ʿarûmmîm, is in danger of losing the fear of God and weakening his devotion to Him. Also of the wise, Jer 8:6–9.

20. See also Jer 8:17, where biting snakes also act as Yahweh's agents.

the snake was more associated with life than with death.²¹ Despite the perennial dangers posed by poisonous snakes, the attitude towards snakes in the ancient world is surprisingly positive.²² Indeed, snakes have the peculiar attribute of shedding their skin, which appears to be a kind of rejuvenation. They are liminal beings, apparently possessing the equivalent of access to the Tree of Life. ²³

So we return to the description of the snake as ʿ*arûm*. The Storyteller has gone out of his way to tell us something about the snake's character, that it was the most ʿ*arûm* of all the animals that God had created. Thus far we can say that the word describes something basically positive about the character of the snake.

This takes us to the second, equally important source for determining the meaning of an unusual word—its immediate context. Gen 3:1 seems to indicate that the snake's nature was established by God Himself. There we're told that the snake is more ʿ*arûm* than "*every land animal* that Yahweh ʾ*elohîm* had made." This refers back to Genesis 2 where God formed the animals as "helpers" for the human. By using the same language as in Gen 2:19 ("And Yahweh ʾ*elohîm* formed from the soil *every land animal*") Gen 3:1 makes it clear that 2:19 includes the snake. Adding the phrase ("that Yahweh ʾ*elohîm* had made") presents the snake and its attribute of being ʿ*arûm* in particular as part of the divine plan in creation, in all likelihood in order to prepare the audience to accept an animal not only with the ability to speak, but also possessing a surprising amount of information. That the snake may turn out to be too smart for its own good says nothing about its character or intentions.

Does this characterization of the snake make it unique among the land animals? According to Gen 3:1, the snake was among the animal species that had been made by God to be helpers to the lone human, and was judicious in comparison with the others. Hebrew syntax differs from that of English in that Hebrew does not distinguish between the comparative and superlative (more vs. most); in biblical Hebrew all comparisons are constructed by the partitive *min* ("from," "among," "beyond") that sets one over against others. It points to something distinctive, whether "more" or unique. The snake as more ʿ*arûm* than all the others makes it

21. Charlesworth, *Good and Evil Serpent*, 324–51 (on Num 21:4–9 and 2 Kgs 18:4); 360–415 (on John 3:14–15).

22. Joines, *Serpent Symbolism*; Charlesworth, *Good and Evil Serpent*.

23. Niditch, *Folklore and the Hebrew Bible*, 44–47.

The Snake

the most ʿarûm of the animals; the phrase characterizes snakes as ʿarûm but limits its meaning to a comparison with others.[24]

There are two possibilities here. In the first, the verbal construction distributes the characteristic to all other members of the class, i.e., to every animal species, only to a lesser degree.[25] On the other hand, in the parallel to this construction in Gen 3:14, the snake is cursed "among all the livestock and among all the animals," not implying that the latter were cursed in any way.

Unfortunately Hebrew syntax alone doesn't allow us to determine with certainty whether the snake is uniquely ʿarûm or simply more ʿarûm than other kinds of animals. However, if we assume the audience to be sufficiently attuned to the way the two verses (3:1 and 3:14) parallel one another, although they are separated by the critical scene in the story, and despite the fact that the clearest instance comes second in the series, we might conclude that, as snakes are singularly "cursed," they are also uniquely ʿarum, so that Gen 3:1 should be understood as "among every (kind of) land animal, the snake was ʿarum."

Taken in context, ʿarûm can only refer to a characteristic of the *species* snake rather than to a quality peculiar to this snake in particular. In the setting of a fable, a trait, whether it be the plodding turtle or the speedy hare, doesn't belong to the individual but to the species of which it is a member, so the punishment of the snake also fittingly applies to all snakes. It is characterized as a member of its species, not as an individual. This, by the way, is an additional argument against identifying this particular snake with Satan, an identification that would have its conduct be uniquely motivated. To see the snake as acting on its own volition or as an agent of Satan ignores the fact that the Storyteller explicitly asks us to see the snake in terms of its nature as a species created by God before He changes that nature for the worse.

To more (or less) clearly understand the meaning of ʿarûm in Gen 3:1, let's return to its immediate context. Gen 3:1 follows 2:25. Before the division of the text into chapters in the medieval period, the two verses were read without the discontinuity that chapter division imposes.

---

24. GKC 119w; 133.

25. To illustrate this, we may compare "Israel loved Joseph among his sons" (Gen 37:3), in which it is implied that Jacob loved all his sons, but favored Joseph above the others. In this case the construction reflects relativity and does not indicate a quality unique to one member of the group. See Cassuto, *Commentary*, 159.

The Storyteller and the Garden of Eden

According to Gen 2:25, "They were naked (ʿarûmmîm), the two of them, the human and his woman, and they were not ashamed." This is followed *immediately* by the statement that the snake was ʿarûm. In the language in which the story was composed the pun is palpable, especially to those listening to the story (or reading aloud), while it's completely lost in translation. The pun calls upon the audience to recognize some connection between the description of the snake as ʿarûm in 3:1 and that of the couple as ʿarûmmîm in 2:25, a connection that turns out to be causal. What the snake knows as a result of its being ʿarûm will affect the human awareness of being ʿarûmmîm.[26]

It's obvious that the desire to make a pun influenced the choice of words here. There can be no doubt whatsoever that ʿarûm was chosen because of its assonance with ʿarûmmîm in the previous sentence.[27] If the Storyteller had been looking for clarity of meaning, the language of biblical Hebrew provided many alternatives. Had he intended to indicate that the snake was wise, he could have used the more common term ḥakam;[28] if he had intended "cunning" or "devious," words meaning more precisely this were close at hand.

The fact that a pun is embedded in these critical verses indicates a lightness of tone (and ambiguity of meaning) that casts some doubt on the idea that the Storyteller envisioned the fable he composed as a tragedy. Contemporary biblical scholars have begun to recognize this. "The story has a mildly ironic and comic character rather than one of unrelieved tragedy and catastrophe."[29] "As a first impression, the author, in treating so heavy a subject as the ultimate origins of current experience, seems to

---

26. "Puns provide contextual support for both meanings of the ambiguity they contain" (Coulson and Severens, "Hemispheric Asymmetry," 184).

27. In Gen 2:25 we find the more unusual spelling ʿarûmmîm. "The selection of the /u/ in Gen 2:25 seems to be governed by the attempt at virtual homonymy towards Gen 3:1" (Stordalen, *Echoes*, 199–200); see also Cassuto, *Commentary*, 143–44.

28. *Targum Onqelos*, the translation into Aramaic (probably dated to the fourth century and recognized in the Babylonian Talmud as authoritative for explicating the Hebrew Bible) renders ʿarûm into Aramaic as ḥakîm (despite the existence of ʿarûm in Aramaic). This obscures the pun but seems to reflect an interpretation of ʿarûm in a positive sense. See Jastrow, *Dictionary of the Targumim*, I:462–63, 1115.

29. Barr, *Garden of Eden*, 12.

have a light touch."³⁰ "Had this been modern literature, it might have been perceived as farce or something similar."³¹

All we can conclude from the way that the snake is initially described in Gen 3:1 is that it intends to address the snake's unexpected abilities to speak and know, rather than serving to depict its motives or moral character. At the same time, in terms of literary style, the pun on ʿarûmmîm and ʿarûm entertains its audience by continuing the characteristic verbal play that began with the creation of ʾadam and ʾiššah.

THE DIALOGUE WITH THE WOMAN: WHAT THE SNAKE SAYS (GENESIS 3:1-5)

As it first speaks to the woman, the snake draws her attention to the trees in the Garden and raises the issue of the divine prohibition. The form of its statement doesn't appear to be a question (as it's usually translated):³² "Indeed God (ʾelohîm) said, you will not eat from every tree of the Garden."³³ It takes God's statement ("From all the Garden's trees be assured that you will eat, but from the Tree of Knowing Good and Bad, when you eat from it, be assured that you will die") and rephrases it as a prohibition, as if He had said, "You won't eat from all the trees in the Garden. There's one that's forbidden."

From a narrative point of view the snake's assertion serves to introduce the dialogue and to focus it on what will follow. It allows the woman to show that she is fully cognizant of the prohibition that she paraphrases, and to which she adds "nor touch it." Adding a prohibition against touching may have functioned to make sure the fruit wasn't eaten; if you don't touch it, you can't eat it. Yet by including "nor touch it," as part of the command the woman ironically adds to her disobedience: she "takes" (by touching) and "eats," while the man only "eats."

The woman is often accused of softening the prohibition by rewording "be assured that you will die" to "lest you die"; this is taken as a sign

30. McEvenue, *Interpreting the Pentateuch*, 65.

31. Stordalen, *Echoes*, 218.

32. The snake's address to the woman begins with a conjunction akin to *moreover* that usually appears with an antecedent (as if continuing a conversation in progress); the antecedent is lacking here (BDB 65a).

33. The man is also present in the scene (3:6) but takes no part. The verbs used by the snake are plural as though addressing them both.

that she is beginning to weaken in her resolve. It rather seems to express how she had processed the threat, as a warning rather than an outright prohibition, and leaves open the possibility that this is the way the threat had been communicated to her, as she wasn't present, didn't even exist, when the prohibition was issued. Either way, the idea that you should stay away from, not even touch, something that could do you grievous harm is not a farfetched conclusion to draw from a serious threat, however expressed.

"*Lest* you die" expresses more a likelihood than a remote possibility. We can compare it to God's concern that if not expelled from the Garden the humans might eat from the Tree of Life ("*lest* he send forth his hand and take also from the Tree of Life and eat and live in perpetuity"). God here addresses the *likelihood* that the humans will eat from the Tree of Life. With "lest you die" the woman doesn't totally negate the risk, but leaves open the possibility that the threatened death will not be realized. Otherwise her decision to eat, inevitable in terms of the story line, would have been suicide.

After the woman gives her version of the prohibition, the snake responds with a strong denial that eating from the tree will result in death and adds what it firmly believes will happen *instead*: "Be assured that you will not die, *because God knows* that your eyes will be opened and you will become like gods, knowing good and bad" (3:4). The syntax here exactly parallels that used by God in the prohibition; in both the speaker expresses confidence that what he is saying is true.

The snake interprets the threat of death to mean that death would occur as a direct result of eating (which would have been its commonsense meaning). It goes on to claim that *God knows that something else will happen*, something that He wants to avoid. This is corroborated by what follows. Eating from the tree does have immediate effects, and these are precisely what the snake claims: the eyes of the pair are opened, and they now have some new cognitive faculty that allows them to know something they hadn't known earlier ("they *knew* that they were naked"). Despite the fact that what they acquire results in a new awareness of their nakedness and a new sense of shame, even God characterizes it as promoting the humans to quasi-divine status ("the human being has become like one of us").

Let's return to the snake's counterclaim ("Be assured that you will not die, rather *God knows* that your eyes will be opened and you will become like gods knowing good and bad"). The words in the text have not received due attention, particularly in light of the theological weight placed upon them. The snake does not claim to have personal knowledge of the effects but rather asserts that "God knows" what the effects of eating will be, and clearly implies that He misstated them in order to keep the humans from eating and becoming "like gods."

According to the snake, these effects will be quite different from that claimed by God; instead of dying, the humans will become "like gods." If the divine prohibition was just a test of obedience, what would be the point of the actual effects of eating described in the text that have nothing to do with death? If the narrative is about a test that the humans fail and then are punished for, there's an awful lot of extraneous material in the story that has to be ignored or devalued—especially the veracity of the snake. In fact the snake's words point to the pivotal event of the story, that the humans become "like gods."

Only rarely is the truthfulness of the snake's statement recognized. It does *not* say that *it* knows what the effect of eating from the Tree of Knowing Good and Bad would be, but that it is certain about what God knows. In consequence, the snake is able to assert with confidence that it will not be death, and in fact they do not die. The snake's words are clear, and everything it says will happen does happen. God's knowledge, according to the snake and the story, is true knowledge. It just doesn't comport with the divine threat. Interpreters tend to ignore the plain meaning of the text because:

> The idea that God would mislead the humans is unacceptable a priori.
>
> The implication that God would deny humans knowledge, whether that knowledge is moral or otherwise, is troublesome from a theological or philosophical perspective.
>
> The theological constructs that have been built upon misinterpretation are too important to allow a plain sense reading of Genesis 3 to prevail.

Over the thousands of years of reading Genesis 2–3, before the twentieth century the number of commentators who recognized that the snake was telling the truth can be counted on one hand,[34] although recently

---

34. Among them, Nachmanides, *Commentary on the Torah*, on Gen 2:9 (thirteenth century); Stanton, *Woman's Bible*, 18 (end of the nineteenth century).

this has begun to change.[35] Those who continue to maintain the idea of the duplicitous snake are forced to defy logic or introduce extraneous ideas. According to von Rad, "the serpent neither lied nor told the truth," whatever that might mean.[36] For Cassuto, the serpent "speaks solely for the purpose of inciting against the will of the Lord God." Cassuto then proposes, "in the ultimate analysis, we have here an allegorical allusion to the craftiness to be found in *man himself*."[37] Applying more contemporary lit-crit language, Sharp writes, "The serpent is the first ironist we encounter in Scripture. Its ironic double voicing speaks truth precisely despite its unreliability."[38] Indeed human cleverness has no limit, especially when it comes to biblical interpretation.[39]

If the divine threat does not refer to death as an immediate effect of eating, but instead entails the loss of immortality and eventual death, it is at best deceptive. It seems to mean one thing, that the fruit is poisonous and that death will swiftly ensue, but in fact means something else, that the humans will die some day. On the other hand, what the snake says is straightforward and everything it says turns out to be true.

Let's look at the story again, keeping in mind its explanatory function. The tone of the story keeps it from being tragic. All is not lost; something has been gained. The human condition is not entirely negative; the impediments to our survival are the result of divine punishment. For what were we punished? By disobeying God's command, we attained a state God did not intend us to reach, we became "like gods." Created to be mortal, created like the other animals of perishable material, we broke through a boundary that separates us from divinity. We became godlike. According to the story, the snake is the agent that initiates the events that

---

35. Pfeiffer, "Wisdom and Vision," 97; Beattie, "*Peshat* and *Derash*"; Barr, *Garden of Eden*, 13; Noort, "Gan-Eden," 25. Views on the question of God's veracity are summarized in Whybray, "Immorality of God," 92–95; Charlesworth, *Good and Evil Serpent*, 315–17, 21.

36. Von Rad, *Genesis*, 87.

37. Cassuto, *Commentary*, 142 (italics original). "Paul Ricoeur made the point that the snake stands for the experience of temptation as a force that comes upon us as if from outside, or from a part of ourselves of which we are ignorant, or which we do not acknowledge; it represents what he called the externality of desire" (Blenkinsopp, *Creation, Un-creation*, 76). See also Fishbane, *Text and Texture*, 22–23.

38. Sharp, *Irony*, 38.

39 Beattie demonstrates the extent to which major twentieth-century commentaries depart from the plain meaning of the text ("*Peshat* and *Derash*").

lead up to this change in our status, despite God's efforts to the contrary. Humbled in its own way, it shares with us in the punishments.

Not unlike the people of Babel, the snake and the humans in Genesis 3 are punished by being alienated from one another, a kind of union-busting on God's part. The implication embedded in the etiology of the dangerous snake is that prior to the divine sentence there had been no enmity between snakes and human beings. This seems a clear indication by the Storyteller that the snake's act was not intentionally hostile to the interests of the humans. We must keep this in mind as we examine the motivations of the various characters in the story.

SEVEN

On the Characters and Their Motivation

Say first what cause
Mov'd our Grand Parents in that happy State,
Favour'd of Heav'n so highly, to fall off
From their Creator, and transgress his Will
For one restraint, Lords of the World besides?
—MILTON, *PARADISE LOST* I 28–32

AS WE FOLLOW A story, we begin to form some idea about its characters, a sense of their motives and their relationship to one another (not to mention a mental image of their age and physical appearance). What the narrative doesn't provide explicitly we supply on our own. This is an unconscious process based on the details we've been given and the cultural biases we impose. Once we form such an impression, when an actor in the story says or does something that contradicts it, we have to retune the image we've constructed.

Characterization in the Hebrew Bible tends to be sketchy at best. The subtlety of the story of the Garden of Eden obliges us to rely on hints and clues to determine the intentions of each of its four characters. The conventional interpretation of the story as "the Fall" is based on assumptions about their motives that may or may not be correct, but can be tested by a close reading. Is the snake necessarily malevolent or God necessarily beneficent? Why do the humans disobey His direct command? Why do they feel shame and why do they hide? None of these questions are clearly answered in a superficial reading, so we're forced to make certain assumptions, constantly checking them against the story as we go along.

In Milton's *Paradise Lost* we're treated to a full-blown emotional depiction of each of the characters, even and most especially the snake-as-Satan (leading William Blake to remark famously that Milton "was of Satan's party without knowing it"). By contrast, there is very little sense of the emotional life of the characters in the actual biblical story. When we as readers fill in the emotional picture, we are often led into contradictions with the story itself. For example, in the portrayal of the scene of the expulsion both Masaccio and Michelangelo depict the man and woman as naked, despite the verse in Gen 3:21 where they have just been clothed. Nakedness in these paintings is symbolic of their new vulnerability in the unprotected world outside the Garden but conflicts with the biblical text. On a deeper level, their crouching posture and the fear and despair in their faces make them all too human.

If, on the other hand, we stay within the confines of Genesis 2–3, the characters remain more like those in a fable, without emotional or psychological depth, and rather less like real individuals. They're presented simply in terms of their goals and desires, the way in which even animals interpret the behavior of others.[1] Given this limitation, we can examine the story for clues about the motives of each of the four characters.

GOD

Because knowledge is power, my child, and those who have it don't intend to share it.

—ANDREA JAPP, *LE SOUFFLE DE LA ROSE*

How is God depicted in the story? First, as discussed earlier, there is the rather unusual way of referring to Him. The name of God used consistently by the narrator is *yahweh 'elohîm*. None of the characters refers to the deity by name except in the critical scene between the snake and the woman, where both use just *'elohîm*. No satisfactory suggestion has been made to explain the variation. Perhaps the idiosyncratic use of the

---

1. Boyd, *Origin of Stories*, 138.

composite Yahweh *'elohîm* in Genesis 2–3 is intended to lay stress on His divinity ("Yahweh, a god") as opposed to the other characters (this distinction being the chief concern of the story in its entirety). It may be that the use of *'elohîm* in spoken dialogue reflects a disinclination to utter the personal name of God that strengthened over time to become an outright prohibition. By contrast, in the creation story in the first chapter of Genesis the deity is referred to as *'elohîm* throughout; the transition to Yahweh *'elohîm* occurs in Gen 2:4b ("on the day Yahweh *'elohîm* made earth and heavens"), one of the reasons to take this half-verse as the beginning of the Garden of Eden story. It doesn't appear likely that the problem of this variant in the divine name will ever be conclusively resolved.

Given all the distinctive characteristics of the story, we shouldn't be surprised to find a unique representation of the deity as well. We've seen that in threatening the man with death, God proves to be the subtle one, conveying one thing when He intends another. This is true whether one adopts the view that the threat refers to the loss of immortality rather than to the imminent death that the warning more than implies ("on the day"), whether it refers to not physical but spiritual death, or whether it's just an empty threat meant to deter the man from eating from that particular tree.

As has often been observed, the characterization of God in Genesis 2–3, especially when compared to that in the first chapter of Genesis, is decidedly anthropomorphic.[2] He is a potter, manually modeling His creatures from the soil (the potter metaphor is used in the Bible to indicate power over the object modeled).[3] He is also a kind of carpenter as he

---

2. "We have no other language besides metaphor with which to speak about God ... Man is created to become like God, and the ultimate justification of anthropomorphic imagery lies in the contribution it makes to the attainment of that goal" (Caird, *Language*, 174, 178). On anthropomorphic depictions of God in the Bible, see Hamori, *When Gods Were Men*, especially 26–54.

3. See above, pp. 87–88, 90n27. The anthropomorphism of the potter image is made even more explicit in Job 10:8, "Your hands shaped me and made me." "Among anthropomorphic metaphors there is a lower correspondence when the metaphor is drawn from man's dealings with the subhuman world" as in the image of the potter and the pot (Caird, *Language*, 154). On the verb *yṣr* "to form" and the forming of the human from clay in biblical and ancient Near Eastern literature, see Westermann, *Genesis 1–11*, 203–5. According to Humbert, the potter image emphasizes the abyss separating creatures from creator (*Études*, 177), and the frequent use of *yṣr* in Second Isaiah serves "to exalt the unique grandeur of Yahweh" (Humbert, "Emploi et Portée Bibliques," 85), to which we may compare Rom 9:20–23. See also Greenstein, "God's Golem."

"builds" the woman from human material, a farmer, planting a garden, and a tailor, fashioning clothes for the man and woman. He walks about in the Garden in the cool of the day; His movements can be heard by the man and the woman. He looks for and speaks with the humans (and the snake). His creative activity is a trial-and-error process in which He has to add something (the help) that He had overlooked in the first go-around, tries the animals, then, when they fail to serve, the woman (2:18–21).[4]

He is also portrayed with human emotions, protective of His divine prerogatives. If knowledge is power, one might say that, in terms of His motive in desiring to limit the human's access to knowledge, He acts as a ruler, reluctant to share that power with His inferiors. The latter is not only clear from the snake's explanation of the reason for the divine threat, "*because God knows* that when you eat from it . . . you will be like gods, knowing good and bad" (3:5), but also from God's own admission, "The human being has become like one of us, knowing good and bad, and now, lest he send forth his hand and also take from the Tree of Life and eat and live in perpetuity . . ." (3:22).[5] The latter quite clearly articulates God's motivation, putting the words in direct speech, as He expels the humans to keep them from approximating to yet another divine advantage. In a story whose focus is on God's reaction to human "godlikeness," we can only find irony in its portrayal of God's humanlikeness.

The deity thus depicted is familiar to readers of other biblical texts, in particular the Tower of Babel episode in Genesis 11. In the two stories His interests and reaction are precisely parallel. In both, He acts to undermine human potential, in Genesis 3 by impeding human beings' ability to do the work for which they were created (and demoralizing them by reminding them of the futility of their efforts), in Genesis 11 by subverting the possibility of collective human effort. The primary difference between the two stories is that the Tower of Babel episode does not involve disobedience.[6] Yet the reaction of God in both stories is quite

---

4. Stordalen finds God "ambivalent" in planting the Tree of Knowing and then prohibiting the humans from eating from it (*Echoes*, 240).

5. The unspoken possibility of a further extension of human godlikeness, represented by the incomplete sentence, may indicate God's unwillingness to put into words something "too awful to contemplate" (Bullinger, *Figures of Speech*, 152).

6. According to the conventional interpretation, the people's intention to build "a tower with its top in the heavens" represents an attempt to breach the physical boundary between the human and divine realms. This interpretation has been challenged by Hiebert ("Tower of Babel"). According to the story Yahweh feared what humans might

similar. In the Garden of Eden the rapport between human being and snake is deliberately ruptured, while in the Tower of Babel, the possibility for human solidarity is crippled by means of dispersion and linguistic differentiation.[7] Both are origin stories that describe aspects of the human condition, ones that are disastrous from our point of view but not from His.[8]

As we've seen, very little attention has been paid to the precise motivation for the divine punishments, rather they have been generally accepted in terms of their etiological function, as explaining the miseries of the human condition. Yet God Himself explains why He acts. To the snake He says, "because you did this." No reason is given to the woman, perhaps because her role is obvious. As for the man, He says to him, "because you heeded [*lit.*, listened to the voice of] your woman and ate from the tree which I commanded you saying you will not eat from it." If the problem had been disobedience, how easily could the Storyteller have had God say to the man "because you didn't heed Me [*lit.*, listen to *My* voice] . . ."

In terms of satisfactory explanations for God's reaction and the ensuing punishments, the explicit reasons that God provides leave much to be desired. The man is punished for allowing himself to be influenced by the woman and for eating the forbidden fruit. God's accusation doesn't clarify His underlying issue with what the man did. Was it because he was swayed by the woman, because he disobeyed by eating, or because of the effect of having eaten? As for the woman, God is even less clear, as He pronounces her punishment with no accusation at all. His failure to provide satisfactory allegations leaves the audience in the dark about what's really motivating Him.

---

accomplish were they allowed to act in concert. An etiological story like Genesis 2–3, it begins from the observation of language diversity and the geographical boundaries between peoples, whose existence it then explains.

7. The redactor incorporated the Tower of Babel story at this point in the larger historical narrative as a prelude to the origin of the people of Israel as distinct from other peoples.

8. Compare, on the book of Job, "The whole book leaves the reader pondering the ironies of life made greater by the undergirding irony of a deity not necessarily well-disposed towards his creatures" (Carroll, "Irony," 326). Job is under the misapprehension that God rewards the good and punishes the wicked (Caird, *Language*, 15). On the depiction of God in Job, Genesis 2–3, and Gen 11:1–9, see especially Whybray, "Immorality of God," 89–112.

On the Characters and Their Motivation

Just as with all the characters in the story we have to come to some conclusion about God's desires and goals. Other than the accusations, the only clues remain in the punishments that He imposes. The kinds of corrective action that He takes reveal what He sees as the problem. We examined this question at length above. Suffice it to say in summary that the punishments function to reduce the stature of the snake, the woman, and the man. God's intention in the punishments is to offset their otherwise superior status among earthly creatures, whether originally God-given in the case of the snake, or God-defying in the case of the humans.

Although many commentators mention the rupture in the relationship between the humans and God, the only decisive and permanent rupture explicit in the text is the one brought about by God, between the humans and the snake. Somewhat more subtle is the rupture between the man and the woman, and between the human being and the soil. In contrast to claiming their essential unity when he first sees her ("bone from my bones, flesh from my flesh"), the man distances himself from the woman as he blames her for his actions, just as he blames God for giving him the woman. Their relationship suffers a decisive rupture through the institution of male domination as a result of the woman's punishment. The conditions imposed by the curse on the soil also impair the relationship between human and soil. For both the human and the woman, the rupture occurs with the material from and for which each was created (*'adam* and *'adamah*, *'iššah* and *'iš*), the last stage in the extended wordplays with which the Storyteller constructed his narrative from the start. In all three cases, the rupture is effectuated by God.

The divine-human relationship remains unchanged. God continues to speak to the humans, dealing with them as He had earlier, on His own terms. No alienation between them is indicated in the story. Someone later (but before the text of Genesis was fixed) felt the need to bring to the fore a more compassionate side of God, demonstrating His concern for the humans He had created by adding, at the end of the story, in the midst of the punishments, the verse in which He clothes the humans (Gen 3:21).[9]

---

9. "What happens in narrative is usually logically related to the story in which the narrative resides. But in the present case this relation is not clear" (Culley, "Action Sequences," 32). See above, pp. 94–96.

The Storyteller portrays God as primarily interested in guarding the boundaries between human and divine, between mortals and gods.[10] He depicts God's particular concern for the human being that He created in multiple ways: the mention of the divine breath that animates the human (omitted in the case of the animals), the portrayal of the generosity with which He provided the human with all He deemed necessary—the woman in particular. Yet His plans were upset when the humans overstepped the line He had set for them, for which they were, in His view, appropriately punished. However, we must keep in mind that the Storyteller was not writing theology, nor does he seem to have much interest in theodicy. He assigns the blame for our current difficulties fairly equally on the deity and the humans who, after all, were warned in no uncertain terms to stay away from the Tree of Knowing Good and Bad.

THE MAN (HUMAN) AND THE WOMAN

You understand . . . the ancient legend of paradise . . . That legend refers to us today, does it not? Think about it. There were two in paradise and the choice was offered to them: happiness without freedom, or freedom without happiness . . . They, blockheads that they were, chose freedom.

—Yevgeny Zamyatin, *We*, Entry 11

There is tension in the story between the detailed description of the events that make up the plot, the scenes that we're given as eye-witnesses, the occasional glimpse into the inner life of the characters, and the fact that the human characters remain nameless throughout, referred to simply as "the human being" (*ha-ʾadam*) and "the woman" (*ha-ʾiššah*). Nameless characters are depersonalized, giving the story the feel of a fable. We are dissuaded from seeing the characters in fables as real individuals and thereby from viewing the story itself as something that really happened.

---

10. In this sense it has much in common with Greek myth. "The idea of gradual progress from a wretched existence, worse than that of the animals, to the glory of the Greek city states tended to emphasize the powers of man. For this had been accomplished largely against the will of the gods, as the Prometheus myths make clear. . . . The prevailing belief appears to have been that man was able to rise above his original brutish state only through trickery and that Zeus had ever since made the life of man precarious in his anger" (Gowan, *When Man Becomes God*, 13).

On the Characters and Their Motivation

As we have seen, when the story of the Garden of Eden was adopted to begin the broader historical narrative in Genesis, the first man and the first woman were transformed into historical individuals and given personal names. After the composition of the story, with its nameless protagonists, the man's name was taken from it, *ha-'adam* became Adam. As for the female character, it took an addition to the text to get her a name. She remains "the woman" until the very end of the story: "The human called his woman Eve (*ḥawwah*) because she became the mother of all life (*ḥâi*)" (Gen 3:20).

It's worthwhile to examine this verse in detail. As a folk etymology, it's obviously based on a (rather farfetched) play on words, but one that differs from other wordplays in the story. Not integrated in any way into the narrative as are the others, it is overt, strained, and lacks the subtlety that characterizes the use of language elsewhere in the Storyteller's work. Stylistically it doesn't fit at all.[11]

Nor does it work in its context. The naming of the woman immediately follows the punishments and interrupts the narration as it moves from punishment to expulsion, all focusing on God's reaction to discovering that the human and the woman have eaten from the Tree of Knowing. This intrusion shifts the narrative abruptly from God pronouncing the punishments to the human doing the naming and then back to God.

Moreover, by making the woman the main character in the crucial scene, the Storyteller attempted to give an explanation for what he perceived to be the oppression of women in his society. As the primary culprit in His eyes, God has just pointed out to the woman her future subordinate status. The story explains this as the upshot of her achievement in getting us higher status among creatures, by placing it under the cloud of disobedience to the will of God. By stressing the highly positive role of the woman as mother the addition in Gen 3:20 contradicts the gist of the woman's punishment that highlights her subordinate status and the trials of maternity.

---

11. It does, however, follow the literary conventions for explaining personal names elsewhere in the Hebrew Bible, particularly in Genesis where entire episodes are built around such (false, and often strained) folk etymologies. See Long, *Problem of Etiological Narrative*; Strus, *Nomen-Omen*; Garspiel, *Biblical Names*; those in Genesis are listed in Bullinger, *Figures of Speech*, 307–8.

It is often claimed that the man's naming the woman in this verse demonstrates his authority over her.[12] Not only is the assumption that naming implies authority vacuous, the entire argument becomes irrelevant when we recognize the verse in which the woman is named is a later addition to the text.[13] The use of the past tense in Gen 3:20 is significant, "And the human called his woman Eve because she *became* the mother . . ." Note that the text does not say "she will become" but "she became"; this takes us out of the story into a future that sees Eve as the progenitrix of all *past* generations. The verb here is in the past tense, clearly indicating that its narrator, unlike the narrator in the remainder of Genesis 2–3, is speaking in retrospect, after procreation had already occurred.[14] The verse can be compared to Gen 2:24 ("That's why a man leaves his father and mother and sticks with his woman and they become one flesh"); in both cases the narrator looks back on the events of the story as relating to a later time (only after the events in the story do men leave their mothers and fathers, the original pair having had no mother or father). In both, the point in time of the observer is out of synch with the narrative time in which the story takes place.

Also, as in the case of Gen 2:24, the intrusion of an addition is signaled by the abrupt change in speaker who here interrupts God as He is pronouncing the punishments. This continues with another addition in 3:21 that describes God (in the third person) clothing the humans. Genesis 3:20 is less apparent an interruption than 2:24, since in the following verses God is no longer addressing the humans but rather refers to them in the third person and collectively in the singular: "See, the human being has become like one of us, to know good and bad, and now, lest he send forth his hand . . ." (3:22).[15] Along with 2:24 and for similar reasons, the naming of the woman as Eve should be regarded as a later addition.

12. This idea that naming implies or asserts authority has received almost unanimous acceptance, but see above, pp. 24–25. On maternal naming, see Pardes, *Countertraditions*, 40–58.

13. Stordalen considers the form of the name and the explanation for it in the text and concludes, "The name in 3:20 attests to the use of earlier sources as well as to the late reworking of this story" (*Echoes*, 209).

14. Even Cassuto, who maintains the unity of the Pentateuch, notes on 3:20, "It may at first seem strange that this verse comes just here . . . These words have been added by the Bible; it is not Adam's own reason, for in that case he should have said: because she *shall be* the mother of all the living" (*Commentary*, 170).

15. There is some awkwardness in the narrative here that has allowed critical analysis

The tone, content, syntax, and time frame of the verse in which the woman receives a personal name clash with the rest of the story, while the style is at odds with that of the narrator of Genesis 2–3 overall. Just as there is no Adam, there is no Eve in the Garden of Eden story. When the man first sees her, he says "it [i.e., her name] will be called woman" (2:23) and so she is throughout, by the man, by the narrator, and by God.

As for the man (*ha-ʾadam*), not only does he lack a personal name, the narrative shows little interest in him as an individual. It is God who notices that "it is not good" for him to be alone. There is no indication as to how he comes by the names he assigns to the animals and the woman. The only sign of his emotional life is his apparent delight at seeing the woman for the first time. The story's silence on his thought process in the critical scene has led to endless speculation about why he chose to violate the divine command that had been given to him directly.[16]

Explanation of the motives of the nameless human characters in this scene is unequally distributed. No motivation of any kind is provided for the man. According to the story, the woman "took from its fruit and she ate, and she gave also to her man with her (*ʿimmah*) and he ate" (3:6b). Some translations simply omit "with her,"[17] while commentaries labor to interpret *ʿimmah* as other than its plain meaning.[18] The intention in omitting "with her" seems to be to stress the greater villainy of the woman

---

of the text in terms of the interweaving of various earlier traditions. Westermann takes Gen 3:20 as "an elaboration" but considers v. 21 as the end of the "earlier stage" of the narrative, thus eliminating the reason for the expulsion in vv. 22, 24 (*Genesis 1–11*, 267–73). This is in line with the theory that the narrative as we have it combines two earlier traditions: one of disobedience and punishment, the other of a plant that confers immortality.

16. "The man, it is true, does to some extent participate in the counteraction—not only in choosing to eat the fruit, but also in his active collaboration in naming the animals and the woman—but on the whole, he is a profoundly passive character throughout the story" (Jobling, *Sense of Biblical Narrative*, 26).

17. E.g., REB; NJPS; TEV; RSV (corrected in NRSV). It's notable that the English translation of Westermann includes "with her" (*Genesis 1–11*, 182) but omits it in quoting Gen 3:6 in his commentary on the verse (249–50); the original German has "bei ihr" in both translation and commentary, although Westermann doesn't directly address the issue of the man's presence (2nd German ed., 1976, 340).

18. E.g., "Expressions of this kind (*ʿim* or *ʾeth* ['with'] with the pronominal suffixes) occur as a rule when a person is said to associate himself in a given action with someone who leads him" (Cassuto, *Commentary*, 148). Another way around the problem was to have the man asleep so that he was there and not there at the same time: "Where was the man when this conversation was going on? Abba Halpun bar Qoriah said, 'he had earlier had sexual relations, and now he was sleeping it off'" (*Gen. Rab.* 19:3).

while obscuring the question of the man's presence. By distancing the man from the scene, the woman can be presented as a temptress, bringing the fruit to the man who was absent during the dialogue with the snake and therefore was "not deceived" (1 Tim 2:14).[19]

If the man is there all along but silent, his act of eating, presented in the text with no depiction of his motive or thought process, can't be entirely attributed to the woman despite his later weak protestation to the contrary ("she gave to me from the tree and I ate"). He simply repeats the narrator's version of events ("she also gave to her man who was with her and he ate") without his admitting his presence while the snake and the woman conversed. In fact, ancient dialogue is incapable of showing more than two people engaged in conversation simultaneously. In consequence, although the text is explicit that the man was present in the critical scene, no particular meaning can be attributed to his silence, which serves the narrative purpose of deflecting attention to the woman, to her thoughts, words, and deeds.

This leads us to consider the woman, the one character in the scene who *is* provided with a motive. She is portrayed as the special creation of the deity, and the audience is led to share the man's reaction in a "poem of ecstasy . . . The norms of judgment in relation to the woman are overwhelmingly positive. She is a totally attractive character . . . The narrator's petitions for approval and identification with all three characters reach a high point in this episode."[20] We see the woman through the man's eyes and feel his emotional response. It is not because she is created last that she completes the creation but because she brings joy into his life. This prepares us rhetorically for what will follow in the very next episode, the woman's dialogue with the snake and her decision to violate the prohibition. Whether she is understood as betraying the man who is so smitten with her, or as helping him even more than God had intended, will depend on how we understand her role in the events that unfold.

In a generally androcentric text the unusual agency of a female character demands attention. The simplest explanation returns us to the etiological function of the story, why women suffer in childbearing

---

19. According to von Rad, "The serpent . . . departs completely from the reader's view, the woman is now alone . . . the one who has been led astray now becomes a temptress" (*Genesis*, 90).

20. Boomershine, "Structure," 116. For Humbert, Gen 2:23 is a "hymne à l'amour" (*Études*, 167); for Gowan, "a love poem" (*From Eden to Babel*, 48).

and why they find themselves subject to male domination. Without active participation in the disobedience, the woman can't merit the specific punishment she receives, one in which she ends up in a state of permanent disadvantage. It is her act of independence that forces God's hand. Somewhat but not entirely overstating the case, Bal writes that the woman "manages to turn the almighty God of Gen. 1 into a character with equal status, equal features, equal feelings."[21]

Just staying within the language of the text, the woman's offense was more egregious than that of the man; knowingly disregarding God's prohibition as she herself defines it, she not only "took and ate" but "also" handed the man the fruit. That this follows the intention of the Storyteller is shown by his making the woman the primary agent of the action only here in the critical scene; otherwise she is depicted as the object presented to the man (2:18–22) or she disappears entirely (3:9–12, 22–24). He structured the story to give the woman greater responsibility in order to account for her lower social status.

While the story maintains total silence on the goals and desires of the man, this is not the case for the woman. Of all the characters her reasoning is most clearly stated. Before we consider this, there are two assumptions commonly made about her motivation that we have to examine. The first is that the woman desired the fruit because it had been forbidden. The second is that she suffered from hubris, a desire to transcend her human status and become a god.

There is no evidence whatsoever in the text to justify the claim that the woman is attracted to the tree because it had been forbidden. Yet the idea persists.[22] On the contrary, as the story makes clear, the woman knew about the tree and the prohibition but ignored it until the snake brought it to her attention. Nor does she understand the fruit as forbidden. Her paraphrase of the threat when describing it to the snake (3:2–3) casts it as a possibility ("lest you die") rather than the certainty expressed by God when He spoke to the man ("when you eat from it be assured that you will die"). By allowing the woman to paraphrase the threat the Storyteller gives her an out; in her evaluation of the situation she is weighing a possible danger rather than an outright prohibition. "What was a commandment with a death penalty becomes a warning of a poisonous tree."[23]

21. Bal, "Sexuality, Sin," 35.
22. Westermann, *Genesis 1–11*, 248–49, and many others.
23. Stordalen, *Echoes*, 200.

Rather than the singular attribute of being forbidden, the story emphasizes the similarity of the Tree of Knowing Good and Bad to the other trees provided for food. It appeared to her to be like all the other trees in the Garden that the narrator initially described as "desirable (*neḥmad*) in appearance and good for eating" (2:9). We're told that "the woman saw that the tree was good for eating and attractive (*taʾawah*) to the eyes" (3:6). In these first two reasons given, equivalent to the description of all the trees in the Garden but reversing their order, the woman determines that the tree is like the others that God had provided them with as food and so was not likely to be poisonous (like the snake, she takes the threat in its literal sense). This factors into her assessment of the snake's claim that the tree would not cause death. She is no more attracted to this tree than she would have been to any of the other trees in the Garden.[24]

It is often argued that the woman chose to eat because she aspired to divinity, that she acted out of hubris.[25] This is a serious accusation and must be examined closely. First of all, eating from the other tree, the Tree of Life, had not been forbidden. Eating from that tree would have also provided the humans with a godlike quality arguably more desirable than that gained from the Tree of Knowing Good and Bad, yet it would not have been hubris to eat from it. In fact the story revolves around explaining how humans got one godlike attribute but not the other, how we came to have such extraordinary cognitive powers but no way to put off death.

Does the portrayal of her thought process betray a desire for divine status? It is her third motive, *neḥmad le-haśkîl*, that has received the most attention and is at the same time the most difficult to interpret and therefore to translate. The phrase repeats "desirable" (*neḥmad*) that is used in 2:9 ("desirable in appearance"), but the question is here, in this instance, desirable for what purpose, what does *haśkîl* mean?

The root from which *haśkîl* is formed has a range of meanings that revolve around the kind of practical knowledge that leads to prosperity or success,[26] quite similar in usage to the word *ʿarûm* used to characterize

---

24. One oddity in the woman's paraphrase of the prohibition is that she doesn't seem to know the *name* of the tree; she simply describes it as "the tree in the center of the Garden." This may be a way of indicating that she perceives it as just another tree.

25. For Mettinger, disobedience to God's command is evidence of hubris, "an act of infringement on the divine realm" (*Eden Narrative*, 56). Defined this way, hubris would characterize us all.

26. The nominal form (*śekel*) refers to practical wisdom and the capacity for good judgment. The verbal form is causative with respect to the active form, in general bring-

the snake in 3:1. Its related noun *śekel* continues to be used today to mean commonsense or know-how (as in 'he has no *śekel*,' no idea how to get anything done). Wherever the noun *śekel* and the verbs that are derived from it appear in the Hebrew Bible they have a strong positive meaning; the related word *maśkîl* appears in the title of many biblical psalms.[27] The verb derived from *śekel* can be translated as "to have understanding or insight or practical knowledge." Like wisdom, *śekel* can be a gift bestowed by God,[28] and is a means of knowing God.[29] Although it is *ḥokmah* that ends up personified as Wisdom in Proverbs, *ḥokmah*, *śekel* and *ʿarûm* overlap in meaning and usage, and in the Wisdom literature all three are opposed to foolishness.[30] The person described as "having *śekel*" (*ha-maśkîl*) can be counted on to do the right thing and therefore to prosper.[31]

It's natural to assume that *neḥmad le-haśkîl* should be understood to refer back to the snake's claim that eating the fruit will make them "like gods," and indeed Yahweh *ʾelohîm* admits that this had in fact occurred ("the human being has become like one of us"). Yet in making her decision the woman relies *in part* on what the snake said. In her mind (for this is what the narrator describes) she paraphrases this (in a verbal construction parallel to the description of all the trees in 2:9) as "*neḥmad le-haśkîl*." This picks up on the second part of the snake's statement (that they would end up "knowing good and bad"), but pointedly omits the first part (that they would "become like gods").

This description of the woman's internal thought process makes no reference to a desire to be godlike, and it is therefore unjustified to at-

---

ing about the root meaning of the verb. On this verbal stem, see Stordalen, *Echoes*, 208 n. 102. In the only other occurrence of the hiphil infinitive construct in the Hebrew Bible, the sinner has ceased "to act wisely, to bring about good" (Ps 36:4); see also Ps 32:8; Prov 16:23; 21:11.

27. Ps 32, 42, 45, 52, 53, 54, 55, 74, 78, 88, 89, 142; cf. "sing *maśkîl* to God," Ps 47:8.

28. 1 Chr 22:12; 2 Chr 2:11; Dan 1:17 (where it is parallel to *ḥokmah*). We can compare *ḥokmah* with the same meaning in 1 Kgs 4:29; 5:12; Prov 2:6.

29. Jer 9:23.

30. *ḥokmah* and *śekel* occur together in Ps 111:10; both are found with *ʿarûm* in Prov 1:2–6; 13: 14–16. "From first to last wisdom for the Jew [sic] . . . meant know-how, and particularly knowing how to live" (Caird, *Language*, 80). For a detailed study of *le-haśkîl*, see Humbert, *Études*, 94–97.

31. On *maśkîl* as knowing God, see Amos 5:13; Ps 14:2; as rewarded by God, see 1 Sam 18:14–15; as having good sense and acting accordingly, see Prov 10:5; 14:35; 16:20; 17:2; Dan 9:25; Job 34:35; as having particular expertise, Jer 50:9; Dan 1:4.

tribute such a motive to her. If the Storyteller wanted to suggest this it would have been easy enough for him to do so. He could have written instead that she found the tree "desirable to become like a god" or even "like Yahweh." Instead, the woman seems to interpret "become like gods" as hyperbole, a phrase that the snake used to indicate that "knowing good and bad" was a higher faculty than what they possessed at the time, an interpretation that turns out to be correct.[32]

The story is quite clear on this point: she did *not* act from hubris, a desire to rise to divine status, although in a very limited sense this is what comes to pass. We have to keep in mind the use of the comparative "like" as well as the plural "gods," which together seem to avoid any intimation that the god*like*ness they did attain involved usurping divine power.[33] There is no indication in the narrative that such power was either desired or achieved. "Having been freely admitted to the Tree of Life and then having eaten from the Tree of Knowledge, the human party comes too close to divinity. Importantly, this effect was unintentional, since neither the human agent nor the narrator (or reader) was aware of this consequence until 3:22."[34] "The woman does appear to make a rational choice (3:6). There seems in the text no sign of titanic pride or rebelliousness about her."[35]

Nor is there any suggestion that the woman is surprised, disconcerted, or substantially transformed by the effect of having eaten. She doesn't appear to view the tree as imparting wisdom (*ḥokmâh*) but rather

---

32. On hyperbole as characteristic of biblical style (and therefore of ordinary language), see Caird, *Language*, 110–17. That humans desire to become like gods is familiar to us from ancient Greece (thus we borrow the Greek word *hubris* to describe it). As modern technology advances, so do the warnings against the powers it grants us. *Our familiarity with the idea doesn't allow us to read it into the woman's thought process in Gen 3:6.*

33. "In the ancient Near East there did exist myths about rebellion against the high god and attempts to usurp his throne, but the rebel is always a lesser deity, never a man" (Gowan, *When Man Becomes God*, 17). Such myths are applied metaphorically to kings, but their desire is for wealth and power rather than knowledge (Isa 14:12–14; 37:23; Ezek 28:2–10; 31:2–18; cf. Isa 10:15). On the biblical language of hubris and pride, see Gowan, *When Man Becomes God*, 29–43; Humbert, "Démesure et Chute," 63–68.

34. Stordalen, *Echoes*, 247.

35. Williams, "Genesis 3," 275. "It therefore seems that it was this tree's capacity to confer the kind of wisdom that comes from growth and maturity which was the principal object of the woman's interest" (Blenkinsopp, *Creation, Un-Creation*, 76). See also Stratton, *Out of Eden*, 88–89.

practical knowledge (*śekel*),³⁶ in fact the very thing that will solve the humans' First Problem, how to deal with the newly acquired sensitivity to being naked ("they sewed together fig leaves and made coverings for themselves").³⁷

The manner in which the story is constructed limited the Storyteller to just one immediate effect of eating from the Tree of Knowing as the primary trait that differentiates humans from other animal species, and it's a tribute to his powers of observation and appreciation of irony that he chose the fact that we alone cannot tolerate being seen naked. He carefully prepared us for this insight by earlier describing the pair as "naked but not ashamed," which immediately puts us in mind of all the other animals in the Garden.

Much too much has been made of this earlier state in terms of a putative original innocence now lost in the fall; no one speaks of the innocence of all the other species that feel no shame at their nakedness (just as the original human beings were able to procreate, like the other animals, without the added ability to "know good and bad"). Here it's more a matter of recognizing nakedness, feeling a need to cover up, and, perhaps equally important, satisfying the need, succeeding at the task, by having the practical knowledge of how to sew.

The woman desires and gets the faculty for knowing that distinguishes human beings from other creatures. This, according to the Storyteller, is a god*like* quality, a source of uniqueness and privilege. How we came to have this quality is the etiological center around which the story revolves. Just as in *Paradise Lost* Eve decides to share the imagined pleasures of the fruit with Adam, in the biblical text the woman shares the new-found faculty with the man by handing him the fruit; the primary difference is that in Milton the woman is deceived whereas in the biblical text she is not (despite her protestations to the contrary).

The woman makes the decision to disobey and eat based on her previous knowledge of fruit trees, a desire to get ahead, and a risk assessment of the danger. "The woman's motives were distinctly within the normal limits and passions of humanity."³⁸ She apparently accepts the snake's portrayal of God's motives, which proves to be correct. What neither the

---

36. Both the pi'el and hiphil forms of *ḥakam* could have been used here more precisely connoting "making wise."

37. Sawyer, "Image of God," 68–69.

38. Barr, *Garden of Eden*, 13.

snake nor the humans can know in advance is God's reaction and the punishments that will ensue.

Having eaten and newly aware of their nakedness, the man and woman hide from God. At this point the woman disappears from the story. God calls out to the man who confesses that he had been hiding because he feared His reaction to his nakedness (3:10). It is noteworthy that he does *not* say that he feared God's reaction to his *disobedience*. Here the Storyteller provides the narrative with an occasion to assert that disobedience was the critical act, an occasion that he lets pass. The man could have immediately confessed (e.g., "I was afraid because I ate from the tree You had forbidden"). This would have been a clear indication that at least the man feared God's reaction to the *act* of disobedience (and not its *result*, that the man knew that he was naked). Instead the man's answer ("I was afraid because I am naked and I hid") suggests to God that the humans *might* have eaten from the forbidden tree.

Like a good judge God eliminates the possibility that the man had been *told* that he was naked by inquiring, Who told you that you're naked? did you eat from the tree that I had forbidden? Why does God ask *two* questions? On its own the second question leaves open the possibility that God is addressing solely the act of disobedience. Both are required to indicate that *God intends to determine the source of the man's knowledge*. Had the man merely been told that he was naked, his knowledge would have been limited to awareness of his nakedness. The second question then poses the alternative, the possibility that he had become aware as a result of eating the fruit of the forbidden tree, in which case his capacity for knowing would have reached "godlike" proportions. Together the two questions point to God's real concern, not the act of disobedience but rather the humans' capacity for knowing that the disobedience entailed. As the sequel shows, it's this new state of affairs that God addresses with the punishments and the expulsion.

The scene is prolonged by the need for further questioning, briefly bringing the woman back for a final appearance. Both the man and the woman avoid taking responsibility, the woman blaming the snake and the man blaming the woman and even God Himself who had provided the woman to him. Syntactically the stress is on the fall guy: "note that the first word of both responses of the man and the woman is the person/animal they want to blame."[39] The man's excuse ("The woman whom you

---

39. Hess, "Roles," 17.

gave to be with me, she gave to me from the tree and I ate") quotes the narrator's description of the event ("and she gave also to her man who was with her and he ate"). However, by inserting into this statement "whom you gave to be with me", the man attempts to shift responsibility to God. Both the man and the woman prevaricate, but on the face of it the man's excuse is more audacious, as he has the effrontery to turn the accusation back on his judge.

God's investigation fails to arrive at the truth. We readers immediately see through the self-serving behavior of the man, casting blame ultimately on the deity; in it we recognize the basic human tendency to shift blame from ourselves onto others. The man's contemptible attempt to exonerate himself obliges the reader to consider also the reliability of the woman's defense—that she had been deceived by the snake. If we as readers reject the one, why should we embrace the other? In fact the narrative leads us to doubt the truth of the woman's claim by juxtaposing it to that of the man.

The notion that the snake's behavior was duplicitous is in good part based upon the woman's attempt at self-defense. The idea that the woman had been deceived by the snake rests on her allegation, although taking the woman's testimony at her word is precisely what the context of blame-shifting asks us *not* to do.

Accepting her version of events also involves ignoring what the story tells us quite clearly. The excuse she gives ("the snake deceived me and I ate") directly contradicts her thought process ("the woman saw that the tree was good for eating and that it was attractive to the eyes and the tree was desirable for imparting intellect"). "The woman's explanation of her offense is equally ironic because of the audience's memory of her meditation on the tree and her subsequent decision to eat its fruit."[40] This is one of many ironies in the story that we ignore at our peril.

When we deny the legitimacy of the woman's excuse we're free to acknowledge that the snake was simply telling the truth, even the possibility that its aim was to benefit rather than to harm. And, we might add, assuming the woman's excuse was truthful has served to legitimate the subsequent accusation of women's gullibility in general: "But I do not permit a woman to teach nor to exercise authority over a man, but to keep quiet. For Adam was formed first, then Eve. Adam wasn't deceived, but

---

40. Boomershine, "Structure," 119.

the woman, deceived, came into transgression" (1 Tim 2:12–14).[41] If she was simply passing the blame to the snake (unjustly), she was behaving exactly as did the man.

How familiar is their conduct? In their dubious rationales for choosing to eat the fruit, their typical humanity shines through. There is no change in human character, no before and after in that respect. Their decision to disobey God's prohibition is often compared to a child's stand against parental authority. The child, incapable of comprehending the parents' instructions, simply owes them unquestioning obedience. If this had been their original state, it's ironic that it is precisely the effect of eating the fruit of the Tree of Knowing Good and Bad that confers on them the kind of maturity that allows them to understand why they *should* obey. The fruit is not just the object of disobedience but also its potential cure. The first man and woman were not extraordinary supercreatures, but rather ordinary human beings who, despite their subsequent punishments, managed to secure for themselves and for the rest of us a higher place in the chain of being.

THE SNAKE

"In this hour you can benefit a thousand ages yet to come. Do you think it better to bear captives or free men, men or gods?"
—Hugo Grotius, *Adamus Exul*, IV.1294–1295 (1601)

Most important for any interpretation of Genesis 2–3 is how we understand the motivation of the snake. Unlike the humans, the snake is not asked to explain itself prior to the punishments, so we're compelled to look for clues elsewhere in the text.

According to the information provided by the narrator, the snake is ʿarûm (judicious) (Gen 3:1a). The Storyteller prepared his audience to suspend disbelief in a talking snake by its initial description, a further indication that ʿarûm should be taken in a positive sense. Its initial statement to the woman (3:1b) has been difficult to analyze semantically. Is it a question, as usually translated, or not? There is no marker for an interrog-

---

41. This is the strongest proof-text for the centuries-long history of women's exclusion from significant roles in Christian churches, continuing even today.

ative, and the conjunction with which it begins presumes that something precedes it, as if we were picking up a conversation already in progress.

In their initial interaction the snake focuses the woman's attention on the negative part of God's command ("from the Tree of Knowing Good and Bad you will not eat from it"), generalizing it to "Indeed ʾelohîm said, you will not eat from every tree in the Garden," true enough, strictly speaking. In contrast, the woman stresses the positive part of the command ("from the fruit of the trees of the Garden we will eat"), following more closely the original mandate ("From every tree of the Garden be assured that you may eat, but from the Tree of Knowing Good and Bad you will not eat from it . . .") When the woman restates what God said, she emphasizes the positive provision of the trees for food, a view of the command that may influence her decision-making process.

This is apparently the purpose of the introduction to the critical scene. Gen 3:1a supplies the snake with credibility to the audience, as having a strongly positive attribute related to wisdom, and 3:1b–3 focuses the scene on the Tree of Knowing Good and Bad (although it is not mentioned by name, only described by the woman as "the tree in the center of the Garden," which is in fact more precisely the location of the Tree of Life in Gen 2:9).[42]

Then, in direct contravention of the divine threat in Gen 2:16 and using identical language and verbal construction, the snake claims that it knows with certainty what God knows about the effects of eating from the Tree of Knowing ("Be assured that you will not die, because God knows that when you eat from it both your eyes will be opened and you will become like gods, knowing good and bad."). Its assertion turns out to be accurate; the negative consequences flow not from eating but rather from the divine punishments that will follow.

The snake is fully aware of God's real motive: very literally, "because God is (in a state of) knowing that on the day of your eating from it, your eyes will be opened and you will become like gods, (in a state of) knowing good and bad" (3:5). The participle describing first God and then the humans as "knowing" is used in both cases as a predicate adjective, establishing a subtle verbal equivalence. If the deity's condition of knowing

---

42. This description of the location of the Tree of Knowing will bring to mind the other tree, the Tree of Life, earlier described as located there, and missing from the story until now.

is permanent and continuous, so will be that of the humans.[43] Unlike the Tree of Life, whose effects had to be renewed by occasional eating, fruit from the Tree of Knowing Good and Bad had to be consumed just once to have a permanent effect on human nature.

The conventional interpretation of the Garden story assumes that the snake's motive was malevolent, that it intended to subvert the relationship between God and the humans, misleading them about the effects of eating from the Tree of Knowing Good and Bad in order to provoke divine wrath. Because there was nothing in the story itself to explain why it would act in this way, fairly early on interpreters came up with the idea, first attested in *The Life of Adam and Eve*, that the snake was really Satan, an angel who had rebelled when God created Adam and ordered the angels to prostrate themselves before him. An entire story was concocted to provide a malevolent motive for the snake, in the case of *The Life of Adam and Eve* going so far as to replace the snake with a fallen angel. The story in *The Life* became the basis for the common belief that the snake was Satan in disguise or acted under his influence, although very few are aware of the existence of *The Life* or its significance for their beliefs.[44]

If we stay within the story itself the only evidence for the snake's malevolence is its characterization as ʿarûm (which in meaning and function is a positive attribute, and which was chosen for its assonance with ʿarûmmîm) and the woman's statement in trying to exculpate herself, that "the snake deceived me and I ate." Here the woman claims malevolence on the snake's part, although, even if it *had* misled her, she would have had no way of knowing whether it had done so intentionally. However, we've already seen in the discussion of the woman's motive that the credibility of her excuse should be taken as equal to that of the man, who blames the deity for giving him the woman in the first place. Actually her credibility is less than his since the story provides us with clear evidence to the contrary in a rare instance of describing in detail a character's thought process (3:6). And if, as it appears, the snake was telling the truth, how was she deceived?

Little attention has been paid to the central clue in the story regarding the relationship between the snake and the humans, that, as part of the snake's punishment, snakes and humans will be enemies from then

---

43. GKC 116n.
44. On *The Life of Adam and Eve*, see above, pp. 107–8.

on (3:15). The divine punishments account for two fundamental characteristics of snakes: their distinctive mode of locomotion and their danger to humans. There is no indication that this corresponds to the situation prior to the punishments; on the contrary, strictly speaking, all the punishments are transformative. If the snake becomes hostile to humans only as a result of a divine decree, we're led to infer that such was not the case prior to that point, and therefore that the snake was *not* acting with malevolence when it informed the woman, accurately, about the effects of eating from the Tree of Knowing Good and Bad. The snake does act as an enabler, encouraging the woman to consider the tree and clarifying what would actually be the effects of eating. However, since its intervention led to an increase of human capabilities that resulted in our unique status among the animal species, its motives cannot be considered harmful either in intent or effect.

Taking this into account we return to Gen 3:1, the first description of the snake. There the Storyteller has made it clear that "the snake was ʿarûm among all the animals of the field *that Yahweh ʾelohîm had made*." Not only is the fear of snakes a result of later divine intervention, the writer has gone out of his way to place the snake among the animals in the divine creation made to be of help to the human being and to point to its exceptional capabilities.

To get around this, interpreters who are invested in finding a demonic presence in the story tend to view the snake as an agent of Satan rather than as evil in itself. The snake is then a creature used by Satan, although the choice of a snake seems odd at best. Why not disguise himself rather as a messenger of God, a type readily found in Genesis?[45]

In fact we see this possibility as early in the textual tradition as *The Life of Adam and Eve*. In the scene in which Satan tricks Eve for the second time, he appears to her as an angel during an act of repentance after the expulsion. There he convinces her that she may cut short her period of repentance because he and his fellow angels have successfully prevailed upon God to forgive both her and Adam. Similarly in the pictorial tradition, the earliest known biblical illustration of Genesis 3 dates to between the eighth and tenth centuries and follows the broad outline of *The Life*

---

45. Gen 16:7-11; 19:1-22; 21:17-18; 22:11-18; 24:7; 28:12; 31:11-13; 32:2-3; also Exod 3:2; 14:19; 33:2; Num 22:22-35; Judg 2:1-4; 5:23; 6:11-22; 13:2-22; 2 Sam 24:16-17; 1 Kgs 13:18; 19:5-7; 2 Kgs 1:3, 15; 19:35; Isa 63:9; Job 4:18; Dan 3:28; 6:22; and also in Chronicles, Zechariah, and Psalms.

The Storyteller and the Garden of Eden

of Adam and Eve. It shows Satan (or his emissary) first masquerading as an angel, then, after having tricked Adam and Eve, as a devil with the traditional forked tail and hooves.[46]

When a fallen angel is substituted for the snake, radically transforming the biblical story, the behavior of the woman leaves the realm of the moral. Depicted in dialogue with an angel instead of a snake she becomes somewhat less blameworthy, while placing a fallen angel in the scene solidifies the assumption that Satan's malevolence towards the humans is the underlying cause of the unfolding events. Yet when Satan replaces the snake, the woman's accusation in Gen 3:13 ("the snake deceived me") and the subsequent punishment of the snake in Gen 3:14–15 make no sense. The substitution reveals the lengths interpretation will go to identify the snake as Satan in the scenario of "the Fall," actually changing the text itself.

Admitting that the snake is just a snake and that it spoke truthfully is a game-changer for interpreting the story of the Garden of Eden. The hostility between snakes and humans in the punishments (imposed by God *after* the dialogue between the snake and the woman) further brings into question the assumption of its malevolence. On the basis of these observations, based strictly on the details of the story, we have to reconsider the snake's motivation in addressing the humans, as difficult as this may prove to anyone invested in the conventional interpretation of the snake as the villain of the piece.[47]

Since there isn't a villain to be found in the Garden of Eden story, there is no villainy either.[48] No one is particularly good or evil; the categories of good and evil are irrelevant. We can't even say that each of the characters acts out of self-interest. God is simply maintaining the order He created, one that makes an absolute distinction between divine and human. The idea that the created order must not be tampered with shows

---

46. Genesis B, embedded in the Junius manuscript of Old English poetry, now in the Bodleian Library, Oxford. Online: Ms. Junius 11, p. 31: http://image.ox.ac.uk/show?collection=Bodleian&manuscript=msjunius11.

47. The conventional reading of the snake as Satan in the interpretation of Genesis 2–3 as "the Fall" has proven to have enormous social utility—the chief engine in the cultural transmission of beliefs, even false beliefs (Gilbert, *Happiness*, 236–45).

48. Using Proppian role analysis, Jobling sees a counternarrative in which Yahweh is the villain, and the snake and woman are the heroes (*Sense of Biblical Narrative*, 26). Sandys-Wunsch views the snake as "a sort of reptilian Prometheus who attained for man his full consciousness" ("Before Adam and Eve," 27).

up elsewhere in biblical texts, in the prohibition against planting different crops in the same field or crossbreeding animals (presumably in order to prevent hybridization) and even a prohibition against wearing clothing of mixed fibers.[49] Divine law is embedded in the laws of nature. The human beings act the way human beings do, trying to make life better at their own peril. We can see this not only when they eat the forbidden fruit but also in the scene in which they try to pass the blame to others. The Storyteller seems to have a rather jaundiced view of human nature, leaving the implicit question in the mind of the audience, are we the best He could do?[50]

---

49. Lev 19:19 mentions all three in one verse, showing that they fell into the same category in their thinking; Deut 22:9–11 includes plowing with different animals yoked together.

50. A question also raised in Qohelet, especially 4:1–4; 7:13, 20, 29. See Whybray, "Immorality of God."

EIGHT

The Storyteller and His Story

Traces of the storyteller cling to the story the way handprints of the potter cling to the clay vessel.

—Walter Benjamin, "The Storyteller"

It is impossible to identify the author of the story of the Garden of Eden, the time and social milieu in which he lived, or his intent in composing it. We can only know him from his work, a story that is remarkably different in style and content from virtually all other writings in the Hebrew Bible. Its author was a master of words who crafted a story to be heard rather than read, generating a narrative from the interconnections of words. His views on the human condition play off the verbal relation between human being (*'adam*) and soil (*'adamah*) and between man (*'iš*) and woman (*'iššah*). He added a long scene, the naming of the animals, so we wouldn't miss the point, although we did anyway.

The sympathies of the Storyteller lay with his audience, one that he could not have imagined would have let him down to the extent that it has over the long history of (mis)interpretation. He presumed that his audience would have a certain competence (to appreciate irony and verbal play)—an expectation that the history of interpretation proves was woefully misplaced. He could not have known that the ambiguities that he left in the story would provide the occasion for radical misreading, or that the clues he left would be ignored. The natural familiarity with its own language and its storytelling traditions that would have allowed the original audience to grasp the nuances of wordplays and idiomatic expressions passed away. Transparency of meaning disappeared and certain ideas about what the story was about hardened into false certitudes.

Thus readers today are doubly disadvantaged. We no longer have full access to the language of the story or to what was the common knowledge of its intended audience. "The method of the biblical narrator requires a constant mental effort on the part of the reader, involving careful thought and attention to every detail of the narrative,"[1] all the more so when the story is built on words and their interrelations, a rhetorical style that is quite foreign to our sensibilities.[2]

With pieces of the language environment no longer available to us, we must struggle with the story in a way unnecessary to its intended audience. There is something lighthearted in its use of language that is difficult to recover and that is entirely lost in translation. Explaining it is akin to explaining a joke, the moment when we "get it" is lost. Yet to study the Bible seriously, wherever that may take us, is to honor the Storyteller, to follow his lead, to find the joy of storytelling and story-hearing, despite distance and the leaden weight of tradition.

The story of the Garden of Eden is one of the only narratives in the Hebrew Bible in which we can see clearly *how* it was composed.[3] Beginning with the image of the first human being formed from clay and with the assonance of ʾ*adamah* and ʾ*adam*, the Storyteller constructed a meditation on what it means to be human, on our uniqueness among creatures, our peculiar qualities and the drawbacks to our existence, composing a story that purports to explain how this all came about.

1. Bar-Efrat, *Narrative Art*, 45.
2. "From the second half of the seventeenth century, the sense that there was some power immanent in words which could allow even their accidental correspondences to suggest meaningful, almost magical, links, started to fade; in its place grew a belief that plainness and transparency were the qualities most to be admired, and consequently that the rhetorical embellishments which encouraged ambiguity were an irritating defect" (Read, "Puns: Serious Wordplay," 87).
3. Modern methodological approaches, whatever their virtues in explicating a text, generally make no claim to have been deliberately employed in the process of its composition. For a survey of interpretive methodologies, see McKenzie and Haynes, *To Each Its Own Meaning*. As specifically related to Genesis 2–3, see Wallace, *Eden Narrative*, 1–28; on structuralist interpretations, see the articles in *Semeia* 18 (1980); for a reader-response interpretation, see Stratton, *Out of Eden*. For a brief bibliography on these methodologies as applied to Genesis 2–3, see Stordalen, *Echoes*, 189 n11.

The Storyteller and the Garden of Eden

Taking off from the initial wordplay, he depicts us as earthbound creatures materially identical to other animals, created by God for a particular purpose, to work the soil from which we were first formed. Although this is how we were created, it is not what we would become. The task of the narrative is to describe the transition from our created state to what we are today.

According to the story, from the beginning we strove to improve our lot, especially our know-how, as the woman reasons in Gen 3:6. In consequence (and in an act of disobedience), we attained a measure of godlikeness, whatever it is that makes us such exceptional creatures, a cognitive faculty that the Storyteller identifies by the idiomatic expression "knowing good and bad." The lesson here seems to be that "one must become divine to be human."[4]

God's response to this was twofold. By means of the punishments, He turned our lives into a struggle for survival, undermined our ability to perform the tasks for which we were created, and disrupted our relationship to the materials of our origin. In terms of the verbal relations that structure the story, each sex becomes subject to, almost a slave to, its material source that is also its verbal origin (*ha-ʾadam* to *ha-ʾadamah*; *ha-ʾiššah* to *ha-ʾiš*). Our tasks become a necessitous burden, our lives more precarious, our condition even less "like gods." Then God goes a step further and eliminates the possibility we once possessed of overcoming mortality (albeit temporarily) by eating from the Tree of Life. His reaction to our accession to a "godlike" status above all other creatures was to reinforce the one aspect that has always separated us definitively from divinity, our mortality.[5]

Yet, as the Storyteller observes, there is also the great irony that the new consciousness that elevates us to godlike status is not an unadulterated good. Its immediate effect is self-consciousness and the awareness that we must cover ourselves. Having to choose just one characteristic that sets us apart from other creatures, he observed that we are the only species that is clothed, indeed that we are virtually incapable of functioning without clothing, at least in the presence of others.

---

4. Niditch, *Chaos to Cosmos*, 37.

5. We can compare the shortening of the human lifespan as an act of retributive justice in Gen 6:3, as God "reaffirms man's mortality" (Gowan, *When Man Becomes God*, 25).

The Storyteller and His Story

We've imagined the Storyteller sitting there, looking around, trying to decide which single aspect of human existence he could use to characterize the difference between human beings and all other species. This is the pleasure conveyed by great art, that it transcends the material at hand and reveals a mind in the very process of creation. By choosing our discomfort with nakedness he leads his audience to reflect on the curious effect it has on human society. Clothing is taken to be the mark par excellence of our elevated status, while at the same time marking our vulnerability, in both a literal and figurative sense.[6]

In making this choice, the Storyteller points to the paradox that it is precisely our godlike cognitive power that results in a sense of shame at being naked and a need to be clothed. It's unclear whether he saw the problem of nakedness as rooted in sexuality; perhaps he simply observed the oddity and cultural significance of human clothing. It's difficult for the modern reader to see a reference to nakedness as anything but sexual; to us it's clear that without clothing social order would be well nigh impossible.

He recognized clothing as a uniquely human phenomenon, just as he recognized male domination as punitive. "The writer, who presumably was a man, knew that men 'ruled over' women, but for him it was a sad fact, a curse . . . He is able to identify with both the man and the woman."[7] This reveals an uncommon mind; fish are usually the last to see (much less critique) the water. It's a sad fact that the story he composed has functioned as the justification par excellence for patriarchal institutions.

Yes, the Storyteller tells us, we are truly exceptional creatures, but this uniqueness comes at a cost. Irony lies at the heart of the story of the Garden of Eden. It's ironic that when humans obtain our unique cognitive capacity its first effect is awareness that they're naked. It can't be denied that here we have a clear case of intentional irony and the failure to recognize it has had serious repercussions on interpretation.

The most mind-bending irony in the story lies in its assertion that the characteristic that makes us so special comes as a result of disobeying God.[8] In contrast to humans' original godlike status in the first chapter

---

6. See above, pp. 76–77, 94–95, 121. On clothing as "an emblem of higher status," see Oden, *Bible without Theology*, 98–105.

7. Tucker, "Creation and Fall," 120.

8. "We can strive to obey God precisely by disobeying the divine command not to know" (Sharp, *Irony*, 42). This sets the story against the Wisdom traditions to which it

of Genesis, where man and woman are created in the image and likeness of God, in the Garden narrative this is achieved only by flouting God's express command. Created in the image of God in Genesis 1, human godlikeness has no downside, while attaining godlikeness against God's will in Genesis 3 has some very disagreeable repercussions.[9]

One of the main stylistic contrasts between the creation as described in the first chapter of Genesis and the origin story in Genesis 2–3 is the lack of irony in the former. We do find irony elsewhere throughout the Hebrew Bible.[10] Its presence, like that of puns or plays on words, draws attention to the personality of the author or speaker. Both irony and wordplay invoke a meaning beyond the plain meaning of individual words; both call upon the audience as interpreters to recognize this meaning and to appreciate it. In this interactive process, the audience plays as much a role as the author.

"Irony in texts has always called for subtlety of reading and acuity of hearing."[11] How did we come by such skills? The experience of contentment generated by stories, and this story in particular, results from an intellectual capacity that, according to the Garden narrative, we came to possess through disobedience.[12] The truly subversive irony of the story of the Garden of Eden is that it never would have been composed, that we wouldn't have been able to appreciate it, if it weren't for the desire to understand, a desire that causes us to disregard the interests of God.

There is irony not only within the story, in the effects of our acquisition of a godlike faculty, but also in the treatment of each of the characters. As in Kafka, whose audience reportedly laughed aloud when he read his stories to them, there are no absolute villains or heroes. Each character in

---

is frequently compared. See Stordalen, *Echoes*, 247–48; Carmichael, "Paradise Myth"; cf. Blenkinsopp, *Pentateuch*, 65–67; Mendenhall, "Shady Side of Wisdom"; Alonso-Schökel, "Sapiential and Covenant Themes," 5–6.

9. For P, the image of God is a permanent attribute of humanity (Gen 1:27; 5:1; 9:6); also Ps 8:6. Humbert understands the idea that we were created in God's image as the source of human exceptionalism, tracing it through the Wisdom literature into Philo (*Études*, 153–75).

10. Irony in the Hebrew Bible is discussed in Sharp, *Irony*; Carroll, "Irony"; Sternberg, *Poetics*; Good, *Irony*.

11. Carroll, "Irony," 325; see also Hutcheon, *Irony's Edge*, 12–13; Booth, *Rhetoric*.

12. "Gen 2:4b—3:24 appears to be better understood not as a fall, but as an awakening. The future, and the imaginative experience of life which we call literature, lie before them" (Burns, "Dream Form," 12).

The Storyteller and His Story

the story has H/his, her, or its own point of view, one no better or worse than the other. By embracing each character the Storyteller leads his audience to accept the irony that lies within the human condition itself and in our relation to God.

In his depiction of our origins, the Storyteller reveals a deep understanding of human nature. First of all, there is the observation that we are social animals ("It is not good for the human being to be alone"). Social isolation is debilitating.[13] Even though the woman's primary role in the story is construed in terms of maternity (as the punishments reflect), God's words are ambiguous (why is it not good exactly?), yet they seem to focus on her presence in the man's life rather than her precise function within it.

For the language-bound human, the recognition of the appropriate companion is expressed in a play on words, 'iššah derives from 'îš. This "counterpart helper" *had* to be a woman, for no other reason than that it was the Storyteller's intention to describe the differing social realities of men and women. The role he assigns to the woman in the story leads us to recognize his most remarkable judgment, that the universal custom of male domination is of questionable justice as it arose as a consequence of a woman's success in obtaining for the human race its distinctive intellect. The failure to recognize this is one of the most tragic constants in the history of interpreting the story.

As "godlike" as we are, the Storyteller seems to enjoy pointing out certain foibles in our character. We are also, from the Storyteller's point of view, a somewhat sorry lot. This is presented with good, lighthearted humor in the humans' response to divine questioning (3:11–13). The man blames God for providing him with the woman while the woman blames the snake. Neither is credible; neither tells the truth. Just as in their decision to disobey, this scene provides "a paradigm of human conduct in the face of temptation."[14] What can we make of a story in which all the characters prevaricate except a talking snake?

By telling a story constructed on and filled with wordplays, the Storyteller addressed his audience in a particular way, preparing it to accept the story *qua* story. His use of wordplays and irony aimed at hold-

---

13. From Aristotle's "man is a social animal" to Gawande, who argues that prolonged enforced isolation constitutes a form of torture ("Hellhole"); see Ska, "'Je vais lui faire un allié.'"

14. Vawter, *On Genesis*, 90–91.

ing the attention of his original audience.[15] If we imagine the story in an oral performance, we can see the audience smiling at the wordplays and enjoying the literary qualities of the tale. One of the great losses in our current approach to the Bible is an inability to see its gentle humor.[16]

Another loss lies in the tendency to ignore the use of irony in biblical texts. The human condition itself, the Storyteller seems to say, is ironic. If instead of the awareness of nakedness he had chosen to say that "knowing good and bad" led to the awareness of eventual death (if he had written, for example, "their eyes were opened and they knew that they would die"), there would be no irony. God had threatened death and death is what they would have gotten. We would then have a poignant story about our loss of immortality in which all the wordplay would have been basically irrelevant and quite possibly tasteless.[17]

Although the Storyteller didn't choose to mention it as the singular result of our new cognitive faculty, we *are* conscious that we will die. "It is the supreme paradox, nonetheless, that the knowledge that was supposed to make man like the immortal gods ends in revealing to himself his hapless mortality."[18] This requires correction. According to the story, the awareness of death doesn't come from "knowing good and bad," but rather from God Himself, who brings up the subject ("because dust you are and to dust you will return") for reasons of His own, as He points to death as the ultimate indignity for the newly godlike.

The story of the Garden of Eden makes no claim to historical truth. This does not make it any less true. Given the inordinate amount of time we spend with fiction in books, film, television, and theater, we seem to need stories; they help us to live, and to die.[19] Children demand them as if they were one of life's necessities. Endlessly fascinating, they are the way in which our minds work. In some sense we are nothing but stories, ranging from the personal story (the one that each of us tells ourselves

15. Boyd, *Origin of Stories*, 396.

16. Alter, "Sacred History," 161; Douglas, "Jokes." Indeed, on two of the only three occasions in which the human speaks he confesses his fear and then points a finger at God.

17. This is not to deny that wordplay occurs in deadly serious texts (especially prophetic texts), but there its use is more limited (what Good calls "punctual") and serves other purposes.

18. Vawter, *On Genesis*, 86.

19. King, *Truth about Stories*; on the importance of stories for the sick, disabled and dying, see Coles, *Call of Stories*.

about who we are) to scientific hypotheses. These, like all stories, are always "'true' and 'untrue' at the same time."[20] I think we can say without a shadow of a doubt that the Storyteller did not believe that the events he was describing actually happened, and that he expected the same of his audience. The story he tells was not intended to be an historical account of how we got to be the way we are, but an exploration of what we are, in all our complexity.[21]

Calling the human characters "the human" and "the woman" throughout gives the narrative the feel of a fable, and the never-again-accessible Eden fits the bill as an over-the-rainbow location.[22] By presenting the story as a fable, complete with talking animal, the audience is invited to take pleasure in the Storyteller's art. He has labored to show human beings as we are, flawed yet superior to other creatures. It's not a sad story, much less a tragic one.

Nor does the Garden of Eden story employ the etiological narrative genre to justify the status quo, as the creation narrative in Genesis 1 does for the observance of the Sabbath in imitation of God's rest on the seventh day.[23] Rather it provides a critique of human nature and implicitly *de*legitimizes male domination as unfair to the woman, who with due deliberation and risk to her life brought us our extraordinary cognitive powers.[24] To accomplish this, to prepare his audience to reconsider ideas embedded in the culture, naturalized in its institutions and practices, he

---

20. Rabinowitz, "Truth in Fiction," 125.

21. "What a close reading of the text does suggest, however, is that the writer could manipulate his inherited materials with sufficient freedom and sufficient firmness of authorial purpose to define motives, relations, and unfolding themes, even in a primeval history, with the kind of subtle cogency we associate with the conscious artistry of the narrative mode designated prose fiction" (Alter, "Sacred History," 149); Mendenhall describes Genesis 2–3 as "a work of utmost artistry and sophistication" ("Shady Side of Wisdom," 320).

22. "Par son allure si générale, le Yahwiste veut certainement transporter le paradis en des regions fabuleuses où, seules, l'imagination et la fantaisie ont accès" (Humbert, *Études*, 20); Noort, "Gan-Eden."

23. On Genesis 1 and the Sabbath, see Robbins, "Time-Telling," 82–86.

24. "If reading must be seen as already beginning with the writing of a narrative and is shaped by the dynamics of the author/character relationship, then the text may determine its meaning to some extent by the way in which the author/character relationship is configured . . . Reading, which recapitulates the act of writing, is a response to the trace which remains in the text of the narrator's response to the protagonist" (White, "Trace of the Author," 60).

reframed man in the first part of the story as serving the needs of the soil from which he was made, and as himself being in need of a woman. This recasting of man takes off from a linguistic argument that is accepted by the audience when it succeeds in resolving the ambiguity in the wordplay—quite a rhetorical device (when it works).[25]

What, then, does all this tell us about the Storyteller? What is his point of view? His interests are anthropological/sociological. The story's sole theological constant is the deity's attempt to keep humans from breaching the boundary between mortal and divine, and, when that fails, to reinforce that boundary by other means. In this sense we can understand Barr's conclusion that the story is intended to lead to an acceptance of mortality.[26] I would amend this to say that the purpose of the story is to allow us to weigh in the balance our mortality, the fragility of our lives, over against our exceptional status in the world, made manifest in our ability to take pleasure in this tale of how we came to be as we are.[27]

The ultimate irony in the Garden of Eden narrative is that the enjoyment we get from a good story is obtained by means of direct contravention of a divine decree. And, as we've seen, the Storyteller placed the woman in the starring role because, working backwards, he wanted to explain what he saw as the humiliation of women in his social world. The subversion of authority, here both divine and male, lies at the heart of the story and our (potential) pleasure in hearing it.[28]

---

25. "The stories were written to do something to people, and our interpretative approach needs to be able to handle— or be handled by—this aspect of them" (Goldingay, "How Far Do Readers Make Sense?," 6).

26. Barr, *Garden of Eden*, 21; also Blenkinsopp, *Creation, Un-creation*, 80–81; Niditch, *Chaos to Cosmos*, 29; Bechtel, "Rethinking the Interpretation," 107–9. To this we may compare Tablet XI of the *Epic of Gilgamesh*: "The denouement of Gilgamesh's quest for immortality is his resigned acceptance of both the death of Enkidu and the fact of his own irrevocable mortality" (O'Connell, "Ironic Reversal," 414).

27. "Y a-t-il un rapport organique entre le thème de la connaissance et celui de l'immortalité, ou sont-ce deux grandeurs sans relation nécessaire l'une avec l'autre? Tout le sens du mythe en dépend" (Humbert, *Études*, 21).

28. Carmichael notes that in the story "the desire for knowledge [is] first channeled through her [a woman]," which is "abnormal in terms of who is most closely connected with the acquisition of knowledge—the males—in the society whose literary work this Genesis myth represents" ("Paradise Myth," 48–49). "The Jewish scriptural canon contains monuments of both radical and reactionary thought" (Davies, "False Pen of Scribes," 139).

The events that the Garden narrative describes are only problematic from God's point of view. Similar to the story of the Tower of Babel and the prologue to the Flood in Gen 6:1–4, the Garden of Eden narrative is based on the theological premise that God has a legitimate interest in maintaining the separation of the human and divine, in limiting the range of human possibilities, no matter the cost. All three illustrate the consequences of bridging that divide, whether potentially in the Tower of Babel episode, by forces outside human control in the Flood story, or inadvertently in the Garden of Eden. Intentionality is irrelevant; the new state of affairs warrants a response that brooks no delay. In each case God's reaction seeks to undo, as far as possible, the potential or real damage created by a situation that blurs the absolute distinction between human and divine.[29]

By overstepping this boundary, human beings now have a cognitive power that is unique among earthly creatures. For this we were punished, not with the loss of immortality (a divine attribute we never possessed) but rather with a more tenuous hold on life. For the newly conscious humans, just as for the snake, the punishments will prove mortifying. Although not dead or newly subject to death, the man and woman find that God has acted decisively to mitigate the damage done to the distinction between us and Him.

From the Storyteller's standpoint, our interests and God's interests do not perfectly coincide. This, by the way, is also implicit in the story of the Tower of Babel to which the present story bears many points of comparison.[30] For both stories, it's a stretch to view God's behavior toward His human subjects as benevolent.[31]

---

29. "This renders a certain rationale in YHWH God's action in the Eden narrative, although his preferences seem perplexing to a modern (or post-modern) reader for whom human autonomy is essential" (Stordalen, *Echoes*, 247). See also Whybray, "Immorality of God," 96–97.

30. From its interest in language (diversity) to its use of wordplay (Babel/*balal*) as a structuring device.

31. According to Pfeiffer, "the myth of the Garden of Eden is the epic of a battle between man and an unfriendly deity. The prime concern of the deity is to safeguard its own superiority with respect to man ... The God of Adam and Eve has as little in common with the God of Israel as the deity of the Book of Job ... Both works are animated by the same protest against the divine indifference to human suffering" ("Wisdom and Vision," 97). Carmichael explains: "Once biblical material was perceived as a unitary work of God-given instruction and guidance, it was inevitable that all actions of the (Israelite) God(s) would come to be interpreted as somehow just, benevolent and in the interests of

The Storyteller and the Garden of Eden

Unlike the work of the Yahwist, the story of the Garden of Eden is not presented unilaterally from God's point of view. "As is well known, biblical narrators practically always associate themselves with the Hebrew God. Not so in this text."[32] Reading the story from God's point of view alone is perhaps the ultimate source of all misreadings. In the light of the reading presented in these pages, we might say that even from His point of view there is no fall; the problem He faces is our *rise* to a "godlike" state.

We began this study from the general consensus that the primary focus of the story is etiological. The Storyteller used the narrative form to dramatize his characterization of the human condition in its positive and negative aspects. His choices reveal an author with a keen insight into human nature and his own social world, one that he describes with Kafkaesque irony. "The aim is not, despite appearances, to explain anything, but to bring to consciousness matters that tend to pass without even minimal reflection."[33]

Once we sweep aside the accreted interpretations and read the text on its own terms, it turns out to be a rather simple story—but its very simplicity belies the demands that the Storyteller has placed on his audience. Only by hearing the story as if we were the audience he had in mind can we hear it speak to us and appreciate what it actually says. Only God, the narrator, and the audience know about the Tree of Life; the characters in the story never get a chance to learn about it. The narrative is constructed so that the existence of a Tree of Life is an idea *for us*.

The events of the story involve a tradeoff. We lost access to the Tree of Life but gained the cognitive faculty that makes us so exceptional. The story works backwards. As an etiological narrative, the really forbidden tree is the Tree of Life, the one we don't have access to, and the forbidden place is the Garden of Eden, where we don't live.

The story asks us to ponder this trade-off. Given what we know now, would we have acted any differently?[34] And if not, is it fair to blame the

---

human welfare" ("Paradise Myth," 47).

32. Stordalen, "Man, Soil, Garden," 24; other instances cited in Carmichael, "Paradise Myth," 47–48. Cf. Mettinger (*Eden Narrative*, 50–52), who finds in Genesis 2-3 a universalization of the Deuteronomistic theme of disobedience, punishment, and, ultimately, exile (a theme, we should note, in which there exists only one side of the story).

33. Carmichael, "Paradise Myth," 48.

34. "It is not obvious that the implied reader should have wished to abandon the present world for that of Eden" (Stordalen, *Echoes*, 466).

woman? This is an altogether remarkable story in the way it was composed, in the issues it raises, and in the way it brings into question the justice of male domination. It is long past time to recognize the Storyteller for the social critic and literary master that he undoubtedly was.

The Garden of Eden
Genesis 2:4–3:24 in Translation*

²:⁴These are the generations of the heavens and the earth (*ha-ʾareṣ*) in their creation.

When (*lit.*, on the day) Yahweh *ʾelohîm* made earth (*ʾereṣ*) and heavens ⁵every shrub of the field was not yet on the earth (*ʾareṣ*) and every plant of the field had not yet sprung up,¹ because Yahweh *ʾelohîm* had not caused rain upon the earth (*ʾareṣ*) and there was no human being (*ʾadam*) to work the soil (*ha-ʾadamah*).

⁶And a mist [?] rose from the earth (*ʾareṣ*) and wet the whole surface of the soil (*ha-ʾadamah*). ⁷Yahweh *ʾelohîm* formed the human being (*ha-ʾadam*) of dust (*ʿapar*) from the soil (*ha-ʾadamah*) and breathed into his nostrils a breath of life (*nišmat ḥayyîm*) and the human (*ha-ʾadam*) became a living being (*nepeš ḥayyah*).

⁸Yahweh *ʾelohîm* planted a garden in Eden in the east and set there the human being (*ha-ʾadam*) He had formed. ⁹And Yahweh *ʾelohîm* caused to spring up from the soil (*ha-ʾadamah*) all [kinds of] trees, desirable in appearance and good for eating, and the Tree of Life in the center of the Garden and the Tree of Knowing Good and Bad.²

---

* I have annotated only those terms that affect the interpretation presented here. Verses that were added later are single spaced.

1. Stordalen understands *śiaḥ ha-śadeh* to refer to wild plants, as opposed to those that will be cultivated for food (*ʿeśeb ha-śadeh*), although eating the latter appears only in the punishments ("Man, Soil, Garden," 12–13).

2. "Bad" rather than "evil," as the latter is overly restricted to the moral sense, ignor-

The Garden of Eden: Genesis 2:4–3:24 in Translation

¹⁰⁻¹⁴Now a river goes out from Eden to water the Garden and from there it divides and becomes four head[water]s. The name of the first is Pishon. It is the one that encircles all the land of the Havilah which is where the gold is, and the gold of that land is good; there [there is] bdellium and the stone of the carnelian. And the name of the second river is Gihon. It is the one that encircles all the land of Kush. The name of the third river is Ḥiddeqel (Tigris). This is the one that goes on the east of Assyria, and the fourth river is Perat (Euphrates).

¹⁵And Yahweh ʾelohîm took the human being (ha-ʾadam) and set him down in the Garden of Eden to work it and to watch over it.³ ¹⁶Yahweh ʾelohîm enjoined the human (ha-ʾadam), saying "From every tree of the Garden be assured that you will eat, ¹⁷but from the Tree of Knowing Good and Bad you will not eat from it, because when (*lit.*, on the day) you eat from it be assured that you will die."

¹⁸And Yahweh ʾelohîm said, "It is not good for the human being (ha-ʾadam) to be alone. I will make for him a counterpart helper (ʿezer kenegdô)."⁴ ¹⁹And Yahweh ʾelohîm formed from the soil (ha-ʾadamah) every [kind of] land animal (ḥayyat ha-śadeh, *lit.*, living being of the field) and every [kind of] bird of the heavens, and He brought [each] to the human (ha-ʾadam) to see what he would call it, and everything that the human (ha-ʾadam) called a living being (nepeš ḥayyah), that was its name.⁵ ²⁰And the human (ha-ʾadam) named every livestock animal, the birds of the heavens and every

---

ing the idiom of which it is a part (see above, pp. 47–48).

3. It is often observed that the verbs here conform to covenant terminology, "to serve (God)" and "to keep (commandments)." The second verb occurs at the very end of the story (3:24) in the sense of "guard."

4. "The translation 'counterpart' captures both the oppositeness and likeness inherent in the Hebrew word kenegdô" (Stratton, *Out of Eden*, 259 n11). "The notion here, I think, is that God wished the earthling to identify someone who could stand by him (see the usage of lenegdô in Josh 5:13), whose company he could share (see menegdô in Ps 10:5), possibly also who could do the same work" (Sasson, "Mother," 212 n16). However, that other species might fill these roles, particularly the latter, is unlikely, and the relevance of Josh 5:13 and Ps 10:5 is dubious.

5. Although the general meaning of the verse is clear, there remains the grammatical problem that the antecedent for the m. pronoun on "its name" can't be nepeš ḥayyah which is f. sg. For a discussion of the possibilities, see Louw, *Transformations*, 133–36.

land animal, but, for the human (*l-ʾdm*)⁶ He/he⁷ did not find a counterpart helper.

²¹And Yahweh *ʾelohîm* caused a torpor to descend upon the human (*ʿal-ha-ʾadam*) and he slept, and He took one of his ribs (*lit.*, sides) and closed up where it had been with flesh. ²²And Yahweh *ʾelohîm* built the rib (*lit.*, side) that He had taken from the human (*ha-ʾadam*) into a woman (*ʾiššah*) and brought her to the human (*ha-ʾadam*).

²³And the human (*ha-ʾadam*) said:
This one (*zoʾt*), this time, bone from my bones and flesh from my flesh,
As for this one (*zoʾt*), it [i.e., her name]⁸ will be called woman (*ʾiššah*)
because from man (*ʾiš*) this one (*zoʾt*) was taken.⁹

²⁴That's why a man (*ʾiš*) leaves his father and his mother and sticks with his woman and they become one flesh.¹⁰

    6. It is possible to read the consonantal text here and in 3:17, 21 as either "to (*or*, as for) the human being" or "to (*or*, as for) Adam." Only on these three occasions the noun *ʾadam* occurs with a prefixed preposition, to which in biblical Hebrew the definite article is assimilated, so the consonantal text (*lʾdm*) could be vocalized as *le-ʾadam* ("to/as for Adam") or as *la-ʾadam* ("to/as for the human being"), with the definite article absorbed into the preposition. The Masoretes (who added vowels to the original consonantal text) vocalized the phrase on these three occasions as the personal name Adam (perhaps following a long-established tradition going back to LXX; see York, "Adam," 15). However these would be the only instances in the text where the personal name would replace the generic "the human being" (*ha-ʾadam*). In every other reference to the first human being in Genesis 2–3, the article is present. Given the use of the personal name Adam in Genesis 4–5, "apparently the Masoretes took the first opportunity offered by the kethib [consonantal text] to treat *ʾādām* as a proper noun" (Lussier, "ʾAdam," 137). The otherwise consistent use of the generic "the human being" and "the woman" makes the Masoretic vocalization questionable, to say the least. "Adam" as a personal name, without prefix or article, does not appear in the consonantal text until Gen 4:25, where it serves to move the primordial story forward to the next generation and, ultimately, to Abraham.

    7. It's unclear whether the subject of the verb here is the human being or Yahweh *ʾelohîm*, although the evidence points to the latter.

    8. Although usually translated "she will be called . . . ," the verb is masculine and refers back to "name," also masculine. The subject of the verb cannot be the woman. This was observed as early as Ibn Ezra's commentary.

    9. The threefold repetition of "this one (*zoʾt*)" will resonate when the woman is accused of doing "this (*zoʾt*)" in Gen 3:13, and tie her very existence to her act of disobedience, becoming quite significant in the history of interpretation.

    10. The verb usually translated as the rather archaic "cleaves to" expresses loyalty (even to God, Deut 4:4; also of the bond of friendship, Prov 18:24), perhaps keying into

²⁵And the two of them were naked (ʿarûmmîm), the human (ha-ʾadam) and his woman, and were not ashamed.

3:1Now¹¹ the snake was judicious (ʿarûm)¹² among every [kind of] land animal (ḥayyat ha-śadeh; lit., living being of the field) that Yahweh ʾelohîm had made. And it said to the woman, "Indeed ʾelohîm said, you (pl.) will not eat from every tree in the Garden." ²And the woman said to the snake, "From the fruit of the trees of the Garden we will eat, ³but from the fruit of the tree that is in the center of the Garden, ʾelohîm said, 'you (pl.) will not eat from it and you (pl.) will not touch it, lest you (pl.) die.'" ⁴And the snake said to the woman, "Be assured that you (pl.) will not die, ⁵because ʾelohîm knows that when (lit., on the day) you (pl.) eat from it both your eyes will be opened and you (pl.) will become like gods [or God] (ʾelohîm),¹³ knowing good and bad."

⁶And the woman saw that the tree was good for eating, and that it was attractive to the eyes and that the tree was desirable for imparting intellect (le-haśkîl), and she took from its fruit and she ate, and she gave also to her man (ʾîšāh) [who was] with her and he ate. ⁷And the eyes of both of them were opened and they knew that they were naked (ʿêrummîm), and they sewed together fig-tree leaves and made coverings for themselves.

⁸And they heard the sound¹⁴ of Yahweh ʾelohîm moving about in the Garden at the breezy time of the day and the human (ha-ʾadam) and his woman hid themselves for fear of (lit., from before)¹⁵ Yahweh ʾelohîm in the

---

"bone from my bones and flesh from my flesh," also an expression of loyalty, in the previous verse.

11. "Now" is inserted here and in 2:10; 3:15, to indicate the change of subject signaled by Hebrew word order, an idea pioneered by Everett Fox.

12. On the meaning of this word, see above, pp. 109–11.

13. Either translation is possible. ʾelohîm can refer to God, or a god (e.g., 1 Kgs 11:25), or to the plural "gods." The translation "gods" takes into consideration Yahweh ʾelohîm's later admission that the human being "has become like one of us" (3:22).

14. The humans hear the sound of His footsteps. For qôl (literally "voice") with this meaning, see 2 Sam 5:24; 1 Kgs 14:6; 2 Kgs 6:32. The idiom "hear the voice" in the sense of "heed, obey" will recur in Gen 3:17.

15. BDB 818a.

midst of the trees of the Garden. ⁹And Yahweh ʾelohîm called to the human (ha-ʾadam) and said to him, "Where are you (m. sg.)?" ¹⁰And he said, "I heard the sound of You (*lit.*, Your voice) in the Garden and I was afraid (ʾira') because I was naked (ʿêrom) and I hid."

¹¹And He said, "Who told you that you're naked (ʿêrom)? From the tree which I enjoined you not to eat from it, did you eat?" ¹²And the human (ha-ʾadam) said, "The woman whom you gave [to be] with me, she gave to me from the tree and I ate." ¹³And Yahweh ʾelohîm said to the woman, "What is this you have done?" and the woman said, "The snake deceived me and I ate."

¹⁴And Yahweh ʾelohîm said to the snake, "Because you did this, cursed (ʾarûr) are you among every [kind of] livestock and among every [kind of] land animal. Upon your belly you will go and dust (ʿapar) you will eat all the days of your life. ¹⁵Now enmity I will establish between you and the woman and between your offspring (*lit.*, seed) and her offspring. It (her offspring) will crush you (yešûpeka) on the head and you will strike it (her offspring) (tešûpennû) at the heel.¹⁶

¹⁶To the woman He said, "Be assured that I will increase your labor/toil (ʿiṣṣabôn) and your conceiving, in pain (ʿeṣeb) you will give birth to children. And you are drawn back to your man (ʾîšek) (*lit.*, your return [tešûqatek] is to your man),¹⁷ and he will rule over you."

¹⁷To the human (l-ʾdm) He said, "Because you heeded (*lit.*, listened to the voice of) your woman and ate from the tree which I enjoined you saying you will not eat from it, cursed (ʾarûrah) be the soil (ha-ʾadamah) on your account. In labor/toil (ʿiṣṣabôn) you will eat all the days of your life. ¹⁸Both thorn and thistle it (the soil) will cause to spring up for you, and you will

---

16. Although the general sense is clear, the precise relationship of the two verbs in this phrase, chosen for their assonance, is not; see Cassuto, *Commentary*, 161.

17. In all ancient translations, the meaning "return" is clear. A study of these translations and the occurrences of tešûqah in texts from Qumran demonstrates that the usual English translation of tešûqah as "desire" is misleading (Lohr, "Sexual Desire?"). See above, pp. 40–44, 63.

eat the plant[s] of the field. ¹⁹In the sweat of your face you will eat food,[18] until your return (*šûbka*)[19] to the soil (*'el-ha-'adamah*), because from it you were taken, because dust (*ʿapar*) you are and to dust (*ʿapar*) you will return (*tašûb*)."[20]

²⁰And the human (*ha-'adam*) called the name of his woman Eve (*ḥawwah*) because she became the mother of all life (*ḥâi*).
²¹And Yahweh *'elohîm* made for the human (*l-'dm*) and for his woman garments of skin and clothed them.

²²And Yahweh *'elohîm* said, "See, the human being (*ha-'adam*) has become like one of us, in knowing good and bad, and now, lest he send forth his hand and take also from the Tree of Life and eat and live in perpetuity (*ḥâi le-ʿolam*) . . ." ²³So Yahweh *'elohîm* sent him from the Garden of Eden to work the soil (*ha-'adamah*) from which he was taken. ²⁴He drove out the human being (*ha-'adam*) and placed on the east of the Garden of Eden the cherubim and the flame of the whirling sword to watch over the path of the Tree of Life.

---

18. On "bread" as a synecdoche for food in general, see Bullinger, *Figures of Speech*, 627. Compare English "break bread."

19. Virtually all translations render this phrase with a finite verb ("until you return"), radically altering the sense of original inevitability conveyed by the infinitive construct.

20. Note the chiastic structure in v. 19b (return to the *'adamah* / taken from it— dust you are / return to dust) with its emphasis on the human's nature *qua* dust.

Bibliography

Abraham, Joseph. *Eve: Accused or Acquitted?* Paternoster Biblical and Theological Monographs. Carlisle, UK: Paternoster, 2002.
Ackerman, James S. "Knowing Good and Evil: A Literary Analysis of the Court History in 2 Samuel 9–20 and 1 Kings 1–2." *JBL* 109 (1990) 41–60.
Albert, Edwin. "Zu Gen 3:17–19." *ZAW* 33 (1913) 1–19.
Alonso-Schökel, Luis. "Sapiential and Covenant Themes in Genesis 2–3." *TD* 13 (1965) 3–10.
Alter, Robert. "Introduction." In *The Literary Guide to the Bible*, edited by Robert Alter and Frank Kermode, 11–35. Cambridge: Harvard University Press, 1987.
———. "Sacred History and the Beginnings of Prose Fiction." *Poetics Today* 1 (1980) 143–62.
Anderson, Gary A., and Michael E. Stone. *A Synopsis of the Books of Adam and Eve*. 2nd rev. ed. Early Judaism and Its Literature. Atlanta: Scholars, 1999.
Arnold, Bill. *Genesis*. NCBC. Cambridge: Cambridge University Press, 2009.
Augustine, Saint. *The City of God*. Translated by Marcus Dodds. New York: Random House, 1950.
———. *The Literal Meaning of Genesis*. Translated by John Hammond Taylor. 2 vols. Ancient Christian Writers 41–42. Ramsey, NJ: Paulist, 1982.
Bailey, John A. "Initiation and the Primal Woman in Gilgamesh and Genesis 2–3." *JBL* 89 (1970) 137–50.
Bal, Mieke. *Lethal Love: Feminist Literary Readings of Biblical Love Stories*. Indiana Studies in Biblical Literature. Bloomington: Indiana University Press, 1987.
———. "Sexuality, Sin and Sorrow: The Emergence of the Female Character (A Reading of Genesis 1–3)." In *Lethal Love: Feminist Literary Readings of Biblical Love Stories*, 104–30. Indiana Studies in Biblical Literature. Bloomington: Indiana University Press, 1987.
———. "The Construction of Reality in Fiction." *Poetics Today* 6 (1984) 21–42.
———. "Tricky Thematics." *Semeia* 42 (1988) 133–55.
Bar-Efrat, Shimon. *Narrative Art in the Bible*. Translated by Dorothea Shefer-Vanson. JSOTSup 70. Bible and Literature Series 17. Sheffield: Almond, 1989.
Barr, James. *The Garden of Eden and the Hope of Immortality*. Minneapolis: Fortress, 1993.
———. "One Man, or All Humanity?" In *Recycling Biblical Figures: Papers Read at a Noster Colloquium in Amsterdam, 12–13 May 1997*, edited by Athalya Brenner and Jan Willem van Henten, 3–21. STAR 1. Leiden: Deo, 1999.
Beattie, D. R. G. "*Peshat* and *Derash* in the Garden of Eden." *IBS* 7 (1985) 62–74.
———. "What Is Genesis 2–3 About?" *ExpTim* 92/1 (1980) 8–10.

Bibliography

Bechtel, Lyn M. "Rethinking the Interpretation of Genesis 2:4b—3:24." In *A Feminist Companion to Genesis*, edited by Athalya Brenner, 77–117. The Feminist Companion to the Bible 2. Sheffield: Sheffield Academic, 1993.

———. "Shame as a Sanction of Social Control in Biblical Israel: Judicial, Political and Social Shaming." *JSOT* 49 (1991) 47–76.

Bergmeier, Roland. "Zur Septuagintaübersetzung von Gen 3:16." *ZAW* 79 (1967) 77–79.

Bird, Phyllis A. "'Bone of My Bone and Flesh of My Flesh.'" *ThTo* 50 (1994) 521–34.

Bledstein, Adrien Janis. "Was Eve Cursed? (Or Did a Woman Write Genesis?)" *BR* 9/1 (1993) 42–45.

Blenkinsopp, Joseph. *Creation, Un-creation, Re-creation: A Discursive Commentary on Genesis 1–11*. London: T. & T. Clark, 2011.

———. "P and J in Genesis 1–11." In *Fortunate the Eyes That See: Essays in Honor of David Noel Freedman*, edited by Astrid B. Beck, 1–15. Grand Rapids: Eerdmans, 1995.

———. *The Pentateuch: An Introduction to the First Five Books of the Bible*. ABRL. New York: Doubleday, 1992.

Bloom, Harold, and David Rosenberg. *The Book of J*. New York: Grove Weidenfeld, 1990.

Boomershine, Thomas E. "The Structure of Narrative Rhetoric in Genesis 2–3." *Semeia* 18 (1980) 113–29.

Booth, Wayne C. *A Rhetoric of Irony*. Chicago: University of Chicago Press, 1974.

Boyarin, Daniel. *Carnal Israel: Reading Sex into Talmudic Culture*. New Historicism 25. Berkeley: University of California Press, 1993.

Boyd, Brian. *On the Origin of Stories: Evolution, Cognition and Fiction*. Cambridge: Belknap, 2009.

Brown, Peter. *The Body and Society*. New York, Columbia University Press, 1988.

Brueggemann, Walter. "From Dust to Kingship." *ZAW* 84 (1972) 1–18.

———. *Genesis*. IBC. Atlanta: John Knox, 1982.

———. "Of the Same Flesh and Bone." *CBQ* 32 (1970) 532–42.

Buchanan, George Wesley. "The Old Testament Meaning of the Knowledge of Good and Evil." *JBL* 75 (1956) 114–20.

Bullinger, E. W. *Figures of Speech Used in the Bible*. 1898. Reprinted, Grand Rapids: Baker, 1968.

Burns, Dan E. "Dream Form in Genesis 2.4b—3.24: Asleep in the Garden." *JSOT* 12/3 (1987) 3–14.

Busenitz, Irvin A. "Woman's Desire for Man: Gen 3:16 Reconsidered." *Grace Theological Journal* 7 (1986) 203–12.

Caird, G. B. *The Language and Imagery of the Bible*. Philadelphia: Westminster, 1980.

Callender, Dexter E., Jr. *Adam in Myth and History: Ancient Israelite Perspectives on the Primal Human*. HSS 48. Winona Lake, IN: Eisenbrauns, 2000.

Carmichael, Calum M. "The Paradise Myth: Interpreting without Jewish and Christian Spectacles." In *A Walk in the Garden: Biblical, Iconographical, and Literary Images of Eden*, edited by Paul Morris and Deborah Sawyer, 47–63. JSOTSup 136. Sheffield: JSOT Press, 1992.

Carr, David A. *Reading the Fractures of Genesis: Historical and Literary Approaches*. Louisville: Westminster John Knox, 1996.

Carroll, Robert P. "Irony." In *A Dictionary of Biblical Interpretation*, edited by R. J. Collins and J. L. Houlden, 325–26. London: SCM, 1990.

Casanowicz, Immanuel M. *Paranomasia in the Old Testament*. 1894. Reprinted, Breinigsville, PA: Kessinger, 2009.

Bibliography

Cassuto, Umberto. *A Commentary on the Book of Genesis*. Vol. 1, *From Adam to Noah*. Translated by Israel Abrahams. Publications of the Perry Foundation for Biblical Research in the Hebrew University of Jerusalem. .Jerusalem: Magnes, 1961.

Charlesworth, James B. *The Good and Evil Serpent: How a Universal Symbol Became Christianized*. Anchor Yale Bible Reference Library. New Haven: Yale University Press, 2010.

Clark, W. Malcolm. "Legal Background to the Yahwist's Use of 'Good and Evil' in Genesis 2-3." *JBL* 88 (1969) 266-78.

Clines, D. J. A. "Noah's Flood: I. the Theology of the Flood Narrative." *Faith and Thought* 100 (1972) 128-42.

———. "Theme in Genesis 1-11." *CBQ* 38 (1976) 483-507.

———. "What Does Eve Do to Help?" In *What Does Eve Do to Help? and Other Readerly Questions to the Old Testament*, 25-48. JSOTSup 94. Sheffield: JSOT Press, 1990.

Cohen, Jeremy. "Original Sin as the Evil Inclination." *HTR* 73 (1980) 495-520.

Coles, Robert. *The Call of Stories*. Boston: Houghton Mifflin, 1989.

Cooper, Jerrold S. "Babbling On: Recovering Mesopotamian Orality." In *Mesopotamian Epic Literature: Oral or Aural?*, edited by Marianna E. Vogelsang and Herman L. J. Vanstiphout, 105-22. Lewiston, NY: Mellen, 1992.

Coote, Robert B., and David Robert Ord. *The Bible's First History*. Philadelphia: Fortress, 1989.

Coulson, Seana, and Els Severens. "Hemispheric Asymmetry and Pun Comprehension: When Cowboys have Sore Calves." *Brain and Language*, 100 (2007) 172-87.

Culley, Robert C. "Action Sequences in Genesis 2-3." *Semeia* 18 (1980) 25-33.

Dahlberg, Bruce T. "The Unity of Genesis." In *Literary Interpretations of Biblical Narratives*, edited by Kenneth R. R. Gros Louis et al., 2:126-33. 2 vols. Nashville: Abingdon, 1974.

Daube, David. *The New Testament and Rabbinic Judaism*. Jordan Lectures in Comparative Religion 2. London: University of London Athlone Press, 1956.

Davies, Philip R. "The False Pen of Scribes: Intellectuals Then and Now." In *Sense and Sensitivity: Essays on Reading the Bible in Memory of Robert Carroll*, edited by Alastair G. Hunter and Philip R. Davies, 117-26. JSOTSup 348. Sheffield: Sheffield Academic, 2002.

Day, Peggy L. *An Adversary in Heaven: Śāṭān in the Hebrew Bible*. HSM 43. Atlanta: Scholars, 1988.

Douglas, Mary. "Jokes." In *Implicit Meanings*, 90-114. London: Henley, 1978.

Dozeman, Thomas B., and Konrad Schmid. *A Farewell to the Yahwist?: The Composition of the Pentateuch in Recent European Interpretation*. SBLSymS 34. Atlanta: Society of Biblical Literature, 2006.

Eliot, T. S. *The Wasteland*. Original edition: New York: Boni and Liveright, 1922.

Evans, J. M. *"Paradise Lost" and the Genesis Tradition*. Oxford: Clarendon, 1968.

Fishbane, Michael. *Biblical Interpretation in Ancient Israel*. Oxford: Clarendon, 1985.

———. *Text and Texture: Close Readings of Selected Biblical Texts*. New York: Schocken, 1979.

Foh, Susan T. "The Head of the Woman is the Man." In *Women in Ministry: Four Views*, edited by Bonnidell Clouse and Robert Clouse, 69-105. Downers Grove, IL: InterVarsity, 1989.

Forsyth, Neil. *The Old Enemy: Satan and the Combat Myth*. Princeton: Princeton University Press, 1987.

Bibliography

Fuchs, Esther. "The Literary Characterization of Mothers and Sexual Politics in the Hebrew Bible." In *Feminist Perspectives on Biblical Scholarship*, edited by Adela Yarbro Collins, 117–36. SBLBSNA 10. Chico, CA: Scholars, 1985.

———. *Sexual Politics in the Biblical Narrative: Reading the Hebrew Bible as a Woman*. JSOTSup 310. Sheffield: Sheffield Academic, 2000.

Galambush, Julie. "ʾādām from ʾădāmā, ʾiššâ from ʾîš: Derivation and Subordination in Genesis 2.4b—3.24." In *History and Interpretation: Essays in Honor of John H. Hayes*, edited by M. Patrick Graham et al., 33–46. JSOTSup 173. Sheffield: JSOT Press, 1993.

Garspiel, Moshe. *Biblical Names: A Literary Study of Midrashic Derivatives and Puns*. Ramat Gan: Bar-Ilan University Press, 1991.

Gawande, Atul. "Hellhole." *The New Yorker*, March 30, 2009, 36–45.

Gilbert, Daniel. *Stumbling on Happiness*. New York: Knopf, 2006.

Gispen, W. H. "Genesis 2:10–14." In *Studia Biblica et Semitica*, edited by Theodoor Vriezen, 115–24. Wageningen: Veenman, 1967.

Glück, J. J. "Assonance in Ancient Hebrew Poetry: Sound Patterns as a Literary Device." In *De Fructis Oris Sui: Essays in Honour of Adrianus van Selms*, edited by Adriann van Selms and I. H. Eybers, 69–84. Pretoria Oriental Series 9. Leiden: Brill, 1971.

———. "Paronomasia in Biblical Literature." *Semitics* 1 (1970) 50–78.

Goldingay, John. "How Far Do Readers Make Sense?: Interpreting Biblical Narrative." *Them* 18 (1993) 5–10.

Good, Edwin R. *Irony in the Old Testament*. Philadelphia: Westminster, 1965.

Goody, Jack. *The Interface between the Written and the Oral*. Studies in Literacy, Family, Culture, and the State. Cambridge: Cambridge University Press, 1987.

Gowan, Donald E. *From Eden to Babel: A Commentary on the Book of Genesis 1–11*. ITC. Grand Rapids: Eerdmans, 1988.

———. *When Man Becomes God: Humanism and Hybris in the Old Testament*. PittTMS 6. Pittsburgh: Pickwick, 1975.

Greenstein, Edward L. "God's Golem: The Creation of the Human in Genesis 2." In *Creation in Jewish and Christian Tradition*, edited by Henning Graf Reventlow and Yair Hoffman, 219–39. JSOTSup 319. London: Sheffield Academic, 2002.

———. "Wordplay, Hebrew." In *ABD* 6:968–71.

Grimké, Sarah. *Letters on the Equality of the Sexes, and Other Essays*, edited by Elizabeth Ann Bartlett. New Haven: Yale University Press, 1988.

Guillaume, A. "Paronomasia in the Old Testament." *JSS* 9 (1964) 282–90.

Hamori, Esther J. *When Gods Were Men: The Embodied God in Biblical and Near Eastern Literature*. BZAW 384. Berlin: de Gruyter, 2008.

Hayter, Mary. *The New Eve in Christ: The Use and Abuse of the Bible in the Debate about Women in the Church*. London: SPCK, 1987.

Hendel, Ronald S. *The Text of Genesis 1–11: Textual Studies and Critical Edition*. New York: Oxford University Press, 1998.

Herlihy, David. *Medieval Households*. Studies in Cultural History. Cambridge: Harvard University Press, 1985.

Hess, Richard S. "Genesis 1–2 in Its Literary Context." *TynBul* 41 (1990) 143–53.

———. "The Roles of the Woman and the Man in Genesis 3." *Them* 18 (1993) 15–19.

———. "Splitting the Adam: the Usage of ʾadam in Genesis I–V." In *Studies in the Pentateuch*, edited by J. A. Emerton, 1–15. VTSup 41. Leiden: Brill, 1990.

Hiebert, Theodore. "The Tower of Babel and the Origin of the World's Cultures." *JBL* 106 (2007) 29–58.

Hillers, Delbert R. "Dust: Some Aspects of Old Testament Imagery." In *Love & Death in the Ancient Near East*, edited by John H. Marks and Robert M. Good, 105-9. Guilford, CT: Four Quarters, 1987.
Humbert, Paul. "Démesure et Chute dans l'Ancien Testament." In *Hommage à Wilhelm Vischer*, 63-82. Montpelier: Causse, Graille, Castelnau, 1960.
———. "Emploi et Portée Bibliques du Verbe *yāṣar* et ses Dérivés Substantifs." *BZAW* 77 (1958) 82-88.
———. *Études sur le Récit du Paradis et de la Chute dans la Genèse*. Mémoires de l'Université de Neuchâtel 14. Neuchatel, Switzerland: Université de Neuchatel, 1940.
———. "La Faute d'Adam." *RTP* 27 (1939) 225-40.
Hutcheon, Linda. *Irony's Edge: The Theory and Politics of Irony*. London: Routledge, 1995.
Jastrow, Marcus. *Dictionary of the Targumim, the Talmud Babli and Yerushalmi, and the Midrashic Literature*. 1903. New York: Judaica, 1989.
Jenni, Ernst. "Das Wort ʿōlām im Alten Testament." *ZAW* n.s. 24 (1953) 1-35.
Jobling, David. *The Sense of Biblical Narrative*. JSOTSup 39. Sheffield: JSOT Press, 1986.
Joines, Karen Randolph. "The Bronze Serpent in the Israelite Cult." *JBL* 87 (1968) 245-56.
———. *Serpent Symbolism in the Old Testament: A Linguistic, Archaeological, and Literary Study*. Haddonfield, NJ: Haddonfield House, 1974.
Kawashima, Robert S. "A Revisionist Reading Revisited: On the Creation of Adam and Eve." *VT* 56 (2006) 46-57.
———. "Sources and Redaction." In *Reading Genesis: Ten Methods*, edited by Ronald S. Hendel, 47-70. Cambridge: Cambridge University Press, 2010.
Kee, M. S. "The Heavenly Council and its Type-Scene." *JSOT* 31 (2007) 259-73.
Kempf, Stephen. "Introducing the Garden of Eden: The Structure and Function of Genesis 2:4b-7." *Journal of Translation and Textlinguistics* 7 (1996) 33-53.
Keynes, John Maynard. "Economic Possibilities for Our Grandchildren." In *The Goal of Economic Growth*, edited by Edmund S. Phelps, 209-14. Rev. ed. Problems of the Modern Economy. New York: Norton, 1969.
Kikawada, Isaac M. "Two Notes on Eve." *JBL* 91 (1972) 33-37.
Kim, Yoo-Ki. *The Function of the Tautological Infinitive in Classical Biblical Hebrew*. HSS 60. Winona Lake, IN: Eisenbrauns, 2009.
Kimelman, Reuven. "The Seduction of Eve and Feminist Readings of the Garden of Eden." *Women in Judaism: A Multidisciplinary Journal* 1/2 (1998) 1-39.
King, Thomas. *The Truth about Stories: A Native Narrative*. CBC Massey Lecture Series. Toronto: Anansi, 2003.
Knibb, Michael A. *The Ethiopic Book of Enoch: A New Edition in Light of the Aramic Dead Sea Fragments*, vol. 2. Oxford: Clarendon, 1978.
Kugel, James L. *Traditions of the Bible: A Guide to the Bible as It Was at the Start of the Common Era*. Cambridge: Harvard University Press, 1998.
LaCocque, André. *Trial of Innocence: Adam, Eve, and the Yahwist*. Eugene, OR: Cascade Books, 2006.
Lanser, Susan S. "(Feminist) Criticism in the Garden: Inferring Genesis 2-3." *Semeia* 41 (1988) 67-84.
Lawton, Robert B. "Genesis 2:24: Trite or Tragic?" *JBL* 105 (1986) 97-98.
Lenzi, Alan. *Secrecy and the Gods: Secret Knowledge in Ancient Mesopotamia and Biblical Israel*. SAAS 19. Helsinki: Neo-Assyrian Text Corpus Project, 2008.
Levenson, Jon D. *Resurrection and the Restoration of Israel: The Ultimate Victory of the God of Life*. New Haven: Yale University Press, 2006.

Bibliography

Levin, Christoph. "The Yahwist: The Earliest Editor in the Pentateuch." *JBL* 126 (2007) 209–31.

L'Hour, Jean. "Yahweh Elohim." *RB* 81 (1974) 524–56.

Livingstone, David N. *Adam's Ancestors: Race, Religion and the Politics of Human Origins.* Medicine, Science, and Religion in Historical Context. Baltimore: Johns Hopkins University Press, 2008.

Lloyd, Genevieve. *The Man of Reason: "Male" and "Female" in Western Philosophy.* Minneapolis: University of Minnesota Press, 1984.

Loader, William. "The Beginning of Sexuality in Genesis LXX and Jubilees." In *Die Septuaginta—Texte, Kontexte, Lebenswelten,* edited by Martin Karrer and Wolfgang Kraus, 300–312. WUNT 219. Tübingen: Mohr/Siebeck, 2008.

———. *The Septuagint, Sexuality, and the New Testament: Case Studies on the Impact of the LXX in Philo and the New Testament.* Grand Rapids: Eerdmans, 2004.

Lohr, Joel N. "Sexual Desire? Eve, Genesis 3:16, and תשוקה." *JBL* 130 (2011) 227–46.

Long, Burke O. *The Problem of Etiological Narrative in the Old Testament.* BZAW 108. Berlin: Töpelmann, 1968.

Louw, Theo A. W. van der. *Transformations in the Septuagint: Towards an Interaction of Septuagint Studies and Translation Studies.* Contributions to Biblical Exegesis & Theology 47. Leuven: Peeters, 2007.

Lussier, Ernest. "ʾ*Adam* in Genesis 1,1–4,24." *CBQ* 18 (1956) 137–39.

Luther, Martin. *Lectures on Genesis: Chapters 1–5,* 198, 203. Translated by George V. Schick. Luther's Works 1. St. Louis: Concordia, 1958.

Maimonides, Moses. *Guide of the Perplexed.* Translated by Shlomo Pines. Chicago: University of Chicago Press, 1963.

Malina, Bruce J. "Some Observations on the Origin of Sin in Judaism and St. Paul." *CBQ* 31 (1969) 18–34.

McEvenue, Sean. *Interpreting the Pentateuch.* Collegeville: Liturgical, 1990.

McKenzie, John L. "The Literary Characteristics of Genesis 2–3." In *Myths and Realities: Studies in Biblical Theology,* 146–81. 1963. John L. McKenzie Reprint Series. Eugene, OR: Wipf & Stock, 2009.

McKenzie, Steven L. and Stephen R. Haynes, eds. *To Each Its Own Meaning: An Introduction to Biblical Criticisms and their Application.* Louisville: Westminster John Knox, 1993.

Meier, Samuel A. "Linguistic Clues on the Date and Canaanite Origin of Genesis 2:23–24." *CBQ* 53 (1991) 18–24.

Mendenhall, George E. "The Shady Side of Wisdom: The Date and Purpose of Genesis 3." In *A Light unto My Path: Old Testament Studies in Honor of Jacob M. Myers,* edited by Howard N. Bream et al., 319–34. Gettysburg Theological Studies. Philadelphia: Temple University Press, 1974.

Mettinger, Tryggve N. D. *The Eden Narrative: A Literary and Religio-Historical Study of Genesis 2–3.* Winona Lake, IN: Eisenbrauns, 2007.

Meyers, Carol. *Discovering Eve: Ancient Israelite Women in Context.* New York: Oxford University Press, 1988.

Miller, Patrick D., Jr. *Genesis 1–11: Studies in Structure and Theme.* JSOTSup 8. Sheffield: University of Sheffield, 1978.

Milne, Pamela J. "Eve & Adam: Is a Feminist Reading Possible?" *BRev* 4/3 (1988) 12–21, 39.

———. "The Patriarchal Stamp of Scripture: The Implications of Structuralist Analyses for Feminist Hermeneutics." In *A Feminist Companion to Genesis,* edited by Athalya

Brenner, 146–72. The Feminist Companion to the Bible 2. Sheffield: Sheffield Academic, 1993.

Moor, Johannes C. de. "The First Human Being a Male? A Response to Professor Barr." In *Recycling Biblical Figures: Papers Read at a Noster Colloquium in Amsterdam, 12–13 May 1997*, edited by Athalya Brenner and Jan Willem van Henten, 22–27. STAR 1. Leiden: Deo, 1999.

Muilenburg, James. "Form Criticism and Beyond." *JBL* 88 (1969) 1–18.

Nabokov, Vladimir. *Speak, Memory: An Autobiography Revisited*. New York: Putnam, 1966.

Naidoff, Bruce D. "A Man to Work the Soil: A New Interpretation of Genesis 2–3." *JSOT* 5 (1978) 2–14.

Neiman, D. "Eden, the Garden of God." *Acta Antiqua Academiae Scientiarum Hungaricae* 17 (1969) 109–12.

Niditch, Susan. *Chaos to Cosmos: Studies in Biblical Patterns of Creation*. Scholars Press Studies in the Humanities 6. Chico, CA: Scholars, 1985.

———. *Folklore and the Hebrew Bible*. GBS. Minneapolis: Fortress, 1993.

———. *Oral World and Written Word: Ancient Israelite Literature*. Library of Ancient Israel. Louisville: Westminster John Knox, 1996.

Noegel, Scott B., editor. *Puns and Pundits: Word Play in the Hebrew Bible and Ancient Near Eastern Literature*. Bethesda, MD: CDL, 2000.

Noort, Ed. "Gan-Eden in the Context of the Mythology of the Hebrew Bible." In *Paradise Interpreted: Representations of Paradise in Judaism and Christianity*, edited by Gerard P. Luttikhuizen, 21–36. Themes in Biblical Narrative 2. Leiden: Brill, 1999.

O'Connell, Robert H. "Ironic Reversal through Concentric Structure and Mythic Allusion." *VT* 38 (1988) 407–18.

Oden, Robert A., Jr. *The Bible without Theology: The Theological Tradition and Alternatives To It*. New Voices in Biblical Studies. San Francisco: Harper & Row, 1987.

———. "Divine Aspirations in Atrahasis and in Genesis 1–11." *ZAW* 93 (1981) 197–216.

Oduyoye, Modupe. *The Sons of the Gods and the Daughters of Men: An Afro-Asiatic Interpretation of Gen 1–11*. Maryknoll NY: Orbis, 1984.

Pagels, Elaine. *Adam, Eve, and the Serpent*. New York: Random House, 1988.

———. *The Origin of Satan*. New York: Random House, 1995.

Pardes, Ilana. *Countertraditions in the Bible: A Feminist Approach*. Cambridge: Harvard University Press, 1992.

Pfeiffer, Robert H. "Wisdom and Vision in the Old Testament." In *Studies in Ancient Israelite Wisdom*, selected with a prolegomena by James L. Crenshaw, 305–13. New York: Ktav, 1976.

Pidoux, Georges. "Encore les Deux Arbres de Genèse 3!" *ZAW* 66 (1954) 37–43.

Pollack, John. *The Pun Also Rises: How the Humble Pun Revolutionized Language, Changed History, and Made Wordplay More Than Some Antics*. New York: Gotham, 2011.

Porter, Frank C. "The Yeçer Hara, A Study in the Jewish Doctrine of Sin." In *Biblical and Semitic Studies: Critical and Historical Essays by the Members of the Semitic and Biblical Faculty of Yale University*, edited by Edward Lewis Curtis, 93–156. Yale Bicentennial Publications. New York: Scribner, 1901.

Rabinowitz, Peter J. "Truth in Fiction: A Reexamination of Audiences." *Critical Inquiry* 4/1 (1977) 121–41.

Rad, Gerhard von. *Genesis: A Commentary*. Translated by John H. Marks. OTL. Philadelphia: Westminster, 1972.

Bibliography

Ramsey, G. W. "Is Name-Giving an Act of Domination in Gen 2:23 and Elsewhere?" *CBQ* 50 (1988) 24–35.
Read, Sophie. "Puns: Serious Wordplay." In *Renaissance Figures of Speech*, edited by Sylvia Adamson et al., 81–94. Cambridge: Cambridge University Press, 2007.
Ries, Julien. "Immortality." *ER* 7:123–45.
Robbins, Ellen. "Day." *NIDB* 2:48.
———. "Time-Telling in Ritual and Myth." *JJTP* 6 (1997) 71–88.
Roberts, J. J. M. "Does God Lie?" In *The Bible and the Ancient Near East: Collected Essays*, 123–31. Winona Lake, Ind.: Eisenbrauns, 2002.
Sandys-Wunsch, John. "Before Adam and Eve—Or What the Censor Saw." *SR* 11 (1982) 23–28.
Sasson, Jack M. "'The Mother of All . . .': Etiologies." In *"A Wise and Discerning Mind": Essays in Honor of Burke O. Long*, edited by Saul M. Olyan and Robert C. Culley, 205–20. Brown Judaic Studies 325. Providence, RI: Brown Judaic Studies, 2000.
———. "The 'Tower of Babel' and the Primeval History." In *I Studied Inscriptions from before the Flood: Ancient Near Eastern, Linguistic, and Literary Approaches to Genesis 1–11*, edited by Richard S. Hess and David Toshiro Tamura, 448–57. Sources for Biblical and Theological Study 4. Winona Lake, IN: Eisenbrauns, 1994.
———. "Wordplay in the Old Testament." *IDBSup*, 968b–70b.
Satlow, Michael L. "Jewish Constructions of Nakedness in Late Antiquity." *JBL* 116 (1997) 429–54.
Savran, George W. "Beastly Speech: Intertextuality, Balaam's Ass, and the Garden of Eden." *JSOT* 64 (1994) 33–55.
———. *Telling and Retelling: Quotation in Biblical Narrative*. Indiana Studies in Biblical Literature. Bloomington: Indiana University Press, 1988.
Sawyer, John F. A. "The Image of God, the Wisdom of Serpents and the Knowledge of Good and Evil." In *A Walk in the Garden: Biblical, Iconographical, and Literary Images of Eden*, edited by Paul Morris and Deborah Sawyer, 64–73. JSOTSup 136. Sheffield: JSOT Press, 1992.
Schmid, Konrad. "Loss of Immortality? Hermeneutical Aspects of Genesis 2–3 and Its Early Receptions." In *Beyond Eden: The Biblical Story of Paradise (Genesis 2–3) and Its Reception History*, edited by Konrad Schmid and Christoph Riedweg, 58–78. FAT 2/34. Tübingen: Mohr/Siebeck; 2008.
Scott, R. B. Y. "Folk Proverbs of the Ancient Near East." In *Studies in Ancient Israelite Wisdom*, selected with a prolegomena by James L. Crenshaw, 417–26. New York: Ktav, 1976.
Sharon, Diane. "The Doom of Paradise: Literary Patterns in Accounts of Paradise and Mortality in the Hebrew Bible and the Ancient Near East." In *A Feminist Companion to Genesis*, edited by Athalya Brenner, 53–81. The Feminist Companion to the Bible 2. Sheffield: Sheffield Academic, 1998.
Sharp, Carolyn J. *Irony and Meaning in the Hebrew Bible*. Indiana Studies in Biblical Literature. Bloomington: Indiana University Press, 2008.
Shectman, Sarah. *Women in the Pentateuch: A Feminist and Source-Critical Analysis*. HBM 23. Sheffield: Phoenix, 2009.
Sjöberg, Ake W. "Eve and the Chameleon." In *In the Shelter of Elyon: Essays on Ancient Palestinian Life and Literature in Honor of G. W. Ahlström*, edited by W. Boyd Barrick and John R. Spencer, 219–25. JSOTSup 31. Sheffield: JSOT Press, 1984.

Ska, Jean-Louis. "Genesis 2–3: Some Fundamental Questions." In *Beyond Eden: The Biblical Story of Paradise (Genesis 2–3) and its Reception History*, edited by Konrad Schmid and Christoph Riedweg, 1–27. FAT 2/34. Tübingen: Mohr/Siebeck; 2008.

———. "'Je vais lui faire un allié qui soit son homologue' (Gen 2:18): A Propos du Terme ʿ*ezer* — 'aide'." *Bib* 65 (1984) 233–238.

Skinner, John. *A Critical and Exegetical Commentary on Genesis*. ICC. Edinburgh: T. & T. Clark, 1910.

Smith, Mark S. *God in Translation: Deities in Cross-Cultural Discourse in the Biblical World*. Grand Rapids: Eerdmans, 2010.

———. *The Early History of God: Yahweh and the Other Deities in Ancient Israel*. 2nd ed. The Biblical Resource Series. Grand Rapids: Eerdmans, 2002.

———. *The Origins of Biblical Monotheism: Israel's Polytheistic Background and the Ugaritic Texts*. New York: Oxford University Press, 2001.

Smith, Morton. *Palestinian Parties and Politics That Shaped the Old Testament*. Lectures on the History of Religions, new ser., 9. New York: Columbia University Press, 1971.

Spong, John Shelby. *A New Christianity for A New World*. San Francisco: HarperSanFrancisco, 2000.

———. *Why Christianity Must Change or Die*. San Francisco: HarperSanFrancisco, 1999.

Stanton, Elizabeth Cady, editor. *The Woman's Bible*. 1895. Boston: Northeastern University Press, 1993.

Sternberg, Meir. *The Poetics of Biblical Narrative: Ideological Literature and the Drama of Reading*. Indiana Literary Biblical Series. Bloomington: Indiana University Press, 1985.

Stordalen, Terje. *Echoes of Eden: Genesis 2–3 and Symbolism of the Eden Garden in Biblical Hebrew Literature*. Leuven: Peeters, 2000.

———. "Genesis 2,4: Restudying a Locus Classicus." *ZAW* 104 (1992) 163–77.

———. "Man, Soil, Garden: Basic Plot in Genesis 2–3 Reconsidered." *JSOT* 53 (1992) 3–26.

Stratton, Beverly J. *Out of Eden: Reading, Rhetoric and Ideology in Genesis 2–3*. JSOTSup 208. Sheffield: Sheffield Academic, 1995.

Strus, Andrzej. *Nomen-Omen: La Stylistique sonore des Noms Propres dans le Pentateuque*. AnBib 80. Rome: Biblical Institute, 1978.

Tennant, F. R. *Sources of the Doctrines of the Fall and Original Sin*. 1903. New York: Schocken, 1968.

Toorn, Karel van der. *Scribal Culture and the Making of the Hebrew Bible*. Cambridge: Harvard University Press, 2007.

Tosato, Angelo. "On Genesis 2:24." *CBQ* 52 (1990) 389–409.

Trible, Phyllis. "Depatriarchalizing in Biblical Interpretation." *JAAR* 41 (1973) 30–48.

———. *God and the Rhetoric of Sexuality*. OBT 2. Philadelphia: Fortress, 1978.

Troost, Arie. "Reading for the Author's Signature." In *A Feminist Companion to Genesis*, edited by Athalya Brenner, 251–72. The Feminist Companion to the Bible 2. Sheffield: Sheffield Academic, 1993.

Tucker, Gene M. "The Creation and the Fall: A Reconsideration." *LTQ* (1978) 113–24.

Turner, James Grantham. *One Flesh: Paradaisal Marriage and Sexual Relations in the Age of Milton*. Oxford: Clarendon, 1993.

Urbach, Efraim E. *The Sages, Their Concepts and Beliefs*. 2 vols. Translated by Israel Abrahams. Publications of the Perry Foundation in the Hebrew University of Jerusalem. Jerusalem: Magnes, 1975.

Bibliography

Van der Merwe, C. H. J. et al. *A Biblical Hebrew Reference Grammar*. Biblical Languages—Hebrew 3. Sheffield: Sheffield Academic, 1999.

Vawter, Bruce. *On Genesis: A New Reading*. Garden City, NY: Doubleday, 1977.

Wallace, Howard N. *The Eden Narrative*. HMS 32. Atlanta: Scholars, 1985.

Walsh, Jerome T. "Genesis 2:4b—3:24: A Synchronic Approach." *JBL* 96 (1977) 161–77.

Watson, Francis. "Recovery and Resistance: Hermeneutical Reflections on Genesis 1–3 and its Pauline Reception." *JSNT* 45 (1992) 79–103.

Werman, Golda. *Milton and Midrash*. Washington DC: Catholic University of America Press, 1995.

Westermann, Claus. *Genesis: A Commentary*. Vol. 1, *Genesis 1–11*. 2. Auflage. BKAT 1. Neukirchen-Vluyn: Neukirchener, 1976.

———. *Genesis: A Commentary*. Vol. 1, *Genesis 1–11*. 3 vols. Translated by John J. Scullion. Minneapolis: Augsburg, 1984.

———. *Genesis: A Commentary*. Vol. 2, *Genesis 12–36*. Translated by John J. Scullion. Minneapolis: Augsburg, 1985.

Whedbee, J. William. *The Bible and the Comic Vision*. Cambridge: Cambridge University Press, 1998.

White, Hugo. "The Trace of the Author in the Text." *Semeia* 71 (1995) 45–64.

Whybray, R. N. "The Immorality of God." *JSOT* (1996) 89–120.

Williams, A. J. "The Relationship of Genesis 3:20 to the Serpent." *ZAW* 89 (1977) 357–74.

Williams, Jay G. "Genesis 3." *Interpretation* 35 (1981) 274–79.

Winnett, Frederick V. "Re-Examining the Foundations." *JBL* 84 (1965) 1–19.

Wolde, E. J. van. "Facing the Earth: Primaeval History in a New Perspective." In *The World of Genesis: Persons, Places, Perspectives*, edited by Philip R. Davies and David J. A. Clines, 22–47. JSOTSup 257. Sheffield: Sheffield Academic, 1998.

———. *Words Become Worlds: Semantic Studies of Genesis 1–11*. Biblical Interpretation Series 6. Leiden: Brill, 1994.

Wyatt, Nicolas. "Interpreting the Creation and Fall Story in Genesis 2–3." *ZAW* 93 (1981) 10–21.

Yee, Gail A. "Gender, Class and the Social-Scientific Study of Genesis 2–3." *Semeia* 87 (1999) 177–92.

York, Anthony D. "Adam." In *Dictionary of Biblical Tradition in English Literature*, edited by David Lyle Jeffrey, 15–20. Grand Rapids: Eerdmans, 1992.

Index of Subjects

Adam, as personal name, 4, 17–20, 126–27, 159n6
additions to the text, 20
    Gen 2:10–14, 28
    Gen 2:24, 31n23, 34–35, 64n19
    Gen 3:20–21, 4, 65, 94–96, 125, 127–29
allegorical interpretation, 11, 12–13, 42n54, 44, 108n9, 118
androgyny, 18, 74, 75n48
"bone from my bones" (Gen 2:23), 31–35, 39, 47
breath of life, 87–88, 89–92, 102, 126
Cain, 2–3, 4n7, 40–43, 65, 94
childbirth and childbearing, 10–11, 43, 61, 63–65
    See also motherhood; procreation
creation story (Genesis 1), 2–4, 14n38, 35, 55, 61n13, 80, 92–93, 122, 147–48, 151
dating of Garden of Eden story, 6–7, 63n17
death and threat of death, 10–12, 28n13, 39n47, 61, 62n14, 64n19, 75–76, 81–104, 106, 116–18, 122, 131–32, 150, 153
    acceptance of death, 150, 152
disobedience, 1, 5–6, 12, 56–58, 60, 66–67, 69, 70–71, 78, 80, 81–82, 84, 94, 95–99, 104, 115, 118, 124, 127, 131, 132n25, 135–36, 138, 146–48, 159n9
dust, 29, 37n36, 38–39, 59–60, 61–62, 68–70, 87–92, 97, 150

Eden, 5, 51, 151
Epic of Gilgamesh, 46, 76n50, 78n58, 81, 100, 102, 152n26
eternal life, 86–87, 100–101
    See also immortality
Eve, as personal name, 3–4, 65, 94, 127–29
expulsion, 2n1, 6, 47, 60n12, 96–97, 100, 103–4, 121, 123, 136
fable, 18–19, 36, 106, 113–15, 121, 126–27, 151
(the) Fall, 1–3, 7–13, 62, 78n60, 105–6, 120, 135, 142, 148n12, 154
fallen angels, 107–8, 140–42
(the) Flood, 2, 3n4, 5, 77, 87, 98–99, 153
folk etymology, 32n24, 33, 127
God
    name of, 16–17, 121–22
    point of view, 66–67, 79–80, 126–27, 153–54
    portrayal of, 80, 96, 98–99, 121–26, 131, 136–37
humiliation, humbling, 39n47, 48, 56n2, 59, 63–64, 68–70, 77, 119, 150, 152
image of God, 4, 80, 147–48
immortality, 45–47, 62, 65n22, 81–104, 128n15, 152n27
    See also breath of life; death; mortality.
irony, 5n12; 7, 21, 34, 43, 65n21, 68–69, 76–77, 114, 115, 118, 123, 124n8, 135, 137–38, 144–54
knowing good and bad. *See* Tree of Knowing Good and Bad

Index of Subjects

Life of Adam and Eve, 3n6, 107–9, 140–42
male domination. *See* woman: subordination of
man
    name of, 32–33, 126–27, 151 (*see also* Adam)
    punishment of, 60–61, 96, 118–19, 124–25, 146
    purpose of, 28–29, 34n28, 35, 44, 56n2, 60–61, 122n2, 146
marriage, divorce (Gen 2:24), 19n13, 31n23, 34, 65n22, 71–75
midrash, 10n28, 18n10, 24n3, 30n19, 32n25, 74n45, 75n47, 82n1, 89n26, 101, 105, 107n8, 108n9, 129n18
mortality, 17, 29, 38, 48, 60–62, 68, 81–104, 146, 150, 152
    See also death; immortality
"mother of all life", 3n5, 28n13, 65, 94–95, 127–28
motherhood, 62, 64–65, 68–69, 94–95, 127, 149
    See also childbirth; procreation
nakedness, 12–13, 35–36, 49, 75–77, 84, 114–16, 121, 134–36, 146–47
    See also shame
naming as authority, 24–25, 29–30, 128
one flesh, 34–35, 64n19, 71–72, 74–75
orality, 7, 52–53, 149–50
original sin, 6, 9, 10, 79, 89n26, 108
patriarchy. *See* woman: subordination of
procreation, 3n5, 24, 34–35, 61, 92–95, 128, 135
    See also childbirth; motherhood
punishments, purpose of, 56–71, 80, 96
Qur'an, 24n3, 43n56, 78n58, 107, 108n10
Satan, 1, 4n7, 12, 78n58, 107–9, 113, 121, 140–42
serpent, 110
    See also snake
sexuality, sexual desire, 12–13, 40, 57, 71–72, 76, 78–79, 84, 92–94, 108, 129n18, 147
shame, 12–13, 36n35, 76–77, 95, 114, 116, 135, 147
    See also nakedness
sin, 3n4, 5–6, 11n32, 12, 41–43, 56–57, 58, 62, 67, 81–82, 86, 107
    See also disobedience; original sin.
snake, 37n38, 102–103, 105–19, 149
    identity of, 42n54 (*see also* Satan; *Life of Adam and Eve*)
    motivation of, 12, 81–82, 118–19, 120, 138–42
    punishment of, 56n2, 59–60, 68, 73, 80, 88–89, 124–25
    veracity of, 35–37, 75, 98, 116–18, 135–38, 149
    See also serpent
Tower of Babel, 55, 98–99, 119, 123–24, 153
Tree of Knowing Good and Bad, 26, 35–36, 45–47, 58, 69, 77–80, 82–86, 106, 126, 132–36, 139–40
    knowing good and bad, 47–48, 75–80, 93–94, 97–98, 115–19, 123–24, 138, 146, 150
Tree of Life, 45–47, 48, 78n58, 93n36, 96, 99–104, 112, 132, 139, 140, 154
Wisdom literature, 46–47, 79, 110–11, 132–33, 147n8, 148n9
woman
    creation of, 23–27, 31–34, 92–93, 96, 122–23, 130, 147–49
    guilt of, 11–12, 81, 99, 106, 108, 108n10, 115–19, 124, 129–36, 138–39, 142–43, 146, 148–49
    name of, 4, 17–20, 23–27, 32–33, 126–29, 151 (*see also* additions to the text: Gen 3:20–21; naming as authority)
    punishment of, 61–71, 80, 96, 125, 146

purpose of, 32–35, 44–45, 56n2, 61, 126, 149 (*see also* motherhood)

subordination of (Gen 3:16b), 25n5, 32, 40–44, 62–71, 130–31, 125, 137–38, 147, 149, 151–52, 154–55 (*see also* male domination; naming as authority)

wordplay, 18, 23–54, 59, 90–91, 115, 127, 144–46, 148, 149, 150–52, 153n30

Index of Hebrew Words and Phrases

ʾadam, 17–20, 126–27, 159n6
    ʾadam and ʾadamah, 18, 28–34, 38–39, 50, 60–61, 74n46, 88–92, 125, 144–46
ʿal-ken, 73
ʿapar, 38–39, 88–92
ʿarûm, 35–37, 109–115
ʿarûmmîm, ʿêrummîm, ʿêrom, 35–37, 114–15
ʾereṣ, 50–51
ʿeṣem me-ʿaṣamai u-baśar mi-bᵉśarî, 39
ʿeśeb ha-śadeh, 157n1
ḥawwah, 3n5, 127, see Eve
ḥomer, 38–39, 90
ʿiṣṣabôn, 37–38, 61

ʾîš, 25
    ʾîš and ʾiššah, 25, 31n23, 32–34, 52
kᵉnegdô, 24, 158n4
neḥmad lᵉ-haśkîl, 132–36
nepeš ḥayyah, 91, 158n5
ʿolam, 99–102
pen, 115–16, 131
ruaḥ ʾelohîm, 87–89, 91–92
śiaḥ ha-śadeh, 64, 157n1
šûbka, 89, 161n17
tardemah, 31n21
tᵉšûpennû/yᵉšûpᵉka, 37n38, 161n16
tᵉšûqah, 40–44, 63
yhwh ʾelohîm, 16–17, 121–22
yṣr, 89n26

Index of Authors

Abraham, Joseph, 62n15
Ackerman, James S., 110n17
Albert, Edwin 83n5
Alonso-Shökel, Luis, 9n24, 148n8
Alter, Robert, 53–54, 72n40, 150n16, 151n21
Anderson, Gary A., 107n6
Arnold, Bill, 56n2
Aquinas, Thomas, 44 n59, 66n27, 67, 93–94
Aristotle, 44n59, 66n27, 149n13
Augustine, 12n33, 34n29, 57, 92, 103
Bailey, John A., 56n2, 76n51
Bal, Mieke, 3n5, 6n15, 18n10, 65n22, 131
Bar-Efrat, Shimon, 9, 74, 109, 145
Barr, James, 18n10, 91, 102n59, 114, 118n35, 135, 152
Beattie, D. R. G., 118n35, 118n39
Bechtel, Lyn M., 36n35, 74n46, 77n53, 89n25, 152n26
Bird, Phyllis A., 14n38
Bledstein, Adrien Janis, 21n19
Blenkinsopp, Joseph, 2n3, 3n4, 5n14, 6n17, 31n21, 42n54, 50n78, 76n50, 79n65, 110n17, 118n37, 134n35, 147n8, 152n26
Bloom, Harold, 21
Boomershine, Thomas E., 95n46, 130n20, 137n40
Booth, Wayne C., 148n11
Boyarin, Daniel, 74n45, 108n9
Boyd, Brian, 13, 77, 121, 150
Brown, Peter, 12n34
Brueggemann, Walter, 31, 39n46

Buchanan, George Wesley, 48n71
Bullinger, E. W., 27n10, 37n36, 99n52, 123n5, 127n11
Burns, Dan E., 148n12
Busenitz, Irvin A., 56n2
Caird, G. B., 10n26, 65n22, 72n38, 78n59, 83n6, 106, 122n2, 122n3, 124n8, 133n30, 134n32
Callender, Dexter E., Jr., 29n15
Carmichael, Calum M., 147n8, 152n28, 153n31, 154n32, 154n33
Carr, David A., 50n78
Carroll, Robert P., 124n8, 148n10, 148n11
Casanowicz, Immanuel M., 27n10, 37n36
Cassuto, Umberto, 26n8, 36n35, 37, 41n52, 42n54, 53n89, 56n3, 65n20, 93n36, 94, 113n25, 114n27, 118, 128n14, 129n18, 161n16
Charlesworth, James B., 11n21, 11n22, 118n35
Clark, W. Malcolm, 47n68
Clines, D. J. A., 2n3, 3n4, 18n9, 34, 56n2, 57n6
Cohen, Jeremy, 89n26
Coles, Robert, 150n19
Cooper, Jerrold S., 52n88
Coote, Robert B., 17n8
Coulson, Seana, 53n90, 114n26
Culley, Robert C., 58n7, 71n35, 125n9
Dahlberg, Bruce T., 2n2

Index of Authors

Daube, David, 72n37, 74n45
Davies, Philip R., 152n28
Day, Peggy L., 107n5
Douglas, Mary, 150n16
Dozeman, Thomas B., 21n20
Eliot, T. S. 102
Evans, J. M., 107n8
Fishbane, Michael, 5n12, 118n37
Foh, Susan T., 43n55
Forsyth, Neil, 107n5
Fox, Everett, 16n7, 160
Fuchs, Esther, 95n44
Galambush, Julie, 25n6
Garspiel, Moshe, 127n11
Gawande, Atul, 149n13
Gilbert, Daniel, 142n47
Gispen, W. H., 28n14
Glück, J. J., 25n7, 27n10
Goldingay, John, 152n25
Good, Edwin R., 7, 148n10
Goody, Jack, 10n27
Gowan, Donald E., 2n1, 5n13, 126n10, 130n20, 134n33, 146n5
Greenstein, Edward L., 27n10, 29n15, 34n29, 38n40, 122n3
Grimké, Sarah, 43n55, 78
Guillaume, A., 27n10
Hamori, Esther J., 122n2
Haynes, Stephen R., 145n3
Hayter, Mary, 68n30
Hendel, Ronald S., 41n52, 45n62
Herlihy, David, 92n34
Hess, Richard S., 8n21, 50n78, 136n39
Hiebert, Theodore, 123n6
Hillers, Delbert R., 59n10
Humbert, Paul, 6n15, 8n22, 16n6, 28n14, 36n33, 44n58, 47n68, 51n86, 71n34, 76n49, 78n60, 86n11, 89n24, 93n37, 100n54, 122n3, 130n20, 133n30, 134n33, 148n9, 151n22, 152n27
Hutcheon, Linda, 148n11
Jastrow, Marcus, 114n28
Jenni, Ernst, 101n58

Jobling, David, 71n35, 129n16, 142n48
Joines, Karen Randolph, 112n22
Kawashima, Robert S., 2n3, 13n37, 18n11
Kee, M. S., 16n3
Kempf, Stephen, 8n21
Keynes, John Maynard, 61n13
Kikawada, Isaac M., 65n25
Kim, Yoo-Ki, 85n8
Kimelman, Reuven, 62n15
King, Thomas, 150n19
Knibb, Michael A., 101n56
Kugel, James L., 15n1
LaCocque, André, 6n17
Lanser, Susan S., 18n11, 62n15
Lawton, Robert B., 73n43
Lenzi, Alan, 16n3
Levenson, Jon D., 62n14, 69n31, 101n57
Levin, Christoph, 21n20
L'Hour, Jean, 16n6
Livingstone, David N., 9n23
Lloyd, Genevieve, 66n27
Loader, William, 33n27, 43n57, 72n37
Lohr, Joel N., 40n50, 43n57, 161n17
Long, Burke O., 127n11
Louw, Theo van der, 25n4, 73n41, 158n5
Lussier, Ernest, 20n15, 159n6
Luther, Martin, 64–65, 69n32
Maimonides, Moses, 34n30, 78n60
Malina, Bruce J., 6n15, 15n1, 82n2, 86n13
McEvenue, Sean, 115n30
McKenzie, John L., 21n18, 52n87
McKenzie, Steven L., 145n3
Meier, Samuel A., 32n24, 64n19
Mendenhall, George E., 6n17, 147n8, 151n21
Mettinger, Tryggve N. D., 6n15, 6n17, 45n61, 56n4, 95n47, 132n25, 154n32
Meyers, Carol, 63n17
Miller, Patrick D, Jr., 6n16, 56n2
Milne, Pamela J., 62n15

Index of Authors

Milton, John, 10–11, 19n12, 31, 79n63, 80n67, 94, 120, 121, 135
Moor, Johannes C., de 18n10
Muilenberg, James, 53
Nabokov, Vladimir, 90
Naidoff, Bruce D., 25n6, 78n57, 88n20
Neiman, D., 5n13, 51n85
Niditch, Susan, 7n18, 112n23, 146n4, 152n26
Noegel, Scott B., 27n10
Noort, Ed, 118n35, 151n22
O'Connell, Robert H., 152n26
Oden, Robert A. Jr., 79n61, 94n41, 147n6
Oduyoye, Modupe, 77n53
Ord, David R., 17
Origen, 11n32, 66n27
Pagels, Elaine, 107n5
Paul, 10–11, 33n27, 72, 82, 83n3, 86
Pfeiffer, Robert H., 3n4, 71n34, 118n35, 153n31
Philo, 11n32, 66n27, 108n9, 148n9
Plato, Platonism, 34, 74–75
Pidoux, Georges, 49n76, 102n60
Pollack, John, 53n90
Porter, Frank C., 89n26
Rabinowitz, Peter J., 151
Rad, Gerhard von, 71n36, 79n61, 118, 130n19
Ramsey, G. W., 30n18
Read, Sophie, 28n11
Ries, Julien, 102n61
Robbins, Ellen, 86n11, 151n23
Sandys-Wunsch, John, 3n4, 16n3, 142n48
Sasson, Jack M., 27n10, 49n77, 93n38, 158n4
Satlow, Michael L., 77n53
Savran, George W., 3n4, 66n26, 106n2
Sawyer, John F. A., 135n37
Schmid, Konrad, 21n20, 97n49
Scott, R. B. Y., 33n26
Severens, Els, 53n90, 114n26

Sharon, Diane, 103
Sharp, Carolyn J., 118, 147n8, 148n10
Shectman, Sarah, 65n23
Sjöberg, Ake W., 46n65
Ska, Jean-Louis, 6n17, 149n13
Skinner, John, 3n5, 5, 11n29, 44n58, 65n21, 89n24, 95n45
Smith, Mark S., 16n3
Smith, Morton, 16n3
Spong, John Shelby, 86n13
Stanton, Elizabeth Cady, 117n34
Sternberg, Meir, 148n10
Stone, Michael E., 107n6
Stordalen, Terje, 5n13, 5n14, 6n17, 8n21, 28n14, 34n28, 38n39, 39n47, 46n63, 50n78, 51, 51n85, 65n21, 80n66, 80n67, 88n20, 93, 96, 98, 101n58, 103, 114n27, 115n31, 123n4, 128n13, 131, 132n26, 134, 145n3, 147n8, 153n29, 154, 154n34, 157n1
Stratton, Beverly J., 18n9, 28n11, 56n2, 134n35, 145n3, 158n4
Strus, Andrzej, 27n10, 28n10, 127n11
Tennant, F. R., 89n26
Tertullian, 11
Toorn, Karel van der, 2n2, 7n19
Tosato, Angelo, 64n19, 71n36, 72n40, 73n42
Trible, Phyllis, 18n10, 25n5, 71n36
Troost, Arie, 21n19
Tucker, Gene M., 71n36, 147
Turner, James Grantham, 71n36
Urbach, Efraim E., 89n26
Van der Merwe, C. H. J., 85n8
Vawter, Bruce, 89n24, 95n46, 149
Wallace, Howard N., 8n22, 52n88, 79n61, 145n3
Walsh, Jerome T., 6n16, 61n13
Watson, Francis, 18n9, 33n27
Werman, Golda, 10n28
Westermann, Claus, 2n2, 3n5, 5n13, 8n22, 13, 28n14, 41n52, 69, 73n43, 78, 78n59, 83n3, 83n4,

179

Index of Authors

86n12, 91, 94n43, 100, 122n3, 128n15, 129n17, 131n22
Whedbee, J. William, 36n34
White, Hugo, 151n24
Williams, A. J., 94n43
Williams, Jay G., 71n33, 134
Winnett, Frederick V., 6n17, 7n18
Wolde, Ellen van, 32n24, 34n29, 72n40
Wyatt, Nicolas, 6n17, 21n20
Whybray, R. N., 86n11, 118n35, 124n8, 143n50, 153n29
Yee, Gail A., 39, 63n18
York, Anthony D., 20n15, 159n6

www.ingramcontent.com/pod-product-compliance
Lightning Source LLC
Chambersburg PA
CBHW062044220426
43662CB00010B/1651